THE SOURCE OF THE RIVER

THE SOURCE OF THE RIVER

THE SOCIAL ORIGINS OF FRESHMEN AT AMERICA'S SELECTIVE COLLEGES AND UNIVERSITIES

Douglas S. Massey

Camille Z. Charles

Garvey F. Lundy

Mary J. Fischer

PRINCETON UNIVERSITY PRESS

PRINCETON AND OXFORD

Copyright © 2003 by Princeton University Press

Published by Princeton University Press, 41 William Street, Princeton, New Jersey 08540

In the United Kingdom: Princeton University Press, 3 Market Place,

Woodstock, Oxfordshire OX20 1SY

All Rights Reserved

Library of Congress Cataloging-in-Publication Data

The source of the river : the social origins of freshmen at America's selective colleges and

universities / Douglas S. Massey ... [et al.]

p. cm.

Includes bibliographical references and index.

ISBN 0-691-11326-2 (alk. paper)

1. College students—United States—Social conditions.   2. Minorities—Education (Higher)—

United States.   3. Academic achievement—United States.   4. Educational equalization—United

States.   I. Massey, Douglas S.

LC208.8 .S68 2003

378.1'98—dc21   2002029344

British Library Cataloging-in-Publication Data is available

This book has been composed in Sabon

Printed on acid-free paper. ∞

www.pupress.princeton.edu

Printed in the United States of America

3 5 7 9 10 8 6 4 2

CONTENTS

LIST OF TABLES AND FIGURES

Tables

Figures

ACKNOWLEDGMENTS

The authors wish to thank the Andrew W. Mellon Foundation and the Atlantic Philanthropies for their financial support of the National Longitudinal Survey of Freshmen and the research that went into this book. Particular thanks go to William G. Bowen and Harriet Zuckerman, President and Vice President, respectively, of the Mellon Foundation, for their support and encouragement throughout. Thanks also go to the Institute for Survey Research of Temple University for its outstanding administration of the NLSF questionnaire, and particularly to Ellin Spector for her expert management of all phases of the survey.

THE SOURCE OF THE RIVER

CHAPTER 1

THE PUZZLE OF MINORITY

UNDERACHIEVEMENT

P RIOR TO the civil rights movement of the 1960s, racial and ethnic minorities were substantially excluded from U.S. higher education. African Americans, in particular, were barred from most colleges and universities by a combination of de jure and de facto mechanisms, and they faced particularly severe barriers at the nation's most selective institutions. If they were able to go to college at all, it was to a historically black college or university. Although several elite private institutions such as Howard, Morehouse, and Spelman provided excellent training for the sons and daughters of the black elite, most African Americans were relegated to underfunded, racially segregated state institutions. The situation was not much better for Latinos, especially in Texas, where Mexican Americans were subject to the sanctions of Jim Crow.

The civil rights movement transformed race relations in the United States and produced vigorous efforts to incorporate African Americans and Latinos into the mainstream of American society. Nowhere was this effort more apparent than in higher education. Led by the nation's elite institutions, American colleges and universities undertook deliberate attempts to recruit minority students through a variety of "affirmative actions." These efforts encompassed a range of mechanisms for enhancing minority recruitment and admissions. Initially, they were justified as an attempt to redress past racial injustices, but as immigration from Asia and Latin America transformed the United States, the rationale shifted from righting past wrongs to representing racial and ethnic "diversity" for its own sake.

The new recruitment and admissions practices had pronounced effects on the racial and ethnic composition of American colleges and universities. The share of nonwhites among U.S. college students increased substantially, going from 16% in 1976 to 27% in 1996 (National Center for Education Statistics 2001). Among African Americans aged 18–24, the share attending college went from 21% in 1972 to 30% in 2000, while the percentage of Latinos attending college went from 17% to 22%. Statistics on Asians have only recently become available, but as of the year 2000 they had the highest rate of college attendance of any racial or ethnic group, with 55% of those aged 18–24 enrolled in school (compared with 36% for whites).

As the decades wore on, however, it became increasingly clear that mere recruitment into former bastions of white academic privilege would not be enough to erase the large gap in educational attainment between Latinos and blacks, on the one hand, and whites and Asians, on the other (Glazer 1997). Despite a variety of retention efforts—increased financial aid, remedial education, special tutoring, peer advising, culturally sensitive dorms, and ethnically supportive student unions—once admitted to institutions of higher education, African Americans and Latinos continued to underperform relative to their white and Asian counterparts, earning lower grades, progressing at a slower pace, and dropping out at higher rates. More disturbing was the fact that these differentials persisted even after controlling for obvious factors such as SAT scores and family socioeconomic status (Bowen and Bok 1998).

The most basic indicator of success in college is graduation. Figure 1.1 shows trends in the percentage of those aged 25–29 who finished at least four years of college from 1977 to 1997. Despite two decades of affirmative action, intergroup differentials in college attainment have hardly changed, and by the end of the 1990s they even appeared to be widening. Through the early 1990s, roughly a quarter of all whites aged 25–29 finished college, compared with just 13% of blacks and around 10% of Latinos. After 1994, however, whites surged upward, reaching 29% by 1997. In contrast, blacks remained stuck at under 15% and Latinos at around 10%.

Longitudinal surveys offer another way to look at educational attainment. These surveys follow the educational progress of a cohort (an entering class) as it progresses through time. The College and Beyond Survey, for example, followed the 1979 and 1989 cohorts of freshmen at selective colleges and universities (see Bowen and Bok 1998). Graduation rates for Asians and whites in the earlier cohort were similar (around 88%) but substantially higher than those reported for Latinos (73%) and blacks (71%). Graduation rates were generally higher for the 1989 cohort, in which Asians displayed the highest graduation rate (96%), followed closely by whites (94%). Surprisingly, the rate for Latinos also rose substantially, reaching 90%, whereas the rate for blacks stagnated in relative terms, lagging behind at only 79%. Graduation rates for minorities were generally higher at more selective institutions (Bowen and Bok 1998).

Despite a multitude of studies, the literature remains inconclusive about the reasons for these persistent differentials. Special programs are being designed and implemented to improve black and Latino retention, but without any real understanding of the underlying causes of their higher dropout rates. One reason for our current lack of knowledge is the scarcity of good data. Studies of minority achievement draw heavily on

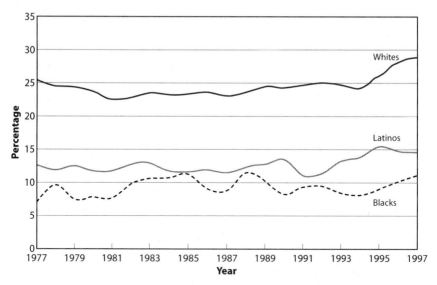

Figure 1.1. Percentage of persons aged 25–29 with four
or more years of college

administrative databases compiled for other purposes or rely on small
convenience samples gathered at particular institutions. Across all studies, moreover, there is a remarkable lack of standardization and sophisti-
cation in design and analysis. As a result, apart from basic measures of
family structure, socioeconomic status, and high school performance, we
know relatively little about the traits and characteristics that members of
different racial and ethnic groups bring with them when they arrive on
campus, or about how such differences in background might affect outcomes in higher education.

   Although we are now four decades into the great social experiment of
affirmative action, no systematic, nationally representative study has yet
sought to investigate the determinants of college success for different
racial and ethnic groups. We sought to redress this gap by surveying representative samples of Asian, Latino, and black freshmen entering a set of
twenty-eight selective colleges and universities in the fall of 1999. The institutions chosen for study were those used by Bowen and Bok (1998) in
their *College and Beyond Survey.* Whereas the goal of Bowen and Bok
was to understand "the shape of the river"—the path followed by minority students as they moved through life after college—ours was to
comprehend the *source* of that river—who the students were, where they
came from, what their characteristics were, and how these characteristics
shaped their academic progress.

In the absence of reliable data, theoretical explanations have proliferated with no good way of choosing between them. For the most part, the various theories that have been proposed to this point are neither logically inconsistent nor mutually exclusive, and for that reason none can be rejected a priori. Probably all contain an element of truth, and the real question is which ones are most powerful in explaining academic performance compared with the alternatives. The only way to answer this question is empirically, using relevant, reliable, and representative data.

Such information is precisely what we sought to provide by launching the National Longitudinal Survey of Freshmen (NLSF). In this volume we use data from the first wave of that survey, in which new students were interviewed as they arrived on campus as freshmen. Our purpose here is to learn all we can about the similarities and differences that whites, blacks, Latinos and Asians bring with them when they walk through the door on the first day of class. We wish not only to document these differences, but to understand the family, neighborhood, school, and peer circumstances from which they arose and, in turn, how they condition academic success during the first term of college. Differing backgrounds may or may not contribute to our understanding of differential rates of academic performance, but it is an obvious place to start. Before we begin our journey toward "the source of the river," however, we first review the different theoretical explanations that have so far been advanced to explain the academic underperformance of minorities in general, and African Americans in particular.

Theories of Minority Underperformance

Social science research on intergroup differences in educational achievement has, for the most part, focused on black-white differentials. Clearly the black-white divide has a special salience given the unique history of slavery, segregation, and discrimination experienced by African Americans in the United States. Since 1965, however, mass immigration has transformed the American reality to render the old notion of the black-white color line increasingly obsolete (Farley 1998; Bobo et al. 2000). The United States now houses a variegated population characterized not by a single, all-encompassing racial duality, but by a multidimensional intersection of changing racial and ethnic continua. Although any label is bound to be an oversimplification of this new, more complex reality, for practical reasons we focus on three groups that together constitute the bulk of what most people consider to be "minorities" in the United States: African Americans, Latinos, and Asians. All three groups are composed not only of natives with many generations of U.S. residence, but also of recently arrived immigrants and their children.

The Theory of Capital Deficiency

Perhaps the simplest and most widely recognized explanation for poor academic performance is that some people, for whatever reason, lack the resources needed for academic success. Such explanations range from the controversial claim that certain racial groups have less inherited intelligence (e.g., Herrnstein and Murray 1996) to more straightforward hypotheses that link poor academic performance to disadvantages stemming from low family income (Jencks et al. 1979; Fischer et al. 1996). Leaving genetic explanations aside, in the jargon of modern social science these explanations generally revolve around different notions of "capital deficiency," where capital comes in a variety of distinct forms.

The most commonly recognized form is *financial capital:* income, assets, and various monetary instruments that together comprise a household's economic resources. Obviously, children born into rich families are at a distinct advantage when it comes to preparing for college. Over the course of their lives, their parents are in a privileged position to purchase academic inputs of higher quality—not simply good schooling, private tutoring, and extracurricular training, but comfortable housing, good nutrition, and access to intellectual stimuli. When problems arise, moreover, wealthy parents can retain an army of specialists to help their offspring overcome whatever learning disabilities they face: educational psychologists, clinical diagnosticians, youth counselors, and child learning specialists.

In recent years, however, social scientists have identified other forms of capital relevant to the education and training of children. *Human capital* refers to the skills, abilities, and knowledge possessed by specific individuals (Schultz 1963; Becker 1964). Education itself is a form of human capital, and years of schooling is its most common indicator (though not without its flaws—see Blalock 1991). Under the precepts of human capital theory, parents invest in their children in the same way that entrepreneurs invest in a company, seeking to maximize their ultimate payoff—in this case the happiness, productivity, socioeconomic status, and prestige of their descendants in society.

Parents who themselves possess large quantities of human capital are in a better position to supervise and manage its acquisition by others (Steinberg 1996; Lareau 2000; Farkas 1996). College-educated parents are more likely than others to read to their children and provide intellectual stimulation within the home. They understand the process of schooling better, are less deferential to teachers and school authorities, and take a more active role in monitoring how their children are being taught and managing their education (Lareau 2000). Hence, one reason that minorities may experience academic difficulties in college is that, owing to a lack of access to education, their parents are less able to prepare them for higher education. Research also shows, moreover, that well-educated black parents are less able to transmit human capital to their children than comparably educated white parents, owing to a legacy of racism and discrimination (Duncan 1969).

Another form of capital is *social capital:* the tangible benefits and resources that accrue to people by virtue of their inclusion in a social structure (Bourdieu and Wacquant 1992). People gain access to social capital through membership in networks and institutions and then convert it into other forms of capital (such as education) to improve or maintain their position in society (Bourdieu 1986; Coleman 1990). When children are connected through ties of kinship or friendship to people who can help them prepare for college—socially, psychologically, culturally, and academically—then those ties constitute a source of social capital.

Finally, *cultural capital* refers to a knowledge of the norms, styles, conventions, and tastes that pervade specific social settings and allow individuals to navigate them in ways that increase their odds of success. This concept originated in the theoretical writings of Max Weber (see Swidler 1986; Macleod 1995) but gained special prominence in the work of Bourdieu (1977), who argued that cultural information passed on informally from one generation to the next helps to perpetuate social stratification. Wealthy children inherit a substantially different body of cultural knowledge compared with working-class children, especially when the latter are members of a racial or ethnic minority. School systems are organized such that the cultural knowledge of middle-class whites is valorized and systematically rewarded, whereas the cultural capital possessed by lower-class minorities is not.

Academia, in particular, is a rarefied social niche with its own customs, traditions, and expectations. Exposure to and prior knowledge of the social conventions of academia can be critical in preparing students for achieving success in a school environment (Farkas 1996). This knowledge may be quite practical—such as knowing why, when, where, and how to study—or it may be more diffuse and loosely related to educational achievement—how to behave in certain social situations, familiarity with certain cultural symbols, knowledge of certain styles of music, food, and dress. The latter are basically shared understandings that enable students to "fit in," be comfortable, and feel like they "belong." DiMaggio and Ostrower (1990) found significant black-white differences in knowledge of Euro-American high culture, which generally suffuses the academic milieu of selective colleges and universities. Alienation from these cultural forms might very well undermine the confidence and, hence, the achievement of minority students from poor and working-class backgrounds.

A major empirical problem for social scientists is that the various forms of capital—financial, human, social, and cultural—are almost always highly intercorrelated (MacLeod 1995). People with financial capital usually also have privileged access to cultural, social, and human capital. Thus, whereas DiMaggio and Ostrower (1990) and Roscigno and Ainsworth-Darnell (1999) have documented clear black-white differences in cultural capital, they also found that these differentials were substantially explained by differences in socioeconomic background. One goal of our study is to measure the forms of capital carefully and separately to disentangle their effects from one another.

Leaving aside the issue of *which* forms of capital are most important in determining educational outcomes, the theory of capital deficiency is generally supported by a substantial body of work documenting the powerful effect that family socioeconomic status has on children's educational achievement. The seminal work here is that of Coleman (1966), whose early results have been substantiated in subsequent work (Hanushek 1989; Miller 1995). Coleman found that differences in achievement among white, black, Asian, and Latino high school students were most strongly influenced by parental education, income, and occupational status, whereas school characteristics had a modest effect on academic achievement.

The Theory of Oppositional Culture

The theory of oppositional culture originated in the work of the anthropologist John Ogbu (1978, 1981). It has also been called the "blocked opportunities framework" (Kao and Tienda 1998) and the "caste theory of education" (Ogbu 1978). Rather than dwelling on individual deficits, Ogbu sought to explain the academic performance of racial and ethnic minorities with reference to broader societal structures and historical processes. He began by distinguishing two kinds of minority groups: voluntary and involuntary. The former include *immigrant minorities,* such as Koreans, Chinese, and Punjabi Indians, who enter the host country freely seeking to improve their material well-being, as well as *autonomous minorities,* such as Jews and Mormons, whose minority status derives from adherence to a belief system that is not predominant in the larger society.

Involuntary minorities include groups such as African Americans, Amerindians, Mexicans, and Puerto Ricans, who were incorporated into American society largely against their will through enslavement, conquest, or colonization and were then relegated to a menial, subordinate status. Whereas voluntary minorities compare themselves to compatriots in their countries of origin to derive a favorable view of the host society, involuntary minorities compare themselves with native majority members and are painfully aware of their disadvantaged status, which generates negative feelings toward mainstream values and institutions. Thus, whereas voluntary minorities see cultural differences simply as obstacles to be overcome in order to achieve success, involuntary minorities view them as symbols of pride and resistance.

Involuntary minorities thus come to perceive knowledge of and participation in the dominant culture and its institutions as a betrayal of group loyalty and a threat to identity. They develop a defiant position vis-à-vis mainstream institutions and feel alienated from schools, learning, and education. Studying hard and excelling in school are seen as culturally illegitimate. Among black high school students, for example, to display intelligence, use standard English, and earn high academic honors is to "act white." For such students, academic success thus comes at a high psychological price: "racelessness." Although their skin may be black, successful African American students are forced to reject a portion of their black identity as part of the "burden of acting white" (Fordham and Ogbu 1986; Fordham 1988, 1996).

These psychological dynamics are also expressed socially. Black parents, for example, communicate a mixed message to their children, telling them that school is important, on the one hand, but simultaneously expressing a distrust of the educational system, on the other, as well voicing doubts about the efficacy of education in shielding their children from racial discrimination. Black peers, meanwhile, view academic success as a threat to group solidarity and negatively sanction students who perform well, calling them "nerds" and "brainiacs," or casting other aspersions on their coolness. Involuntary minorities thus tend to develop a collective oppositional culture, a frame of reference that actively rejects mainstream behaviors to undermine academic achievement.

Ogbu and Fordham developed their ideas based on ethnographic fieldwork they conducted in racially segregated American high schools. Other ethnographers have sought to confirm their results by studying different groups in different settings. Solomon (1992), for example, studied West Indian students in Toronto and found considerable resistence to academic success, especially among males. Even though West Indians are voluntary immigrants to Canada, Solomon argued that exposure to discrimination and isolation led to the formation of an oppositional identity. Waters (1999), meanwhile, identified two different patterns of assimilation among second-generation West Indians in New York: one group identified with native black Americans and adopted an oppositional identity that led to academic underachievement, whereas another group identified with immigrants and were more academically successful.

In his study of Latinos, Suarez-Orozco (1991) found that the various national-origin groups behaved in ways consistent with Ogbu's theory depending on whether they were voluntary (Cubans, Dominicans) or involuntary immigrants (Mexicans, Puerto Ricans). Likewise, Matute-Bianchi (1986) found that the children of recently arrived Mexican immigrants generally displayed proschool attitudes that led to academic achievement; but those born or raised in the United States developed oppositional identities as *chicanos* or *cholos* that undermined their educational progress.

Other ethnographers, however, found students to be more discerning and sophisticated in their rejection of mainstream culture. Carter (2001), for example, reported that black and Latino students rejected certain styles of speech, dress, and music as "acting white" but nonetheless valued behaviors conducive to academic success, such as studying hard, getting good grades, and making the honor roll. Although O'Connor (1997) found that black students indeed adhered to a collective "black" identity, it did not include hostility to academic success. Based on her fieldwork among the Navajo, Deyhle (1995) argued that oppositional culture was inappropriate in explaining their resistance to education, which she traced to their marginalization in the economy and to distinct elements of their cultural heritage, which derived from centuries-old traditions rather than opposition to European culture per se.

If attempts to verify oppositional theory from ethnographic research have yielded a mixed record, efforts to verify it quantitatively have been even less successful. Cook and Ludwig (1998) found that, controlling for socioeconomic status, academically successful black students surveyed in the National Educational Longitudinal Survey (NELS) were no less popular than others, and that, on average, black students were no more alienated from school than were whites. Indeed, on some dimensions they were even *more* invested in academic success. Although Ainsworth-Darnell and Downey (1998) obtained similar results, Farkas, Lleras, and Maczuga (2002) criticized them for including all schools in their analysis rather than focusing on segregated institutions. They also found problems with their dependent variable (self-reported "popularity"). In several analyses using as an alternative dependent variable "frequency of hostile attacks," they found that black students in high-minority and high-poverty schools were more likely to be put down or made fun of for doing well academically. The strength of these findings, however, have been questioned by Downey and Ainsworth-Darnell (2002).

In their study of NELS data, Kao, Tienda, and Schneinder (1996) found that blacks and Latinos had aspirations closely matching those of whites, but that they earned significantly lower grades, suggesting a pattern of underachievement. In contrast, Asians had much higher aspirations than whites who earned the same grades, suggesting a pattern of overachievement. For them, peer culture apparently places a heavy emphasis on educational attainment, and, if anything, Asian students suffer a danger of "choking" under the relentless pressure for stellar grades and superior accomplishment (Kao 1995; Cheryan and Bodenhausen 2000). Unlike black parents, moreover, Asian parents do not send a mixed message about the importance of education (Sue and Okazaki 1990). Whereas Asian parents may be skeptical about the degree to which education will forestall discrimination, they do not communicate this skepticism to their children to the same degree as black parents do (see also Kao and Tienda 1998)

When Kao, Tienda, and Schneider (1996) considered the relationship between peer evaluation and academic performance, however, they found little evidence of any social bias against academically successful minorities, be they Asian, Latino, or African American. They also found that blacks and Latinos used their own groups as a reference to form peer evaluations and did not have identities defined in *opposition* to whites. Kao and Tienda (1998) subsequently reported that repeating a grade level greatly dampened the college aspirations of Latinos and blacks, although most of the intergroup differences were accounted for by differences in family resources.

The Theory of Stereotype Threat

The theory of stereotype threat was developed by the psychologist Claude Steele (1988, 1992, 1998). It argues that members of certain minority groups are prone to underperform academically because of an unconscious fear of living up to negative stereotypes about their group's intellectual capacity. Stereotype threat is a possibility whenever a person is at risk of fulfilling a negative stereotype associated with his or her group. If the threat is strong enough, it may interfere with performance, and long-term exposure leads to disidentification as a psychological defense mechanism: the domain in which the threat occurs is dropped as a basis for self-esteem (Steele and Aronson 1995; Aronson, Quinn, and Spencer 1998).

African Americans are stereotyped as being intellectually inferior in U.S. society (witness Herrnstein and Murray 1996), and black students are keenly aware of the prevailing negative valuation of their mental abilities. Every time black students are called upon to perform academically in the college setting, they are at risk of confirming this negative valuation, both to themselves and to others. The threat may be particularly salient in selective colleges and universities, where minority students are widely perceived (rightly or wrongly) by white faculty and students to have benefitted from a "bending" of academic standards because of affirmative action.

Failing to perform up to expected standards is psychologically distressing because it implies that the stereotype is, in fact, correct: the student *is* intellectually inferior to other students. Rather than face the risk of such distress, black students downplay the importance of academic success as a standard of self-worth and put less effort toward academic achievement. If they fail, they can then tell themselves that they really did not try their hardest and that academic outcomes are not important anyway.

The theory of stereotype vulnerability rests on three basic assumptions. First, it assumes that people are highly motivated to think well of themselves and have others do the same. Second, it assumes that anxiety about the possibility of performing badly increases the likelihood of a poor performance. Third, it assumes that disidentification—psychological disengagement from the domain in question—is the long-term outcome of exposure to such anxiety. Disidentification should not be confused with the related but more general concept of devaluation, which refers to the abstract perception of a domain as unimportant. Disidentification involves the specific removal of the domain as a measure of self-esteem (Crocker and Major 1989). It is well documented, for example, that African Americans generally value education—indeed, they value it more than other racial and ethnic groups. Despite this valuation, African Americans consistently underperform academically, yet they nonetheless have high self-esteem (Mruk 1999). This is the case, Steele would argue, because academic performance is not a central domain in which African Americans construct self-esteem: they have *disidentified* with academic achievement as a metric of self-worth.

Experiments undertaken to test the theory of stereotype vulnerability have generally yielded supportive findings (Steele and Aronson 1995; Josephs and Schroeder 1997; Aronson, Quinn, and Spencer 1998). In these experiments, one group of students is prompted so as to reduce stereotype threat before undertaking a test or intellectual task, while another is left alone or primed to increase stereotype threat. Results invariably show an inverse relationship between the degree of stereotype threat and intellectual performance. A major question, however, is the degree to which these results can be generalized outside the laboratory.

To examine stereotype threat in the real world, Steele et al. (forthcoming) instituted a special program for African American students at the University of Michigan. Students were recruited into the program, but rather than stigmatize them by making the program appear as an attempt to compensate for shortcomings, they were told that being in the program was an honor. They attended weekly seminars to get to know each other and share common experiences and then participated in specific "master workshops" to expose them to advanced material. After several years, results showed that program participants earned better grades and were less likely to drop out than other black students.

The Theory of Peer Influence

The theory of peer influence basically states that academic aspirations and achievement are strongly shaped, especially in adolescence, by social pressures emanating from the people that students encounter in their schools and classrooms (Coleman 1961). According to Hallinan (1983), peer effects can be classified into two broad categories: contextual and proximate. *Contextual peer effects* are those stemming from the social, demographic, or economic composition of a student body. *Proximate peer effects* are those stemming from the influence of specific people in a friendship network. Studies of proximate effects generally begin by enumerating the individuals in a person's social network and then consider how their values, beliefs, and aspirations influence the academic aspirations or achievement of the student.

Contextual peer effects operate through two mechanisms: reference group processes and interpersonal processes. The former occur because other students present in a classroom or school tend to establish group norms, offer concrete role models, and provide a yardstick for social comparison (Festinger 1954; Kelley 1967; Merton and Rossi 1968). Interpersonal processes operate because the values and standards of peers are transmitted interpersonally through specific interactions between individuals within a social environment (Hallinan 1983: 221).

The literature on proximate peer influence contends that proximity is a necessary, though not sufficient, condition for interpersonal attraction and, hence, influence. When two people are proximate in a social structure, their likelihood of interaction and mutual influence increases (Hallinan 1982: 290). Research on proximate effects generally compares the attitudes and behaviors of students with those of specific peers and infers influence from observed similarities. Sewell, Haller and Portes (1969), for example, delineated three potential sources of interpersonal influence—teacher encouragement, parental encouragement, and friends' college plans—of which they found the latter to be most important. Hallinan (1983) likewise found that students were more likely to attend college if their friends expected to go to college, regardless of socioeconomic status, and that the strength of the peer effect generally increased from the freshman to senior year of high school.

A serious empirical problem in studies of peer influence is self-selection. In general, young people choose friends who are similar to themselves, with comparable goals, aspirations, and outlooks (Kandel 1978; Epstein and Karweit 1983; MacLeod 1995). Other things being equal, students with high educational aspirations seek out friendships with others who share similar expectations for educational success, whereas students with low academic aspirations seek out others with low expectations for success. If we observe a correlation between the aspirations of individuals and the aspirations and performance of their peers, is it because of peer influence or self-selection into the peer group? Whereas some investigators argue that peer effects primarily reflect selection processes (Brown 1990), others conclude that they remain strong even after selection effects are controlled (Savin-Williams and Berndt 1990).

Kao (2001) attempted to control directly for selection effects using longitudinal data. She found that peer effects strongly influenced educational aspirations: Asians had greater educational success, in part, because they were more likely to have academically oriented friends. She also found that black students were more sensitive to friends' beliefs and behaviors than others. In contrast to the predictions of Ogbu, however, black peers were no less supportive of educational success. Rather, they were more strongly disposed to outside work, which was more detrimental to their academic achievement than for other groups.

Steinberg (1996) also considered intergroup differences in peer influence and found that Asian students outperformed other groups despite being exposed to "less than perfect" parenting. In contrast, black students performed significantly worse than others despite more positive parenting. Steinberg explains difference in terms of peer influence. Asian students were far more likely than others to have friends who placed a great emphasis on academic achievement; the friends of black and Latino students placed least emphasis on schooling, while whites were in-between.

Attachment Theory

Tinto (1993) argues that the process of dropping out of college is much like the processes of departure from other human communities—leaving generally reflects an absence of effective integration and the social support it provides. Thus, departing students are those who are insufficiently attached, socially and academically, to the institution in question. In Tinto's words, "an institution's capacity to retain students is directly related to its ability to reach out and make contact with students and integrate them into the social and intellectual fabric of institutional life. It hinges on the establishment of a healthy, caring educational environment which enables all individuals, not just some, to find a niche in one or more of the many social and intellectual communities of the institution" (pp. 204–5).

Attachment is influenced by individual factors, of course, such as a student's motivation for earning a college degree and his or her degree of commitment to achieving it. But integration is not solely an individual-level phenomenon; it necessarily involves an *interaction* between the individual and the institution. Student departure may be conceptualized to have three interactional dimensions. The first is *adjustment*, or the process by which students become acclimated to the social and academic environment of the college or university. Students who come to campus underprepared academically will find adjustment particularly stressful, as will those whose prior socialization and life experiences differ markedly from those of other students. Both groups experience an elevated risk of leaving school. The final stage of adjustment is integration, wherein a student comes to feel a sense of belonging at the institution.

A second interactional source of leaving school is *congruence,* which is the degree of fit between the student's preferences and interests and those of the institution. As before, incongruence can occur in either the social or the academic realm. Academically, it occurs whenever students feel a mismatch between their level of preparation and the level at which courses are taught (too easy or too hard), or when they have ideological differences with the material being presented. Social incongruence occurs whenever students perceive that their own beliefs, values, and behaviors are at odds with those of other students. *Isolation* is the final interactional source of student departure. Students who do not make close personal connections with faculty or students on campus are naturally less attached to the institution and consequently give up less when leaving. Isolated students have few social ties binding them to the institution and are thus more likely to leave. Many students remain in school despite a lack of interest or disillusionment with their studies because that is where their friends are (Johnson, Crosnoe, and Elder 2001).

Critical Theory, Segregation, and School Effects

Critical theory accounts for differential educational outcomes in terms of specific institutional arrangements that reproduce inequality. Bowles and Gintis (1976), for example, argue that schools are not neutral sites designed to provide all students with equal educational resources. Rather, they are institutions created by the dominant social classes to inculcate a curriculum corresponding to the class position of the students, thus reproducing socioeconomic inequality over time. To put it crudely, parents of upper-class children have no interest in devoting resources to the education of lower-class children, so that poor and working-class students end up going to lousy schools to receive a lousy education to prepare them for the lousy jobs they will hold as adults (see also Willis 1977). This basic line of reasoning has been extended beyond social class by postmodernist theorists, who argue that academic institutions are also structured along the lines of race and ethnicity to generate inequality (Davies 1995).

It has long been known that the quantity and quality of educational resources available to students are structured not only by socioeconomic status but by school segregation. An abundant literature going back to Coleman (1966) documents the ongoing reality of racial and ethnic segregation in American schools (Orfield 1993), and studies continue to show a particularly high degree of segregation and isolation for blacks and Latinos (Orfield and Eaton 1996). Racially segregated schools are, on average, of significantly lower quality on a variety of academic and nonacademic dimensions (Kozol 1991; Orfield 1993).

Thus, one potential explanation for the underperformance of blacks and Latinos in U.S. colleges and universities is that the schools they attend as children and teenagers prepare them less well for collegiate work by providing lower-quality education, or that their schools actively harm their capacity for learning by exposing them to deleterious and maladaptive environments characterized by violence, social disorder, and concentrations of poverty. Although research has found that school characteristics have rather modest effects on educational outcomes once socioeconomic status and selection effects are controlled (Coleman 1966; Burtless 1996), no study has yet examined the degree to which the social and academic environment experienced in high school influences academic achievement in college.

Differences in College Preparation

Whatever the causes of minority underperformance in college—capital deficiency, oppositional culture, stereotype vulnerability, peer influence, institutional attachment, or school segregation—it is clear that measurable differences in academic preparation exist among whites, blacks, Asians, and Latinos by the time they graduate from high school. One of the most widely used indicators of college preparation, for all its flaws, is the SAT I: Reasoning Test, or SAT. As can be seen in figures 1.2 and 1.3, average verbal and math SAT scores have improved for all racial and ethnic groups in the past twenty years. Among blacks, math scores rose by 34 points and verbal scores by 24 points between 1976 and 1995, the largest increases observed for any group. Despite their improvement, however, African Americans still lag well behind whites and Asians. Whites generally earn the highest average verbal scores (448 in 1995), whereas Asians earn the highest average math scores (538 in 1995). Latinos fall in-between blacks and Asians on verbal scores, and between blacks and whites on math scores.

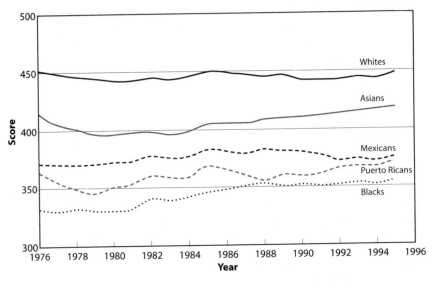

Figure 1.2. Average verbal score on SAT, 1976–1996

The use of SAT scores to indicate the degree of preparation for higher education has come under considerable criticism over the years. Not only are they said to be culturally biased (Taylor 1980), but research has consistently shown them to be imperfect and inconsistent as predictors of college performance (Bowen and Bok 1998; Crouse and Trusheim 1988; Kane 1998; Vars and Bowen 1998). For example, the relationship between SAT scores and academic performance is generally weaker for blacks, Latinos, and women than for whites, Asians, and men. African Americans, in particular, earn lower grades in college than one would predict given their SAT scores, and the *degree* of underperformance increases as SAT scores rise (Nettles 1991; Bowen and Bok 1998). Whatever is happening to undermine the academic performance of African Americans, it cannot be attributed to differences in SAT scores alone.

A second widely used indicator of college preparation is the number of Advanced Placement (AP) credits earned in high school. AP courses have increased in both prevalence and variety over the past decade. Between 1984 and 1997, for example, the number of students taking an AP examination increased nearly threefold, going from 5% to 13% among all twelfth graders (Condition of Education 2000).

There are strong incentives for college-bound students to take AP courses. First, those who take them may sit for a special exam, which if passed allows the student to receive college credit. AP scores are scaled

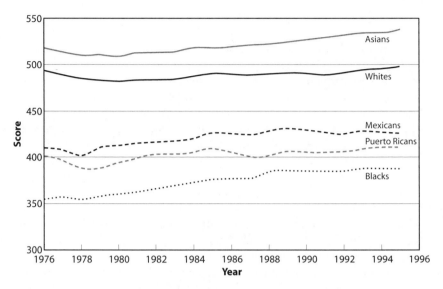

Figure 1.3. Average mathematics score on SAT, 1976–1996

from 1 to 5, with 5 being the highest possible score. Most colleges and universities accept a score of 3 or above and give one academic credit in the relevant subject.

A second reason for the growing popularity of AP courses is that they signal a rigorous curriculum of study (Condition of Education 2000). As with SAT scores, there are significant intergroup differences in AP exam-taking. In 1984, for example, 5% of white eleventh and twelfth graders took at least one AP exam, compared to just under 1% of African Americans and 2% of Latinos. Although the percentage had risen for all groups by 1997, blacks and Latinos continued to lag far behind Asians and whites (Condition of Education 2000).

In addition to SAT scores and AP credits, sound college preparation is also indicated by having taken advanced science and mathematics courses in high school. A study of high school transcripts conducted by the National Center for Education Statistics (1995) revealed a growing exposure to these subjects among high school graduates. As before, however, there were marked racial and ethnic differences. Whereas two-thirds of Asians in 1992 had taken advanced algebra, biology, and/or chemistry, only 44% of blacks and 51% of Latinos had taken advanced algebra, and 42% of blacks and 45% of Latinos had taken biology and chemistry. By way of comparison, 62% of whites had taken advanced algebra, and 56% had taken biology and chemistry.

Assembling the Puzzle

That African Americans and Latinos are, on average, less well prepared for college than whites and Asians, and that they achieve at lower rates once they enter higher education, are not controversial claims. What is contentious and unresolved is the explanation for these intergroup differences. According to the theory of capital deficiency, blacks and Latinos have less access to various forms of capital—financial, human, social, and cultural—than whites and Asians (no doubt reflecting the legacy of discrimination and segregation), and these deficiencies translate directly into lower levels of academic preparation and poorer performance in college. According to the theory of oppositional culture, minorities such as blacks and Puerto Ricans devalue the institutions and products of the oppressor society, including its schools and education. As a result, academic achievement is perceived as "acting white" and is negatively sanctioned. The theory of stereotype vulnerability argues that the stereotype of black intellectual inferiority renders black and Latino students fearful of fulfilling the myth, causing psychological distress that they lower by disidentifying with education. Peer group theory holds that powerful adolescent subcultures emerge to challenge adult authority systems and that students who are susceptible to peer pressures rebel by underperforming academically. Attachment theory argues that school leaving stems from a lack of social and academic integration. Finally, a variety of critical theories argue that American society is structured such that certain minority groups are allocated by discriminatory processes to schools that offer inferior educational resources, leaving them ill-equipped to cope with the demands of higher education.

As already stated, these explanations are not mutually exclusive, and our task is to sort through them empirically to see which ones are most important in determining academic success or failure, here defined as performance during the first semester in college. In doing so, we focus on particular social arenas at different phases of life—childhood, early adolescence, and the late teenage years. Chapter 3 considers the family origins of NLSF respondents, exploring differences between whites, blacks, Asians, and Latinos with respect to household structure, family composition, home resources, and parental attitudes and behaviors. Chapter 4 broadens the purview to examine the nature of the neighborhoods in which the respondents came of age, considering the extent of racial and ethnic segregation as well as degree of exposure to various forms of social disorder and violence. Chapter 5 moves on to consider the characteristics of schools attended by students at different ages, focusing on the educational resources offered as well as on social and demographic composition. Chapter 6 takes an in-depth look at the social world of the teenager, exploring the values, perceptions, characteristics, and behaviors of high school peers. Finally, in chapter 7 we describe the values and aspirations of the students themselves as they are about to embark on a new journey through higher education and, ultimately, life.

Having documented in some detail the differing social, economic, and cultural backgrounds of white, black, Latino, and Asian freshmen, in chapter 8 we begin to sort out the independent contributions made by different background factors in determining preparation for college along a variety of dimensions: academic, financial, social, and psychological. In chapter 9 we measure how differences with respect to both background and preparation come together to determine a student's academic success in the first semester of college. A final chapter summarizes what we have learned from our close examination of the initial wave of the NLSF and sets the stage for analyzing successive follow-up surveys. Before we enter into the complexities of analysis, however, in the next chapter we describe the sample of students we compiled and the nature of the information we gathered from them.

CHAPTER 2

SAMPLE AND METHODOLOGY

THE NATIONAL longitudinal survey of Freshmen was developed to provide comprehensive data to test different theoretical explanations for minority underachievement in higher education. Rather than prejudging the validity of any single point of view, we sought to develop a broad database capable of testing each conceptual model, assessing its explanatory power, and specifying the circumstances under which it might apply. Specifically, the NLSF sought to measure the academic and social progress of college students at regular intervals to capture emergent psychological processes hypothesized by investigators such as Steele and Ogbu, while measuring the degree of social integration and intellectual engagement suggested by Tinto, and to control for pre-existing background differences with respect to social, economic, and demographic characteristics.

To realize this vision, we proposed to survey equal-sized samples of white, black, Asian, and Latino freshmen entering selective colleges and universities. The baseline survey would consist of face-to-face interviews that compiled detailed information about the neighborhood, family, and educational environments students experienced *before* entering college. The survey would also assess their attitudes, aspirations, and motivations *at the time of entry.* We proposed to follow the baseline survey with a shorter telephone survey conducted during the spring term to gather information from the same students about their social, psychological, and academic experiences on campus.

We planned to follow these first-year surveys with additional telephone interviews conducted during the spring term of each of the subsequent three years, using a survey instrument based on the one used in the first year. By combining retrospective data captured in the baseline survey with prospective information compiled in years one through four, we sought to create a longitudinal database stretching from childhood through college graduation. Such a design would provide a basis for linking precollege experiences to behaviors and psychological states emerging in the course of higher education, and for sorting out the direction of causality between determinants and outcomes. Those dropping out of college or transferring to another institution would be followed, interviewed, and retained in the survey to avoid building selection biases into the sample.

The Pilot Survey

Obviously a longitudinal survey of this nature would be quite expensive to administer. We therefore sought to pretest questionnaires and survey procedures before launching a large-scale, nationwide survey. During the academic year 1997–98, we worked to develop drafts of interview schedules that were informed by a review of the research literature and by in-depth interviews undertaken with students, faculty, and administrators at the University of Pennsylvania. These efforts yielded two provisional survey instruments: a baseline questionnaire designed to be administered to freshmen early in the fall term and a follow-up telephone survey to be administered to the same respondents in the spring term.

The pilot survey was administered in the fall of 1998 by Temple University's Institute for Survey Research to freshmen at the University of Pennsylvania. It enabled us to evaluate the validity of questionnaire items and to program the baseline instrument as a Computer Assisted Personal Interview (CAPI) and the follow-up instrument as a Computer Assisted Telephone Interview (CATI). The pilot survey also provided important data to support methodological analyses on the accuracy of self-reports.

We endeavored to interview *all* entering African American and Latino freshmen at Penn, along with comparably sized samples of Asian and white freshmen. In August 1998 we obtained from the Penn Registrar a list of 130 African Americans and 98 Latinos who had enrolled for the fall term, along with samples of 130 whites and 130 Asians. The list we received included the name, social security number, campus address, campus phone number, and campus e-mail address for each student, along with his or her permanent address and telephone number. The investigators initiated the project by sending a letter to all students who had been selected. It explained the goals of the study, solicited their cooperation, and alerted them to the fact that they would soon be approached by ISR personnel. Interviewers from ISR then began to contact students to set up appointments for the face-to-face interviews.

In general, Penn freshmen proved to be very cooperative, giving us an overall completion rate of 74%. African Americans exhibited the highest rate of participation at 82%, and Latinos were the lowest at 65%. Asian and whites students were roughly the same at 72%. Although Latinos displayed the lowest completion rate, this outcome reflected unusual difficulties in locating respondents and scheduling interviews rather than outright refusals. Once contacted, only 7% of Latinos refused outright, compared with 9% for blacks and 10% for Asians. Whites had the highest refusal rate at 15%. Midway through the spring term we began to administer the follow-up telephone survey to those interviewed in the fall.

Once students had agreed to participate in the study, we found that virtually all of them agreed to be interviewed again. Of students interviewed in the fall, 98% were successfully reinterviewed in the spring term.

Results from the Pilot Survey

As part of the pilot survey, students signed release forms granting us permission to access information from their college application and financial aid forms. For those students granting us permission, we linked to administrative records from the university. The matched data were then used to assess the accuracy of self-reported data on a variety of issues. In the spring telephone survey, for example, we asked students about grades earned in the fall semester, and by linking these data with official grade reports from the Registrar, we were able to measure the accuracy of the self-reports. This analysis is shown in table 2.1.

Each column of the table represents the grade that respondents reported earning during the fall semester, and each row represents the grade recorded by the Registrar. The diagonal percentages (highlighted in boldface) give the percentage of cases where the self-report agreed exactly with the grade recorded by the Registrar. The off-diagonal percentages indicate disagreements, with the size of the discrepancy increasing as one moves away from the diagonal cells. Those above the diagonal represent grades that were overreported by respondents; those below, grades that were underreported. For example, freshmen at Penn reported having earned 270 A's (a perfect 4.0) in the fall term. Of these *reported* A's, roughly 87% were "true" A's, and 13% were overreports (the actual grade was lower). Mostly the errors were small and indicate small rounding upward (of the 13% of grades that were overreported, 9% simply reported an A− as an A).

In general, the diagonals suggest a high degree of reliability in self-reporting. The diagonal percentages are very high at the two extremes of the distribution (100% at F and 87% at A, reflecting floor and ceiling effects, respectively); they decline as we move toward the center. The least consistency lies in the C-to-D range (1.0–2.3), with diagonal percentages ranging from 50% to 76%. Overall, there was perfect agreement between self-reports and recorded grades in 82.8% of cases, and the correlation coefficient between reported and recorded grades was .894. Thus, if we wish to study the effects of respondent characteristics on grades relying only on self-reports, parameter estimates would be attenuated somewhat by measuring error, but not seriously. The self-reports thus appear to be good proxies for actual grades, and if one rounds to the closest letter grade (A−'s become A's, B−, and B+'s become B's, etc.), most of the inconsistencies disappear and the correlation rises to .98.

TABLE 2.1

Comparison between self-reported fall grades and grades actually earned and recorded by university registrar

Actual Fall Grade	Self-Reported Fall Grade									
	0.0	1.0	1.3	2.0	2.3	2.6	3.0	3.3	3.6	4.0
0.0	**100.0**	7.7		1.0				0.6		
1.0.		**76.9**	33.3	2.9			1.0	0.6		0.4
1.3		7.7	**50.0**	1.0		2.3	0.5	1.2		
2.0				**72.6**	13.5	6.9	1.5	0.6		
2.3				3.9	**73.1**	9.2	1.5	1.7		1.1
2.6				12.8	5.8	**74.7**	9.8	1.7	0.7	0.7
3.0		7.7	16.7	4.9	3.9	3.5	**81.4**	11.0	0.6	1.5
3.3				1.0	3.9	2.3	3.4	**81.5**	2.0	0.7
3.6							0.6	0.6	**90.9**	8.9
4.0						1.1	0.4	0.6	5.6	**86.7**
Number	5	13	6	102	52	87	204	173	153	270

Source: Penn Pilot Survey, 1998

To test for the existence of intergroup differences in the accuracy of grade reporting, we regressed the recorded grades on self-reported grades and included a set of dummy variables indicating race/ethnicity. The results are shown in table 2.2. If there were no errors at all in the self-reports and no differences between groups, we would achieve a straight-line formula with a slope equal to 1.0 and an intercept of 0. The intercept of 0.25 indicates that the basic tendency for students is to overreport their grades (not surprisingly). Since white freshmen are the reference group, the value of .25 means that they tend to overreport by an average of a quarter of a point. The coefficient for Latinos is close to zero and nonsignificant, meaning that they overreport to the same extent as whites. The coefficients for African Americans and Asians are both significantly negative, however, indicating that their tendency to overreport grades is less than that of whites. Blacks overreport least, followed by Asians.

In general, the average error is small no matter which group one considers—less than a quarter of a grade-point—and the group-specific effects are even smaller. In theory, if we can assume that the pattern of grade misreporting at Penn prevails at other selective schools throughout the country, then we are on firm ground in using the equation estimates shown in table 2.2 to adjust self-reports to yield intergroup consistency. But given the size of the discrepancies, the net adjustment would probably be small in any event, and the self-reported grades would certainly be measured more reliably than many other variables in the survey (school and neighborhood racial composition, attitudes, parents' income, etc.).

The pilot survey also asked students to estimate the grades they would *eventually* earn in their spring-term courses. Since the follow-up interviews may have occurred before midterms or class assignments had been

TABLE 2.2
Estimated OLS regression of actual on self-reported grades
controlling for race and ethnicity

Variable	Regression Coefficient	Standard Error	P-Value
Self-Reported Grade	0.924	0.015	0.001
Race/Ethnicity			
White	–	–	–
Black	−0.127	0.028	0.001
Asian	−0.079	0.028	0.001
Latino	−0.008	0.031	0.820
Intercept	0.250	0.052	0.001
R^2	0.802		

Source: Penn Pilot Survey, 1998

handed in, these estimates may have been based on nothing more than an educated guess. The correspondence between these estimates and the recorded grades is shown in table 2.3. Not surprisingly, they are considerably less accurate than those reported in table 2.1.

The average correspondence between the reported and recorded grades is only 29%, and the maximum is only 46%. More than half of the students who estimated that they would get an A in a course actually earned something lower, and in this case the discrepancies do not cluster tightly around the diagonal. Of those estimating an A, only 64% got an A or an A−. The discrepancies naturally worsen as one moves away from the two extremes of the grade distribution. Of the 269 people who expected to earn a B in a course, only 24% actually did so (11% earned a B+ and 26% earned a B−), meaning that a total of only 61% came within one increment of the grade they would eventually earn.

In general, then, students estimating their spring-term grades were not able to do so with much accuracy. The correlation between actual and recorded grades was just .575, suggesting that any attempt to use these self-reports in multivariate estimation would yield a considerable attenuation of the relationship through unreliability. Based on the results of the pilot survey, therefore, we appear to be on solid ground in using the reports of fall-term grades as outcome measures to study the determinants of academic success, but on methodologically shaky terrain in using the spring-term estimates.

The pilot survey also offered us a means of calibrating the accuracy of self-reports about socioeconomic background by linking to records provided by Penn's Office of Student Financial Assistance. Unlike the records of the University Registrar, which cover all students enrolled at Penn, records from the Office of Student Financial Assistance pertain only to those students who applied for financial aid. Of the 281 students who applied for financial assistance (about 78% of the sample), roughly half (141) gave us permission to access the information in their financial aid application, which reports parental income and home value, two items we specifically asked about in the pilot survey.

Table 2.4 compares average parental incomes calculated from student self-reports with averages computed using data from the financial aid form (see top panel). On average, the rate of error was only 4.7% and the correlation between the two series was .70. Nonetheless, there are sizable differences across groups. Asians seem to have the least accurate perception of how much their parents made, overestimating family income by an average of 14% and displaying a correlation of only .65 between self-reported income and that reported on the financial aid application. Whites were also relatively inaccurate, overstating their parents' income by 8% and displaying a correlation of only .47 with the figures reported on the

TABLE 2.3

Comparison between self-reported estimate of spring grades and grades actually earned and recorded by university registrar

Actual Spring Grade	Self-Reported Estimate of Spring Grade									
	0.0	1.0	1.3	2.0	2.3	2.6	3.0	3.3	3.6	4.0
0.0		100.0		7.6		6.0	2.2	1.2	0.5	0.9
1.0.				13.2	9.1	7.7	2.2	1.2		0.3
1.3				7.6		5.8	0.4		0.5	0.3
2.0				35.9	36.4	28.9	15.2	6.7	2.7	2.5
2.3				13.2	45.5	15.4	16.7	3.7	3.8	4.1
2.6				20.8	9.1	13.5	21.6	17.1	7.8	5.4
3.0				1.9		11.5	20.8	26.2	15.1	11.0
3.3						7.7	9.3	23.8	19.5	12.0
3.6						3.9	7.1	11.0	24.9	18.6
4.0							4.5	9.2	5.6	44.8
Number	0	1	0	53	11	52	269	164	185	317

Source: Penn Pilot Survey, 1998

TABLE 2.4
Comparison between financial data reported on financial aid application
and that self-reported by respondents

Variable	Reported on Aid Form	Self-Report	Error	Correlation	N
Parents' Income	$65,950	$69,071	4.7%	0.70	141
Whites	$67,823	$73,516	8.0%	0.47	31
Asians	$70,885	$80,577	13.7%	0.65	13
Latinos	$61,088	$64,250	5.2%	0.78	34
Blacks	$66,635	$67,111	0.7%	0.76	63
Parents' Home Value	$172,968	$196,749	13.8%	0.78	100
Whites	$176,243	$244,870	38.9%	0.79	23
Asians	$197,517	$236,667	19.8%	0.80	12
Latinos	$179,442	$206,596	15.1%	0.86	25
Blacks	$159,675	$150,950	−5.5%	0.72	45

Source: Penn Pilot Survey, 1998

application form. Latinos and blacks were generally more accurate in estimating their parent's income, possibly because there was less of it. Latinos display an average error rate of 5% and achieve a correlation of .78, while for blacks the error is only .7% and the correlation is .76.

Although the correlation between self-reported home values and those estimated on the application form are much higher and considerably more uniform, the tendency to overestimate is even more marked than for income (see bottom panel of table 2.4). On average, Penn freshmen overestimated the value of their parents house by nearly 14%. As before, black self-reports were more accurate than those of other groups, followed by Latinos, then Asians and whites.

In general, then, we see that students tend to inflate their parents' incomes and home values and that the tendency to do so is least for blacks and Latinos and greatest whites and Asians. Although correlations between the figures reported on application forms and those reported by respondents are fairly strong, coefficients of .70 for income and .78 for home value indicate considerable unreliability of measurement. In general, unreliability undermines the strength of observed relationships, so to the extent we observe that parental income affects student outcomes, our data will understate the degree of that relationship.

The National Sample

Given the high response rates and encouraging results achieved from the Penn pilot survey, we made a few modifications to the survey instruments and prepared to administer them to a nationwide sample of college fresh-men in the fall of 1999. The institutions we chose to sample mirror those examined by Bowen and Bok (1998) in their *College and Beyond Survey*. Our principal modification was the addition of the University of Califor-nia at Berkeley, which is not only a large and selective institution (cur-rently rated as number one among public universities by *U.S. News and World Report*), but also a school that recently abandoned its historical commitment to affirmative action (as a result of Proposition 209, which was approved by California's voters in 1995).

Drawing our sample from among the institutions already studied by Bowen and Bok offered us several advantages. First, Bowen and Bok are past university presidents (of Princeton and Harvard, respectively), and they had already established collaborative relationships with the presi-dents of these institutions, giving us an initial foot in the door. Second, as the current president of the Mellon Foundation (a primary funder of the NLSF), Bowen was in a position to approach college presidents person-ally to secure their approval and support. An overture from the president of a large foundation with a history of funding in higher education natu-rally would be received more favorably than one emanating from the pro-ject investigators alone. Finally, the collection of data from students in in-stitutions whose graduates had already been surveyed by Bowen and Bok would open up fruitful possibilities for later comparative analysis.

The thirty-five schools that we asked to participate are listed in table 2.5. The sample was stratified by the relative size of the black student body. In-stitutions with relatively large black student populations (1,000+) were assigned a target sample size of 280 respondents (70 in each of four racial/ ethnic groups); those with black student populations of 500–1,000 got a target size of 200 interviews (50 in each group); those with 100–500 black students had a target size of 80 respondents (20 in each group); and those with fewer than 100 black students were assigned a quota of 40 in-terviews (10 in each group). The historically black schools were given a target of 70 interviews per institution.

In July 1999 each college or university president received a letter from William Bowen explaining the nature and purpose of the NLSF and so-liciting support for our interviewing on campus. Included in the mailing was a letter from the investigators reiterating Bowen's request and ex-plaining that in order to participate, the institutions would need to pro-vide, in August of that year, a list of the prospective members of the fresh-man class with each person's name, race, Hispanic origin, date of birth, permanent address, phone number, campus address, campus phone num-ber, and e-mail address, if available.

In most cases our entreaties were favorably received. Only five presi-dents declined outright to let their institutions participate in the study

(Duke, Vanderbilt, Wellesley, Hamilton, and Xavier). A major disappointment, however, was the response received from four historically black institutions we had targeted for study. Although only Xavier declined to participate outright, we were able to secure a sample of freshmen in only one historically black institution. Despite the fact that the presidents of both Morehouse and Spelman agreed on behalf of their institutions to participate, the Registrar's Office at both colleges could not provide a list of freshmen from which we could draw a sample. This left only Howard University to represent historically black institutions.

The final institutional participation rate was 80%. The loss of seven institutions out of thirty-five cut our expected sample size from a planned 4,160 to only 3,550 students. To make up for the lost cases we increased the number of interviews conducted at other institutions. In all, we approached 4,573 respondents across twenty-eight institutions. Of these, 3,924 completed the survey, for an overall response rate of 86%, which by the standards of survey research is very high, particularly for a long (more than two hours) face-to-face interview that for all intents and purposes was unpaid (respondents received a token payment of $15 for participating). The final sample included 959 Asians, 998 whites, 1,051 African Americans, and 916 Latinos. To be eligible for inclusion in the sample, a respondent had to be enrolled at the institution in question as a first-time freshman and be a U.S. citizen or resident alien. Foreign and returning students were excluded from the sample.

By any criteria, the twenty-eight institutions constitute an elite sample. To indicate institutional quality, table 2.6 presents median SAT scores for entering freshmen along with the percentage who were in the top decile of their high school class, the institutional acceptance rate, and the annual alumni giving rate. Across the twenty-eight institutions, the median combined SAT score of freshmen was 1243, and 71% were in the top 10% of their graduating class. The median SAT ranged from a low of 1105 at Howard to a high of 1465 at Yale. The percentage at the top of their graduating class ranged from 18% at Howard to 98% at Berkeley. The most selective school in the sample was Princeton, with an 11% acceptance rate, and the least selective was Miami University of Ohio, with an acceptance rate of 79%. The average acceptance rate was 40%, indicating the generally high degree of selectivity in the institutions under study. For the most part, these schools were strongly supported by their alumni. The average rate of participation in annual giving was 37%, ranging from 9% among Howard alumni to 66% among Princetonians.

As with the pilot survey, we subcontracted with Temple University's Institute for Survey Research to undertake the actual interviewing. They employed the CAPI protocols developed earlier. Once we received approval for the study from a college or university president, we contacted institu-

TABLE 2.5

Sampling plan for National Longitudinal Survey of Freshmen in selective colleges and universities

Categories and Schools	Target Sample	Final Sample	White	Asian	Latino	Black
Historically Black Colleges						
Howard University, Washington, D.C.	70	60	0	0	0	60
Morehouse College, Atlanta, Ga.	70	0	Declined to participate			
Spelman College, Atlanta, Ga.	70	0	Declined to participate			
Xavier University, New Orleans, La.	70	0	Declined to participate			
Schools with 1,000+ Black Students						
University of Michigan, Ann Arbor, Mich.	280	362	78	86	102	96
University of North Carolina, Chapel Hill, N.C.	280	268	72	78	32	86
University of California, Berkeley, Ca.	280	304	80	72	82	70
Schools with 500–1,000 Black Students						
Columbia University, New York, N.Y.	200	237	54	54	79	59
Duke University, Durham, N.C.	200	0	Declined to participate			
Emory University, Atlanta, Ga.	200	197	63	53	29	52
Miami University, Oxford, Ohio	200	204	55	47	51	51
Northwestern University, Evanston, Ill.	200	224	54	62	51	57
Penn State University, Univ. Park, Pa.	200	261	66	69	65	61
Stanford University, Palo Alto, Ca.	200	216	50	50	59	57
Tulane University, New Orleans, La.	200	221	61	49	50	61
University of Pennsylvania, Philadelphia, Pa.	200	220	65	52	52	51

Schools with 100–500 Black Students

Georgetown University, Washington, D.C.	80	89	23	21	22	23
Oberlin College, Oberlin, Ohio	80	79	20	20	19	20
Princeton University, Princeton, N.J.	80	86	26	20	20	20
Rice University, Houston, Tex.	80	97	25	20	26	26
Tufts University, Sommerville, Mass.	80	83	20	20	20	23
University of Notre Dame, South Bend, In.	80	91	20	24	20	27
Vanderbilt University, Nashville, Tenn.	80	0	Declined to participate			
Washington University, St. Louis, Mo.	80	90	29	20	20	21
Wellesley College, Wellesley, Mass.	80	0	Declined to participate			
Wesleyan University, Middletown, Conn.	80	94	22	26	25	21
Williams College, Williamstown, Mass.	80	91	22	25	24	20
Yale University, New Haven, Conn.	80	89	23	26	20	20

Schools with <100 Black Students

Barnard College, New York, N.Y.	40	57	13	13	14	17
Bryn Mawr College, Bryn Mawr, Pa.	40	37	9	11	6	11
Denison University, Granville, Ohio	40	39	11	10	8	10
Hamilton College, Clinton, N.Y.	40	0	Declined to participate			
Kenyon College, Gambier, Ohio	40	41	11	11	9	10
Smith College, Northampton, Mass.	40	41	10	10	11	10
Swarthmore College, Swarthmore, Pa.	40	47	16	10	10	11
Total	4,160	3,924	998	959	916	1,051

TABLE 2.6

Indicators of institutional quality for colleges and universities included in the
National Longitudinal Survey of Freshmen

Categories and Schools	Median SAT	% Freshmen in Top 10% of Class	Acceptance Rate	Alumni Giving Rate
Historically Black Colleges				
Howard University	1105	18	56	9
Schools with 1,000+ Black Students				
University of Michigan, Ann Arbor	–	63	64	13
University of North Carolina, Chapel Hill	1250	68	39	31
University of California, Berkeley	1315	98	27	18
Schools with 500–1,000 Black Students				
Columbia University	1400	87	14	32
Emory University	1355	90	42	39
Miami University	–	32	79	21
Northwestern University	1385	83	32	29
Penn State University, University Park	1190	42	49	21
Stanford University	1455	88	15	37
Tulane University	1292	52	78	21
University of Pennsylvania	1400	91	26	40

Schools with 100–500 Black Students				
Georgetown University	1350	78	23	30
Oberlin College	1325	59	50	43
Princeton University	1450	92	11	66
Rice University	1415	86	27	39
Tufts University	1340	70	32	30
University of Notre Dame	1345	83	35	48
Washington University	1355	79	34	37
Wesleyan University	1365	70	29	49
Williams College	1410	84	23	60
Yale University	1465	95	16	49
Schools with <100 Black Students				
Barnard College	1315	73	37	40
Bryn Mawr College	1300	61	59	52
Denison University	1215	52	69	43
Kenyon College	1295	50	68	47
Smith College	1280	52	56	47
Swarthmore College	1418	82	22	56
Average	1243	71	40	37

Source: U.S. News and World Report, September 1, 2000

tional administrators to obtain a list of freshmen to use as a sampling frame. We then randomly selected students by race and ethnicity and forwarded the names to ISR for assignment to interviewers.

We had expected operations to proceed smoothly once college presidents had endorsed the project, but instead of getting the lists in August or September, in most cases the process dragged out for months (the last list arrived in February!). Institutions varied greatly in their procedures for granting access to student data. A few institutions (mostly small liberal arts colleges) sent us the list of incoming freshmen without hesitation; others required additional reviews at their own institutions (by lawyers, deans, research directors, etc.). And even though all instruments, consent forms, introductory letters, and human subjects protocols had been reviewed and approved by the University of Pennsylvania's IRB, many institutions required us to submit our materials to their own human subjects committees for independent evaluation. In some cases we were required to modify our consent forms and introductory letters and to provide additional information about data management and storage procedures.

Once we began to communicate directly with registrars and deans about creating the sampling frame, other problems arose. Although most institutions followed our specifications and provided the contact information we requested, some forwarded post office boxes instead of addresses. Others omitted telephone numbers, dates of birth, or gender, which were used to verify the subject's identity. Whereas most schools provided adequate numbers of freshmen to complete the target number of interviews in each ethnic category, a few did not, requiring us to make efforts to compensate for shortfalls by exceeding the target in schools supplying longer lists of potential respondents.

A final barrier we faced was learning about and complying with each institution's rules governing the behavior of interviewers on campus. Each institution had its own procedures for gaining access to student dorms, acquiring telephone numbers, and complying with campus security regulations. In most cases, we could not know these policies in advance, and they only became apparent once personal contact with students was attempted. In several cases, interviewing had to be suspended until the principal investigator and/or survey director could speak to school administrators to learn about the institution's requirements and institute field procedures to ensure compliance.

To prepare for data collection, ISR mailed an introductory letter to prospective respondents signed by the project investigators that explained the purposes of the study and asked for their cooperation. The letter included a Verification and Appointment Form that students were requested to fill out and send back in a prepaid envelope. This form asked students to indicate the most convenient time for an interviewer to call and to verify or record their contact information (phone number, address, e-mail). During the baseline interview, respondents were asked to provide additional tracking data to ensure their inclusion in the annual follow-up interviews. Specifically, we requested that they provide the names of two individuals who would be likely to know the student's location if he or she were to move. Participants were encouraged to provide the names, address, and telephone numbers of close relatives or long-time friends rather than other students.

The delays and barriers encountered in gaining access to students created numerous administrative problems for ISR. Delays often meant that trained interviewers were left waiting with nothing to do, and expensive laptop computers (used for CAPI) sat idle in the field. Considering the many problems and difficulties we encountered while working with twenty-eight different schools and twenty-eight institutional environments located in far-flung corners of the country, our response rate of 86% is very high indeed. The rate of response did vary, however, between groups. African Americans generally evinced the highest response rate (89%) and whites the lowest (83%); Latinos and Asians were in-between, roughly at the mean of 86% (see table 2.7). The response rate for females (86.3%) was slightly above that for males (85.1%).

During the spring of 2000, we sought to reinterview all respondents captured in the baseline survey to learn about their experiences since entering college. Rather than a lengthy face-to-face interview, however, the follow-up survey was conducted by telephone and was considerably shorter. Ultimately, 95% of the original baseline sample was reinterviewed. As table 2.8 indicates, the follow-up rate again varied from group to group, although not as markedly as in the baseline. Latinos and whites were nearly identical at 96% and 95.9%, respectively, whereas blacks displayed a follow-up rate of 94.3% and Asians had a rate of 93.7%. Thus, the follow-up rate was not only remarkably high; it was also relatively consistent from group to group.

TABLE 2.7
Refusal and completion rates for fall 1999 baseline of
National Longitudinal Survey of Freshmen

	Total	White	Asian	Latino	Black
Completed Interview	85.8%	83.0%	85.8%	85.5%	88.9%
Refused	14.2	17.0	14.2	14.5	11.1
Number Selected	4,573	1,202	1,118	1,071	1,182

TABLE 2.8
Rates of participation in spring 2000 follow-up survey,
National Longitudinal Survey of Freshmen

	Total	Asian	White	Latino	Black
Completed Follow-Up	95.0%	93.7%	95.9%	94.3%	96.0%
Number in Baseline	3,924	998	959	916	1,051

Questionnaire Content

As already mentioned, the baseline questionnaire underwent extensive pretesting and was programmed for CAPI administration using a laptop computer. A printed form of the final version is presented in appendix A. The baseline survey was designed to gather extensive information about the respondent's life prior to entering college and to measure in some detail his or her initial attitudes, motivations, and perceptions. Our retrospective assessment of prior life experiences focused on three key environments—home, school, and neighborhood—at three important junctures in the life course: at age 6, when respondents were just beginning primary school; at age 13, as they entered adolescence and were in middle school; and during their senior year in high school (age 17 or 18), as they were preparing to leave for college.

At each point in the life cycle, we compiled a household roster to determine the respondent's family and household situation. Respondents listed everyone in their home at the time, giving their age, sex, employment status, and whether or not they were enrolled in school. We then asked detailed questions about parental involvement in the formation of human capital (whether parents checked homework, attended PTA meetings, conferred with teachers, etc.), social capital (the extent of parental contact with friends and control over social activities), and cultural capital (how often parents took respondents to plays, concerts, museums, etc.). We also asked about different parenting styles (how often respondents were rewarded or punished, whether limits were imposed on TV watching, and the extent to which they were assigned household chores).

After reporting on their household situation, respondents were asked to describe the school they attended: whether it was public or private, its approximate racial composition, the kind of extracurricular activities it offered, and the relative incidence of various kinds of social disorder and delinquency (fighting, smoking, drinking, drug taking, tardiness, skipping classes, cutting school, etc.). Respondents also reported what they did during summer vacations (whether they went to sleep-away or day camp, attended summer school, or embarked on a family vacation). Finally, we asked about conditions in the neighborhoods where the respondents lived at ages 5, 13, and 18, where a neighborhood was defined as the three-block radius around their home. In addition to estimating the approximate racial composition, they reported on the incidence of social disorder and violence.

The baseline survey asked a variety of more detailed questions about home, school, and neighborhood conditions during the senior year. Respondents reported on the frequency with which they and their parents read books, newspapers, and magazines; watched TV; and used computers or other educational resources. They reported on the number and variety of amenities in the home, whether or not they had their own room, and the existence and nature of parental curfews. A battery of questions focused on the child-rearing practices employed by parents. To assess the character of schooling, we asked respondents to rate the quality of various academic and extracurricular resources, the amount of time spent in different classes, the difficulty of these courses, and the grades they received. A special module focused on the attitudes, beliefs, and behaviors of each respondent's high school peers, assessing the relative valuation of different personal, social, and educational activities as well as the degree to which each respondent was sensitive to such valuations. We also had respondents estimate the racial and ethnic composition of their friendship networks.

Having reported in some detail on their lives prior to entering college, respondents were then asked to contemplate their current thoughts and feelings. First they rated the importance of the factors they considered in deciding where to attend college. They also described their educational aspirations and estimated the likelihood that they would complete various educational milestones. Next, respondents answered a set of standard questions about their racial and ethnic attitudes: stereotypes, perceptions of social distance, perceptions of discrimination, assessments of the extent to which their fate was tied to the fate of various groups, and their personal racial and ethnic identification. The questions on racial attitudes were followed by standard questions on self-esteem and self-efficacy. The questionnaire concluded by asking about respondents' social, economic, and demographic background. Of all questions posed in the survey, those on racial attitudes gave respondents the most discomfort, a sentiment that was particularly strong among white and Asian respondents.

Given its comprehensive nature, the baseline survey was long and complicated and generally took at least two hours to administer. In contrast, the spring follow-up survey was shorter, more focused, and designed to be administered as a Computer-Assisted Telephone Interview. It asked about respondents' experiences since entering college and only took 30–40 minutes to complete. It began by asking students to describe the courses for which they had registered, the ones they had dropped, and the grades they had received or planned to receive, Then they described their current living arrangements and their work, study, and social habits. One module led respondents through an hour-by-hour accounting of their waking hours on the most recent Tuesday. Another asked them to estimate the total number of hours spent in various activities during the latest Monday-Friday period and then repeated the exercise for the most recent Saturday-Sunday block. Finally, respondents estimated the relative incidence of different behaviors in the classroom and around campus, and whether or not any problems had arisen to interfere with their studies.

The interview then turned to financial issues. Students estimated how much money they needed to finance their first year at college, and to report how much came from various sources (parental and family contributions, grants, fellowships, savings, loans, work). If students had worked, they were asked to report the number of hours per week, the wages received, and the kind of job held. They also reported amounts of money sent to and received from family members, as well as access to credit cards paid by themselves and their parents.

These financial questions were followed by a series of items assessing respondents' attitudes toward different aspects of college life: how well they were doing in courses; how well they felt they had been prepared for college; how hard they found their coursework; their sensitivity to the views of professors and classroom peers; their motivation for academic success. We also sought to assess how important various social and academic outcomes were to their parents and peers. Finally, after ascertaining respondents' perceptions of racial and ethnic prejudice and the nature of intergroup relations on campus, we asked them to estimate the racial composition of their professors, classes, and friendship networks. The follow-up module ended with a series of questions about romantic relationships and dating behavior.

Freshmen at Selective Colleges and Universities

ISR forwarded to us cleaned files containing data from the baseline survey in late August 2000, enabling us to construct a basic demographic and socioeconomic portrait of the cohort of freshmen entering the nation's selective colleges and universities in the fall of 1999. Analyses can be carried out using either weighted or unweighted data. Since different fractions of students were sampled across various groups and schools, the raw, unweighted data are not representative of the entire cohort. The appropriate weight given to each case is the inverse of the sampling fraction. All of the tabulations in this book rely on weighted data, but results are virtually identical when unweighted data are used.

Demographic Background

Table 2.9 considers the demographic characteristics of black, white, Asian, and Latino students interviewed by the NLSF. Women constitute more than half of incoming students in all racial/ethnic groups. The predominance of women reflects circumstances nationally, where women now comprise a majority of students in higher education. This apparent feminization is exacerbated somewhat in the NLSF by the fact that it includes two women's colleges (Barnard and Bryn Mawr) but no all-male schools (which have virtually ceased to exist). Nonetheless, the gender distribution for whites is fairly close to parity (53% female, 47% male).

TABLE 2.9
Indicators of respondents' demographic and racial/ethnic background,
National Longitudinal Survey of Freshmen, 1999

Indicator of Background	Whites	Asians	Latinos	Blacks
Gender				
Male	47.1%	44.5%	45.8%	32.8%
Female	52.9	55.5	54.2	67.2
Ratio of Females to Males	1.12	1.25	1.18	2.05
Racial Origins				
White Non-Latino	96.3	0.2	2.5	0.4
Black Non-Latino	0.1	0.0	0.0	75.4
Black Latino	0.3	0.0	12.9	1.7
White Latino	0.0	0.0	48.9	0.1
Asian	0.79	1.5	0.3	0.4
Mixed Race	1.7	7.4	28.2	17.0
Other	0.7	0.8	6.8	5.0
Immigrant Origins				
Respondent Born Abroad	3.7	32.2	17.3	9.1
Mother Born Abroad	8.4	90.8	45.3	22.1
Father Born Abroad	8.9	89.7	52.3	23.4
Religion				
Catholic	33.1	17.2	70.8	17.3
Protestant	40.1	26.5	13.5	70.7
Jewish	12.2	0.1	5.5	0.5
Muslim	0.3	4.8	0.0	1.7
Hindu	0.1	12.3	0.3	0.1
Buddhist	0.1	10.5	0.1	0.1
Religious Commitment				
Religious (0–10 scale)	5.3	5.3	5.5	6.4
Observant (0–10 scale)	5.3	5.5	5.6	6.3
% Attending Weekly Services	21.0	28.9	24.5	25.9

The most extreme gender imbalance is observed among black freshmen, of whom only one-third were male! For every black male entering the elite segment of U.S. higher education, in other words, there were, on average, two black females (2.05). Assuming this cohort is representative of preceding cohorts, the demography of African Americans in higher education sets serious constraints on racial endogamy in campus dating. Although Wilson's (1987) "marriageable male hypothesis" was developed to explain the decline of marriage among poor, inner-city African Americans, it ironically applies equally well, and perhaps even better, to heterosexual blacks in the most elite stratum of American higher education.

Other minority groups face similar demographic constraints, but they are much less extreme. Among Latino freshmen, 54% were women (yielding a ratio of 1.18 women per man), whereas 56% of Asians were female (for a ratio of 1.25 women per man). If the mating pool were to be confined strictly to campus and to be both monogamous and endogamous, then 51% of black women, 20% of Asian women, and 15% of Latino women would be forced to remain romantically unpaired, compared with just 11% of white women.

In drawing the sample, we used the racial and ethnic classifications adopted by the institutions themselves, which generally follow federal guidelines. On the survey, however, we asked the respondents *to identify themselves* in terms of race, national origin, birthplace, and religion. As the data in table 2.9 reveal, the "black" population of freshmen is far from being homogenous. Indeed, African American freshmen attending elite schools are a rather diverse lot. Roughly a quarter of all black freshmen had a foreign-born parent, and 9% were themselves born abroad. Some 17% reported themselves as being of mixed race, and 2% said they were Latino. Since the rate of black-white intermarriage is currently around 5%, and nationwide only 3% of African Americans are foreign born (Farley 1996), both immigrant and racially mixed origins are substantially overrepresented among black freshmen at elite institutions. In terms of religion, 71% of black freshmen identified themselves as Protestants; 17% said they were Catholic; and 2% were Muslim.

Compared with blacks, whites are far more homogenous in terms of racial identity: 96% identified themselves simply as non-Hispanic whites. Only 4% were born abroad, and just 9% had immigrant parents. Whites were more diverse with respect to religion: 40% were Protestant, 33% were Catholic, and 12% were Jewish. Given that Jews constitute 3–4% of the U.S. population, they, too, are substantially overrepresented in the elite segment of American higher education.

Asians are relatively homogenous in the sense that 92% identified themselves as being purely of some "Asian" race (only 7% reported mixed racial origins). Naturally, this classification masks a great deal of diversity with respect to national origin. Although not shown in the table, 35% of the Asian cohort identified themselves as Chinese, 17% as Indian, 16% as Korean, 6% as Vietnamese, 4% as Filipino, and 2% as Japanese. Around 7% said they were racially mixed, and around 13% reported that they belonged to some "other" Asian origin. Reflecting the importance of immigration to the Asian American population, nine out of ten freshmen reported an immigrant parent, and a third (32%) were themselves born abroad. Reflecting the diversity of national origins, Asian religious affiliations were also quite diverse: 27% reported themselves to be Protestant, 17% Catholic, 12% Hindu, 11% Buddhist, and 5% Muslim.

Latinos are diverse not only with respect to national origins, but also in terms of race, at least using the broad categories of table 2.9. Only 3% reported themselves simply as "white," although nearly half (48.9%) said they were "white Latino," meaning that a majority subscribed to some sort of "white" racial identity. Another 28% said they were of mixed race, and 13% said they were "black Latinos." Not surprisingly, Latinos are predominantly (71%) Catholic, although 14% said they were Protestant, and 6% reported themselves as Jewish.

In terms of national origins, 29% of Latino freshmen were Mexican, 17% were South American, 9% were Puerto Rican, 2% were Cuban, 4% were Central American, and 1% were Dominican. Some 28% said they were of mixed origins, and the remaining 10% were in some "other" category. Since Mexicans constitute more than 60% of all Latinos nationwide, they are severely underrepresented in elite colleges and universities. In contrast, South Americans and Puerto Ricans are overrepresented. This imbalance probably reflects the dissimilarity between the geographic distribution of elite institutions and the geographic distribution of Latinos in the United States. Whereas selective colleges are disproportionately located in the Northeast, where South American and Caribbean Latinos predominate, Mexicans are disproportionately located in the West. Of the twenty-eight elite institutions represented in our sample, only three are west of the Mississippi River (Stanford, Berkeley, and Rice).

Socioeconomic Background

Table 2.10 provides a rough socioeconomic profile of the NLSF cohort. As one might expect, blacks and Latinos tend to come from a substantially less privileged background than whites or Asians. Whereas 84% of the fathers and 77% of the mothers of white freshmen were college graduates, only 60% of the fathers and 54% of the mothers of black freshmen had graduated from a college or university. Thus, a substantial share of black freshmen at elite institutions are first-generation college students, whereas among whites this circumstance is quite rare. Likewise, 80% of

TABLE 2.10
Indicators of respondents' socioeconomic background, National Longitudinal Survey of
Freshmen, 1999

Indicator of SES	Whites	Asians	Latinos	Blacks
Father				
Is College Graduate	83.8%	80.3%	66.3%	59.6%
Has Advanced Degree	54.1	53.6	34.0	29.6
Managerial/Professional Occupation	77.6	71.0	60.6	62.7
Is Currently Working	94.8	93.9	93.9	91.2
Mother				
Is College Graduate	77.4	67.9	51.6	53.9
Has Advanced Degree	36.5	27.5	23.1	25.2
Managerial/Professional Occupation	67.0	57.2	56.1	61.0
Is Currently Working	76.4	76.1	79.2	87.3
Siblings				
Has Siblings 18+ Not HS Grads	2.4	5.2	11.9	10.0
Has Siblings 25+ Not College Grads	28.1	21.5	48.1	52.1
Financial Status				
Household Ever on Welfare	4.4	8.5	12.5	16.7
Applied for Financial Aid	63.1	68.3	81.3	88.1
Parents Own Home	94.7	85.7	85.0	72.2
Household income $100,000+	51.0	42.1	33.5	24.7
Median Income (in $000s)	$88	$63	$63	$43
Value of Home (in $000s)	$308	$352	$241	$196

the fathers and 69% of the mothers of Asian freshmen had graduated
from college, compared with 66% of Latinos' fathers and only 52% of
their mothers.

The contrast in class background becomes sharper when one considers
advanced degrees. Whereas absolute majorities of white and Asian fathers
had some kind of advanced degree (54% of each group), postgraduate education was confined to a distinct minority of fathers among black and
Latino freshmen (30% of the former and 34% of the latter). Among white
freshmen, even a sizable share of mothers held advanced degrees: 37%,
compared with 28% among Asians, 25% among blacks, and 23% among
Latinos.

In sum, whereas the typical white or Asian freshman clearly comes from
a professional or managerial class background, this is not the case for a
sizable share of Latino and African American freshmen. Nearly four-fifths
(78%) of the fathers of white students worked in a managerial/profes-
sional occupation and 71% of Asian fathers did so; the figure was just
63% for black freshmen and 61% for Latino freshmen.

These class differences are reflected in broader economic indicators. Whereas 95% of white freshmen came from a family that owned a home, the figure was only 72% for African Americans (compared with 85% for Latinos and 86% for Asians). In other words, more than a quarter of all black freshmen came from families that had no opportunity to build wealth in the form of home equity, compared with just 6% of whites, 14% of Asians, and 15% of Latinos. Moreover, as Conley (1999), Oliver and Shapiro (1995), and Yinger (1995) have all documented, the ongoing reality of racial residential segregation undermines the ability of black homeowners to build equity through the appreciation of home value. Among freshmen with home-owning parents, whites lived in houses worth roughly $308,000 compared with just $196,000 for blacks. Asian freshmen, in contrast, reported homes worth more than those of whites ($352,000), while the homes owned by the parents of Latino students were valued much less, at $252,000.

As a result of differences in home ownership and value, the vast majority of white and Asian freshmen come from families with a substantial cushion of wealth, whereas many Latino and especially black students lack this benefit. The expected home value for whites (i.e., housing value times ownership rate) was $289,000, more than twice the black figure of $133,000 and 30% greater than the Latino figure of $200,000. Asians, meanwhile, had an expected home value of $352,000.

Not only do black and Latino freshmen have less family wealth to rely upon, they also have substantially lower incomes. Whereas half (51%) of all white freshmen came from a household with an income over $100,000, only 25% of blacks and 34% of Latinos did so (compared with 42% of Asians). Likewise, whereas 17% of African American freshmen and 13% of Latino freshmen came from a family that had been on welfare at some point in the past, the figures for white and Asian freshmen were small: only 4% and 9%, respectively. Accordingly, the vast majority of black and Latino students had applied for financial aid (88% of the former and 81% of the latter), whereas 38% of white freshman and 32% of Asian freshman came from families that were paying the full cost of an elite education. Were it not for financial aid, the vast majority of blacks and Latinos would be unable to attend these selective schools.

The foregoing data imply that a large share of African American and Latino freshmen lack class resources that are routinely available to whites and Asians as they make their way through college and university. Latino and black freshmen can thus be expected to be more vulnerable than their white or Asian counterparts to exogenous economic shocks and idiosyncratic circumstances that inevitably arise in the course of life. Most minority families lack the cushions of wealth and income—not to mention the buffers of confidence and self-assurance accrued through generations of wealth and income—typical of other students enrolled at elite institutions of higher education.

Implications of Compositional Differences

The socioeconomic composition of freshmen in the nation's elite schools carries some rather troubling implications about the dynamics of interaction along racial and class lines. For many Asian and white freshmen, who come from a relatively homogenous and privileged background, it means that the first and perhaps only people of lower-class origins they will interact with will be black or Latino. The relative number of whites and Asians of low socioeconomic status are simply too small in number to constitute a cohesive group or symbolic presence on campus. As a result, some of what whites and Asians conclude are "black" traits are likely to be markers of class rather than race, and, likewise, what black and Latino students conclude is "white" is actually a culture of intense class privilege.

The socioeconomic composition of black and Latino freshmen also sets up the possibility of significant intragroup tensions along class lines. Whereas whites and Asians interacting among themselves can take for granted certain commonalities of lifestyle, background, values, and culture in interacting with other white and Asian students, black and Latino students cannot take common class standing for granted at all. Rather it is likely that many intraracial interactions will necessarily cut across class lines, creating the possibility of contentious debates over the "authenticity" and "legitimacy" of class-based black and Latino styles.

Class heterogeneity among blacks and Latinos can also be expected to create confusion in the minds of white and Asian students who come to college with limited interracial experience. After interacting with a minority student of lower-class origins, a naive white student might draw certain conclusions about the values, outlook, and expectations of African Americans, only to gravely offend a black student of high socioeconomic status when these conclusions are applied to the next interaction, leaving the black student thinking that the student is racist and the white student confused.

Perhaps the most distinctive feature of the demography of black freshmen at elite institutions is their sex ratio. Whereas white freshmen were relatively evenly balanced between men and women, there was a rather striking dearth of men among African Americans. The gender split of 33% male and 67% female yielded a ratio of about two females per male. This imbalance implies that a large portion of the future black elite will be female. Moreover, if we assume that college is a primary venue for mate selection, and that other college graduates constitute the primary marriage pool for the college-educated, then without marriage across racial or educational lines, a sizable portion of the future black elite will consist of unmarried women. Although Asians and Latinos also displayed a relative dearth of males, it was not nearly as severe as that observed among blacks: 45% of Asian freshmen and 46% of Latino freshmen were male, yielding ratios of 1.3 and 1.2 women per man, respectively. In contrast to blacks, moreover, both of these groups displayed rather high rates of intermarriage with whites.

Thus, a quick look at the socioeconomic and demographic characteristics of NLSF respondents indicates basic differences between whites and Asians, on the one hand, and blacks and Latinos, on the other. Whether or not these overall differences correspond to broader differences in background and experience will be the subject of the next several chapters, and whether these differences help us to account for differences in college preparation and performance will be the final issue that we address.

CHAPTER 3

FAMILY ORIGINS

A S THEY GROW older, children successively experience an increasing array of ecological contexts—social settings that include widening sets of people, materials, ideas, and experiences. The character of these changing ecological contexts—and how they are experienced—plays an important role in shaping the sort of person a child eventually becomes (Bronfenbrenner 1979). Basic ecological contexts include neighborhood, school, work, and peer settings, but the earliest and most enduring ecological context is the home itself, which includes the people, things, attitudes, and behaviors encountered within a child's household of origin. The home environment is particularly important in the lives of preschool and early school-age children. For those not in daycare, the immediate household is virtually the only ecological context they experience, and even for children who spend a portion of their time in a structured institutional setting, home and family are crucial mediating influences.

Research has shown that experiences accumulated within the home environment exert a powerful influence on children's social, emotional, and intellectual development (Dunn 1983; Hayes, Palmer, and Zaslow 1990; Brooks-Gunn and Chase-Lansdale 1991; Hofferth and Phillips 1991; Guo and Harris 2000). Salient characteristics of the home include the number and age of household members, the nature and quality of their interrelationships, the condition of the dwelling, and the social and material resources it contains. Social relationships within the home may be horizontal (with others of the same age and authority) or vertical (with someone of greater age and maturity), and they may embrace both kin and nonkin (Hartup 1989).

Given that the home environment has such a powerful influence on the cognitive, social, and emotional development of young people, it is important to measure and control for differences in family background in studies of academic attainment, especially if there is a possibility that household circumstances might differ across groups. We have already documented significant socioeconomic differences between African Americans and Latinos, on the one hand, and whites and Asians, on the other. Prior research has found sharp class differentials with respect to the nature and quantity of parental investments in children (Duncan and Brooks-Gunn 1997; Brooks-Gunn, Klebanov, and Duncan 1996; Chase-Lansdale and

Gordon 1996), and equally sharp cross-class differences in styles and practices of child-rearing (Kohn 1969) and parental attitudes (Kluegel and Smith 1986; Lamont 1992).

It is thus important to consider differences in the home environment as possible sources of racial and ethnic variation in later academic performance. The NLSF questionnaire queried respondents in some detail about their home and family situations, focusing on three salient points in the life course: age 6, when respondents were just entering primary school; age 13, when they were embarking upon adolescence and beginning to cope with the greater demands of middle school; and ages 17 or 18, the senior year of high school when respondents were preparing to go off to college.

Household Composition over the Life Course

The stability of social relationships and the consistency of interactions with adults have important effects on the social and emotional development of children. Other things being equal, marital dissolution and family instability undermine children's social, behavioral, and cognitive development, particularly if the disruptions occur early in childhood (McLanahan and Sandefur 1994). Given data available from the NLSF, we can construct a fairly detailed picture of the home and family environment experienced by our respondents at three key phases of the life course.

Family Situation at Age 6

Table 3.1 considers the respondent's family situation at the beginning of primary school, roughly at age 6. The top panel contains information about the household as a whole; the two middle panels present characteristics of fathers and mothers separately; and the bottom panel contains information on co-resident siblings, who constitute potential role models. This table reveals very clear differences between groups with respect to household composition even at this early stage in the life cycle. Whereas 93–94% of whites and Asians were living with two biological (or adoptive) parents at age 6, only 85% of Latinos were doing so, and among blacks the figure was just two-thirds (69%).

Despite the absence of one parent from nearly a third of all black households, the mean household size was identical to that of whites (3.4 persons), meaning that African American homes contained more of other sorts of relations. Among all groups, African Americans were most likely to live with nonnuclear family members (21%). In addition, 13% of black respondents reported that their household contained a part-year occupant, compared with only 8% of whites. Although co-residence with

TABLE 3.1
Composition of household in which respondent lived at age 6

Item	Whites	Asians	Latinos	Blacks
Household				
Mean No. of Members	3.4	3.6	3.6	3.4
% with Two Biological Parents	92.9	94.4	84.9	68.8
% with Stepparent	1.7	1.0	3.1	3.3
% Containing Part-Year Members	8.4	12.3	11.8	12.9
% Containing Nonnuclear Family	5.4	19.6	15.9	21.3
Father				
% Present in Household	93.2	95.5	87.6	71.9
Mean Age	37.3	38.1	37.2	37.2
% Working Full Time	97.0	96.7	95.2	94.3
% Working Part Time	1.4	1.5	2.2	2.0
% in School	5.3	4.6	6.5	5.8
Mother				
% Present in Household	99.1	98.3	99.1	96.8
Mean Age	35.3	35.0	33.8	33.5
% Working Full Time	38.3	44.1	47.2	76.2
% Working Part Time	21.8	16.1	14.7	8.7
% in School	5.0	4.7	9.0	10.2
Siblings				
Mean Age	6.1	6.5	7.1	7.6
% Aged 5–17 in School	99.5	97.8	98.1	98.5
% Aged 18–22 in College	88.4	98.9	74.4	73.1

nonnuclear family members was also quite common among Asians and Latinos, this fact reflects their foreign origins rather than family instability per se, as immigrant families are frequently called upon to accommodate arriving relatives (see Massey, Alarcón, Durand, and González 1987).

As young children, virtually all respondents lived with their mother. Across groups, the percentage never dipped below 97%. Differences in living arrangements stemmed primarily from the absence of the father. Although 93% of white respondents and 96% of Asians lived with their father at age 6, only 88% of Latinos and 72% of blacks did so. Apart from his presence or absence, however, there were few differences with respect to the father's characteristics. Irrespective of race or ethnicity, the typical father was 37 or 38 years old and worked full time when respondents were 6 years old.

Among mothers, however, there were large differences in rates and patterns of labor-force participation. Whereas just 38% of white mothers worked full time, the figure was 44% for Asians and 47% for Latinos, while fully 76% of black respondents reported that their mothers worked full time when they were age 6! Compared with the mothers of other groups, those of white respondents were more likely to be working part time. Whereas 22% of whites reported a mother working part time when they were 6, just 9% of blacks did so. The figures for Latinos and Asians were in the 15–16% range.

Among respondents' siblings who were present at age 6, nearly all those of school age (5–17) were enrolled in school, and virtually all siblings of college age (18–22) were likewise enrolled in a college or university among Asians, as were 88% of college-age white siblings. But among blacks and Latinos, less than 75% of college-age siblings were attending a college or university. Thus, blacks and Latinos were somewhat less likely than others to have an older sibling who could serve as a college-going role model.

Thus, as early as age 6 we observe significant differences in household composition between groups. Black respondents, in particular, were far more likely than others to report an absent father, suggesting that they experienced a smaller total investment of parental time. To illustrate, suppose that a typical 6-year-old spends 11 hours per day sleeping (8 P.M. to 7 A.M.) and 6 hours per weekday at school (8:30 A.M. to 2:30 P.M.). Given these assumptions, each respondent could potentially absorb up to 122 hours of total parental time per week, yielding 488 hours per month for a two-parent household (assuming no vacations or holidays).

These 488 hours of *potential* investment, however, are reduced by parental absence and labor-force participation. We assume that parents who leave the household through marital disruption spend no time with their children (an oversimplification to be sure, but in the case of fathers painfully close to the truth—see Furstenberg and Cherlin 1991) and that full-time workers do not see their children for the first three hours after school. Given the observed group-specific patterns of parental absence and employment, these assumptions mean that the total investment of parental time would be reduced to around 370 hours per month for whites and 374 hours for Asians, decreases of around 25% from the maximum potential. Latinos, in contrast, would experience a 31% reduction in parental time to 338 hours per month, and black parental time would drop by 51%, to just 237 hours per month.

Changes by Age 13

Table 3.2 continues to track differences in the home by focusing on family conditions as the respondent entered middle school at around age 13. Basically, we see an exacerbation of trends visible at age 6. Among all

TABLE 3.2
Composition of household in which respondent lived at age 13

Item	Whites	Asians	Latinos	Blacks
Household				
Mean No. of Members	3.4	3.6	3.5	3.3
% with Two Biological Parents	85.5	91.1	75.3	57.3
% with Stepparent	5.9	1.5	6.7	8.7
% Containing Part-Year Members	7.3	12.2	8.4	7.7
% Containing Nonnuclear Family	6.5	19.8	10.2	17.2
Father				
% Present in Household	87.8	92.1	77.3	60.3
Mean Age	44.3	45.1	44.1	44.1
% Working Full Time	95.5	94.4	93.7	92.3
% Working Part Time	2.4	2.1	1.1	2.3
% in School	5.2	3.9	7.1	7.2
% Not Working	2.0	2.2	3.6	4.4
Mother				
% Present in Household	97.7	98.3	97.4	94.2
Mean Age	42.3	42.2	40.8	40.6
% Working Full Time	45.3	53.2	52.5	79.5
% Working Part Time	28.8	30.1	27.7	9.7
% in School	25.4	15.0	17.9	9.3
Siblings				
Mean Age	14.9	15.7	15.7	16.7
% Aged 5–17 in School	98.9	99.4	98.9	99.8
% Aged 18–22 in College	94.3	99.8	91.5	87.7

groups, the percentage of respondents living with two parents fell, the share of those living with a stepparent increased, and the percentage living without a father rose. Rates of change in household composition were considerably greater for blacks and Hispanics than for whites and Asians. By age 13, only 57% of black respondents still lived with both parents, and just 60% reported a father present. Among Latinos, 75% lived with both parents, and 77% reported a father in the household. In contrast, 91% of Asian respondents still lived with both parents, and 92% had a father present; the respective figures for whites were 86% and 88%.

We also see a shift in parental employment patterns as households age. The percentage of fathers employed full time dropped slightly, reaching 96% for white respondents at age 13, 94% for Asians and Latinos, and 92% for blacks. Among mothers, however, the share working full time *increased*. Among white mothers the percentage goes from 38% to 45%, whereas for blacks it goes from 76% to 80%. The respective shifts were 44% to 53% in the case of Asians and 47% to 53% in the case Latinos. The rate of part-time employment also increased among mothers as respondents aged, with the percentage reaching 29% for whites, 30% for Asians, 28% for Latinos, and 10% for blacks. In other words, as children age, mothers' labor-force participation rates progressively rise.

There were also strong contrasts between groups with respect to mother's school attendance. Whereas a quarter of all white respondents reported having a mother in school at age 13, the figure was just 9% for blacks, 15% for Asians, and 18% for Latinos. Among siblings present at age 13, nearly all those of school age were currently enrolled in school, and the vast majority of college-age siblings were attending a college or university: 100% for Asians, 94% for whites, 92% for Latinos, and 88% for blacks. The absence of sibling role models noted at age 6 thus seems to have moderated somewhat by age 13.

On the Eve of College

During their senior year in high school, respondents were aged 17 to 18 and were going through the process of applying to college. The composition of homes during this time is the subject of table 3.3. As families continued to age, household sizes generally fell, presumably because older siblings had left home. The decrease was most pronounced among blacks, whose household size reached 2.6 persons, compared with 2.9 for whites, 3.0 for Latinos, and 3.1 for Asians. Although divorce and separation continued to take a toll on family stability, the change between 13 and 18 was not as dramatic as that between 6 and 13. Nonetheless, by senior year only about half of black respondents (52%) and two-thirds of Latino respondents (68%) were still living with both parents, compared with 81% of whites and 87% of Asians.

Although the full-time employment of fathers continued to fall, it nonetheless remained at high levels for all groups (93–94% for whites and Asians and 90% for blacks and Latinos). Likewise, the labor-force participation of mothers continued to increase to the point where absolute majorities of all groups were employed full time: 51% of whites, 57% of Asians, 61% of Latinos, and 81% of blacks. Whereas the share of white, Asian, and Latino mothers attending school dropped, the share of black mothers in school rose slightly, from 9% at age 13 to 14% at age 18. Among siblings of college age, around 90% of whites and Asians were enrolled compared with 83% of Latinos and 78% of African Americans. Thus, some of the shortfall in collegiate role models seems to have reemerged for Latinos and blacks on the eve of college attendance.

TABLE 3.3
Composition of household when respondent was a senior in high school

Item	Whites	Asians	Latinos	Blacks
Household				
Mean No. of Members	2.9	3.1	3.0	2.6
% with Two Biological Parents	81.1	87.1	68.4	51.6
% with Stepparent	2.6	2.0	4.4	3.1
% Containing Part-Year Members	13.7	15.0	10.7	9.9
% Containing Nonnuclear Family	5.4	16.3	9.4	13.9
Father				
% Present in Household	84.2	88.5	72.3	56.0
Mean Age	48.3	49.0	48.2	48.1
% Working Full Time	93.6	92.6	90.0	90.0
% Working Part Time	1.8	2.1	3.0	2.6
% in School	2.9	2.4	7.0	6.1
% Not Working	4.0	3.7	4.8	4.7
Mother				
% Present in Household	96.1	97.5	94.8	92.9
Mean Age	46.3	46.2	44.9	44.6
% Working Full Time	51.1	57.0	61.1	81.0
% Working Part Time	26.8	18.0	16.4	7.7
% in School	7.7	6.6	12.8	13.9
Siblings				
Mean Age	15.7	16.1	16.7	17.6
% Aged 5–17 in School	99.1	98.9	99.8	99.3
% Aged 18–22 in College	87.6	89.9	83.0	78.1

Child-Rearing Strategies

As any parent will point out, it is not simply the *quantity* of parental time
that matters, but also the *quality*. What parents actually do with children
and how they do it are very important in determining social, behavioral,
and cognitive outcomes. Thus we included a battery of questions about
the specific child-rearing techniques that the parents of respondents prac-
ticed while they were growing up. We were particularly interested in the
degree to which parents involved themselves in promoting their children's
education, acquisition of cultural knowledge, social relationships, and intellectual independence. We also considered the strictness of parental discipline and the extent to which parents rely on shame and guilt as tools
for child raising.

Human Capital Formation

Human capital refers to skills and abilities that make a person more productive and more valuable economically, the classic example being education (Becker 1964). Table 3.4 considers parental involvement in various facets of human capital acquisition when respondents were aged 6, 13, and 17–18. According to Guo and Harris (2000), cognitive stimulation within the home is the single most important mechanism by which parents promote the intellectual development of their children, so the first measure we consider is the frequency with which parents read to respondents at age 6.

TABLE 3.4

Parental involvement in formation of human capital when respondent was age 6, age 13, and a senior in high school

Age and Item	% Saying Parent Did Often or Very Often			
	Whites	Asians	Latinos	Blacks
Age 6				
P Read to R	79.4	43.6	63.0	59.5
P Helped R with Homework	69.8	54.1	65.6	79.0
P Took R to Library	57.9	55.4	47.1	52.6
P Put R in Summer School[a]	14.0	11.6	10.6	14.1
P Put R in Educational Camp[a]	3.1	13.5	7.9	6.0
P Put R in Enrichment Program[a]	5.0	6.6	3.4	5.3
Age 13				
P Helped R with Homework	28.2	20.1	30.1	32.0
P Took R to Library	33.7	39.7	32.4	38.4
P Put R in Educational Camp[a]	8.6	11.2	19.5	12.7
P Participated in PTA	38.1	16.8	31.6	31.7
High School Senior				
P Helped R with Homework	6.9	4.0	8.8	7.7
P Met with R's Teachers	11.0	6.9	15.0	17.9
P Read Daily Newspaper	83.4	75.7	72.9	68.8
P Read Sunday Newspaper	87.9	74.0	77.1	77.1
P Read Weekly News Magazine	57.0	43.4	48.1	42.6
M Pushed R to Do Best[a]	96.1	93.8	93.5	95.0
M Helped R with Schoolwork[a]	73.1	58.4	64.1	62.9
M Encouraged R after Poor Grades[a]	90.3	90.6	91.3	88.8
F Pushed R to Do Best[a]	96.8	93.7	95.1	96.1
F Helped R with Schoolwork[a]	65.7	35.2	60.1	66.7
F Encouraged R after Poor Grades[a]	91.8	91.1	91.7	91.7

[a]Percentage answering "agree" or "strongly agree" instead of "often" or "very often."

The data reveal significant intergroup differences. Whereas 79% of white freshmen said that their parents read to them often or very often as young children, only 44% of Asian respondents did so. Black and Latino respondents fell about midway between these two extremes, with 60% and 63% being read to as children, respectively. At the same time, 58% of whites said their parents took them to the library often or very often at age 6, compared with 55% of Asians, 53% of blacks, and just 47% of Asians. When asked how often parents helped respondents with their homework, African Americans said 79% did so often or very often, compared with 70% for whites, 66% for Latinos, and 54% for Asians.

We also asked respondents whether their parents put them into a summer educational program at age 6. Although the percentage reporting such an action was generally small, there were nonetheless consistent differences between groups. Whereas only about 4% of whites and blacks said their parents put them into a summer school, the frequency was 11% for Asians and Latinos. Asians were most likely to attend an educational camp, with 14% reporting such attendance, followed by 8% of Latinos, 6% of blacks, and just 3% of whites. However, only a small percentage of any group (under 7%) reported attending a summer enrichment program, and intergroup differences were rather small.

Whereas the most striking intergroup disparity at age 6 was that white parents read more often to their children, by age 13 very few parents in any group were still reading to their children, so we focused on other parental actions, as shown in the middle panel of table 3.4. Black parents continued to be most likely to help respondents with their homework, with 32% reporting such help often or very often, followed by Latinos and whites at 30% and 28%, respectively, and Asians at just 20%.

Black and Asian parents were more likely to take their children to the library than white or Latino parents, although differences were modest. Roughly 39% of blacks and Asians said their parents brought them to a library often or very often, compared with 33% of whites and Latinos. Latino parents were most likely to place their children in a summer educational camp (20%), followed by blacks (13%), Asians (11%), and whites (9%). White parents participated most frequently in parent-teacher associations, however: 38% did so compared with just 17% of Asian parents. Hispanic and black parents also evinced relatively high levels of PTA involvement at around 32%.

Given the recency and salience of the respondent's senior year, we asked the largest number of questions about parental behavior during this phase of the life cycle. Responses to these items are summarized in the bottom panel of table 3.4. By the age of 17 or 18 very few parents were still helping their children with homework (the range was 4% to 9%, with Asians lowest and blacks highest). There was also little variation in the degree of moral support coming from parents. Upwards of 90% of all respondents reported that their mother and father pushed them to do their best and encouraged them when they received poor grades.

Significant differences emerged, however, when respondents were asked whether their mother and father helped them with schoolwork they didn't understand. Whereas nearly three quarters of whites (73%) agreed that their mother helped them, only 58% of Asians did so, compared with 63–64% of Latinos and blacks. Likewise, roughly two-thirds of whites and blacks reported getting help from fathers, compared with just 35% of Asians. Latinos were only slightly behind whites and blacks, with 60% reporting fatherly assistance. Asian parents were also least likely to have met with teachers (just 7% did so), whereas black parents were most likely to have done so (18%), followed by Latinos (15%) and whites (11%).

A good part of a parent's influence on children occurs through example, and the cultivation of cognitive skills is no exception. Children with parents who read regularly are more likely to read themselves. Among NLSF respondents, white respondents were consistently more likely than others to report parental reading. For example, the percentage of whites who said their parents read a daily newspaper often or very often was 83%, whereas for blacks it was only 69%. Latinos and Asians came in at 73% and 76%, respectively. Similarly, the percentage of parents who read a weekly news magazine often or very often was 57% for whites compared with 43% for blacks and Asians and 58% for Latinos. Finally, whereas nearly nine out of ten white parents (88%) read a Sunday newspaper often or very often, the figure was closer to three quarters for the other groups (74% for Asians and 77% for blacks and Latinos).

Although there is some inconsistency among the items shown in table 3.4, they generally suggest a pattern whereby white parents are most intensively involved in cultivating the human capital of their children and Asian parents are least involved. We confirmed this conjecture by creating a summary index of parental involvement in human capital formation. The details of how we constructed the index are summarized in appendix B, table B1. Basically, for each item we assigned a numerical value to indicate the relative frequency with which a parental behavior was reported to have occurred (0 = never, 1 = rarely, 2 = sometimes, 3 = often, and 4 = very often). The values were then added across items to create a summated ratings scale.

The resulting index of parental involvement had a theoretical range of 0 to 104 and a reliability coefficient of .830 (Cronbach's alpha). Average scores for the various groups are graphed as a bar chart in figure 3.1. As can be seen, the degree of parental involvement in human capital formation (i.e., the degree to which parents involved themselves in promoting the intellectual development of their children) was greatest for whites and

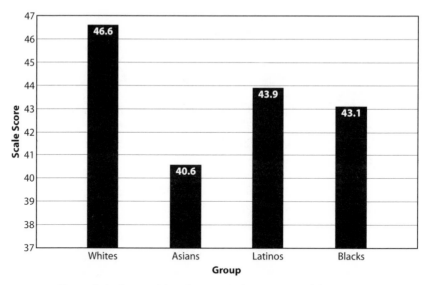

Figure 3.1. Parental involvement in human capital formation

least for Asians. The scale score of 46.6 for white parents was 15% greater than that of Asian parents (40.6). Latinos and blacks fell in-between, with scale scores of 43.9 and 43.1, respectively.

Cultural Capital Formation

Cultural capital refers to habits of dress, speech, comportment, and think-ing that may not themselves directly enhance productivity, but which fa-cilitate entry into privileged social and economic settings (DiMaggio 1982; Bourdieu 1986; Lamont and Lareau 1988; Farkas 1996). Much of the knowledge that will later prove useful in navigating the shoals of higher education is not taught in the classroom, but in other, more infor-mal ways. Parents have always been key actors in imparting cultural knowledge, not just about how to dress, talk, and behave, but also about the many things that college-educated people are "supposed to know." One means by which parents can impart such knowledge of culture to their children is by taking them to museums and cultural events.

Table 3.5 assesses the degree to which parents engaged in such behav-iors at three points in the life cycle. At age 6, relatively few respondents were taken to an art museum by their parents. Only 16% of Latinos re-ported being taken to an art museum often or very often, and the fre-quencies were even lower for other groups: 13% for blacks, 12% for whites, and 10% for Asians. Thinking that art might be too sophisticated

TABLE 3.5

Parental involvement in formation of cultural capital when respondent was age 6, age 13, and a senior in high school

Age and Item	% Saying Parent Did Often or Very Often			
	Whites	Asians	Latinos	Blacks
Age 6				
P Took R to Art Museum	11.5	9.9	16.1	12.9
P Took R to Science Center	21.5	15.1	15.5	20.5
P Took R to Zoo or Aquarium	30.5	23.2	31.5	36.7
Age 13				
P Took R to Art Museum	11.8	6.2	12.1	8.2
P Took R to Science Center	12.0	8.2	10.7	9.2
P Took R to Plays or Concerts	32.2	16.3	22.3	23.4
High School Senior				
P Took R to Art Museum	7.4	3.0	7.8	3.0
P Took R to Plays or Concerts	22.0	10.5	15.8	13.1

for 6-year-olds, we inquired about attending science centers, zoos, and aquariums. We reasoned that by taking their children to these venues, parents would at least get them in the habit of going to exhibits.

Higher percentages of respondents did recall being taken to these places at age 6. Most common was going to a zoo or aquarium. Some 37% of black respondents said they were taken to a zoo or aquarium often or very often, compared with 32% of Latinos, 31% of whites, and 23% of Asians. Figures were somewhat lower for science centers, with 21–22% among both whites and blacks reporting attendance at such a venue often or very often, compared with 15–16% of Asians and Latinos.

Parental involvement in museum going did not increase much by age 13. Generally 12% or fewer respondents reported being taken often or very often to either an art museum or a science center, and intergroup differences were rather small. By middle school parental involvement in cultural formation seems to have shifted to the realm of plays and concerts. A third of whites (32%) reported being taken to a play or concert often or very often when they were age 13, followed by blacks and Latinos at 22–23% and Asians at 16%. A similar pattern of group contrasts persists in high school. As seniors, 22% of whites were taken to a play or concert often or very often, compared with 16% of Latinos, 13% of blacks, and 11% of Asians. Very few respondents went to art museums at age 18, but once again reported frequencies were least for Asians and African Americans.

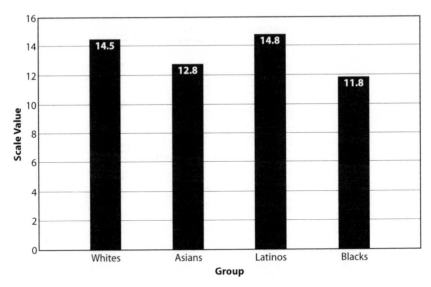

Figure 3.2. Parental involvement in cultural capital formation

Obviously the items in table 3.5 offer a limited assessment of parental involvement in the creation of cultural capital, but when combined to form a summated ratings scale (see appendix table B2), they yield a reliable scale ($\alpha = .886$) that varies from 0 to 44. A bar chart of parental involvement in cultural capital formation is presented in figure 3.2. Although intergroup differences are modest, white and Latino values are around 15, whereas black and Asian scores are closer to 12. Thus white and Latino parents appear to be more involved in the cultural education of their children than do African Americans and Asians.

Social Capital Formation

As children age, peers become increasingly important as a social context, especially in adolescence. Although the ability of parents to control their children's friendships and associations may be limited (see Rich 1998), most observers would probably agree that monitoring a child's social behavior remains an important part of parenting. In table 3.6 we examine the degree to which parents involve themselves in the formation of social capital, which consists of resources emanating from ties between people (Coleman 1988), in this case friendships the respondent reported in adolescence (ages 13 and 18).

Once again we see a sharp contrast between Asians and other groups. Only 21% of Asian respondents said their parents talked to their friends

TABLE 3.6

Parental involvement in formation of social capital when respondent
was age 13 and a senior in high school

| Age and Item | % Saying Parent Did Often or Very Often | | | |
	Whites	Asians	Latinos	Blacks
Age 13				
Talked to R's Friends	54.4	20.9	46.7	43.6
High School Senior				
Parents Talked to R's Friends	52.8	21.1	47.3	43.9
Mother Knew R's Friends[a]	80.9	65.4	73.1	69.0
Father Knew R's Friends[a]	95.4	89.7	92.8	90.7

[a]Percentage answering "agree" or "strongly agree" instead of "often" or "very often."

often or very often, either at age 13 or during their senior year in high
school. In contrast, well over half of white parents (54%) spoke to their
children's friends with this frequency at both ages; the figure for blacks
was about 44%, and for Latinos it was 47%. There were few intergroup
differences in the degree to which respondents's fathers were reported to
know their friends. In each case, 90–95% agreed that their father knew
their friends. Sharper contrasts were found with respect to mothers.
Whereas 81% of white respondents said their mother knew their friends,
only 66% of Asian respondents and 69% of black respondents reported
the same, compared with 73% of Latinos.

As before, we combined the items shown in table 3.6 to form a summated ratings scale of parental involvement in social capital formation with
a potential range of 0 to 18 and a reliability of .778 (see appendix table
B2). Figure 3.3 graphs the mean score for each group; as one would expect
from the above discussion, whites display the highest level of parental involvement in social capital formation. The average white score of 11.6 is
26% greater than the Asian value of 9.2. Latinos are between these two
extremes at 10.7, but blacks are on the low side with a score of 9.9.

Cultivation of Intellectual Independence

An important attribute for success in higher education is independence of
thought and mind. In moving from high school to college, one shifts from
the simple mastery of organized material to the deployment of prior learning in new and creative ways. To the extent that students have been encouraged by their parents to think and act for themselves, they will be better prepared for the intellectual challenges of university life. Thus the
NLSF questionnaire asked a battery of questions to assess the degree to

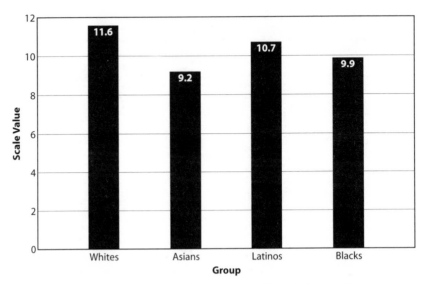

Figure 3.3. Parental involvement in social capital formation

which parents granted respondents independence and intellectual autonomy while they were growing up. Responses to these items are summarized in table 3.7

Intellectual independence develops gradually over the life course. We
asked whether parents checked at ages 6 and 13, to see if respondents had
done their homework, and whether they rewarded them for good grades.
By valuing homework and intellectual achievement early on, parents, we
felt, would lay a sound foundation for the later construction of autonomy.
In general, black respondents reported the greatest parental involvement.
Eighty-three percent reported that at age 6 their parents often or very
often checked to see whether they had done their homework. In contrast,
only 65% of Asians did so. For whites and Latinos, the figures were 79%
and 74%, respectively.

Black parents were also most likely to reward respondents for earning
good grades. Whereas 71% of black parents rewarded high grades, the
frequency was 48% for Asians, 53% for whites, and 59% for Latinos. Although the degree of parental involvement on this indicator dropped by
age 13, the pattern of intergroup differences remained the same.

As high school seniors, most respondents said their parents pushed
them to think independently, although Asians were slightly lower than the
other groups. Only 85% said their mother pushed them to think independently compared with 91–94% of the other groups. For fathers, the
respective figures were 86% for Asians and 94–95% for the others.

TABLE 3.7
Parental cultivation of intellectual independence when respondent was age 6, age 13, and a senior in high school

	% Saying Parent Did Often or Very Often			
Age and Item	Whites	Asians	Latinos	Blacks
Age 6				
P Checked R's Homework	78.9	65.4	74.1	82.6
P Rewarded R for Good Grades	53.1	47.6	59.4	70.5
Age 13				
P Checked R's Homework	44.2	32.6	47.1	50.3
P Rewarded R for Good Grades	40.1	33.5	49.4	58.1
High School Senior				
M Thought Should Give in on Arguments[a]	19.5	37.4	26.3	25.7
M Pushed R to Think Independently[a]	93.6	85.1	90.6	92.0
M Explained Reasons for Decisions[a]	65.9	57.7	55.8	49.2
M Thought Shouldn't Argue with Adults[a]	52.6	69.8	61.7	73.3
M Thought She Was Always Right[a]	37.6	50.9	50.5	50.6
M Told R Would Understand When Older[a]	24.0	41.9	36.2	44.6
F Thought Should Give in on Arguments[a]	23.6	42.3	31.8	28.7
F Pushed R to Think Independently[a]	94.6	85.6	93.5	93.2
F Explained Reasons for Decisions[a]	65.9	57.1	60.7	48.9
F Thought Shouldn't Argue with Adults[a]	63.1	78.8	69.7	84.2
F Thought He Was Always Right[a]	29.1	48.3	40.8	45.8
F Told R Would Understand When Older[a]	27.9	51.4	45.5	53.3

[a]Percentage answering "agree" or "strongly agree" instead of "often" or "very often."

Stronger intergroup differentials emerged when we asked about specific parental attitudes and behaviors related to the respondent's independence, such as giving in on arguments, not arguing with adults, and getting reasons for parental decisions.

For example, only 20% of whites agreed that their mother believed that one should give in on arguments, and 24% agreed with this description of their father. In contrast, 37% of Asian mothers and 43% of Asian fathers were reported to hold this belief. The corresponding figures for blacks were 26% for mothers and 29% for fathers, whereas for Latinos they were 26% and 32%, respectively. Moreover, whereas 66% of whites said their mother or father offered reasons for their decisions, only 49% of blacks did so, compared with 57% of Asians. Among Latinos, 56% said their mother offered reasons for decisions, and 61% said this about their father.

Whites were also relatively unlikely to have parents who "thought they were always right." Only 37% of white respondents said this of their

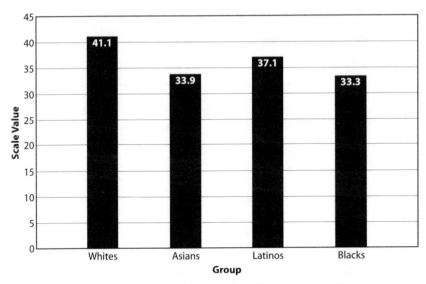

Figure 3.4. Parental cultivation of intellectual independence

mother, and just 29% of whites said it of their father. Among other groups around 50% reported having a mother convinced of her own rectitude, while 48% of Asians reported this trait of their fathers, compared with figures of 46% for blacks and 41% for Latinos.

White parents were also less likely to endorse the view that one shouldn't argue with adults or to fall back on the time-honored parental bromide that "you'll understand when you grow up." Blacks and Asians were generally at the other extreme, with Latinos in the middle. Consistent with this general pattern, when we coded the items numerically and combined them to create a 64-point index measuring the parental cultivation of intellectual independence (see appendix table B3), we found that whites were highest at 41 and blacks and Asians were lowest at 33–34, while Latinos were in-between at 37 ($\alpha = .719$). These indices are graphed in figure 3.4. The differential between the lowest and highest values is on the order of 20%.

Strictness of Discipline

Another facet of child rearing is strictness of discipline, and this issue is assessed by the items shown in table 3.8. At age 6, very strong and clear differences are evident among groups on this dimension of child rearing. In general, black parents enforced the strictest discipline, followed by Latinos and Asians, while white parents were consistently the most per-

TABLE 3.8
Strictness of parental discipline when respondent was age 6, age 13, and a senior in high school

	% Saying Parent Did Often or Very Often			
Age and Item	Whites	Asians	Latinos	Blacks
Age 6				
P Punished R for Bad Grades	11.0	20.4	21.1	28.9
P Punished R for Disobedience	32.6	38.6	43.7	64.4
Age 13				
P Punished R for Bad Grades	40.1	33.5	49.4	58.1
P Punished R for Disobedience	23.5	22.5	31.8	44.8
P Limited R's Time with Friends	5.01	5.51	5.3	14.6
High School Senior				
P Punished R for Bad Grades	5.3	7.1	13.1	14.8
P Punished R for Disobedience	10.2	10.3	17.9	22.8
P Limited R's Time with Friends	3.6	10.7	8.4	7.5
M Forbade Things When Displeased[a]	8.5	16.0	18.2	14.7
M Made Life Miserable Poor Grades[a]	90.3	90.6	91.3	88.8
F Forbade Things When Displeased[a]	7.5	14.91	3.7	9.8
F Made Life Miserable Poor Grades[a]	14.4	24.5	23.5	25.4
Curfew 11 PM or Later on Weeknight[a]	70.2	66.8	61.2	63.0
Curfew 1 AM or Later on Weekend[a]	67.5	61.0	63.1	65.8

[a]Percentage answering "agree" or "strongly agree" instead of "often" or "very often."

missive. For example, nearly two-thirds (64%) of black respondents said they were punished often or very often for disobedience, compared with just 33% of whites. Latinos came in at 44% and Asians at 39%. Likewise, whereas 29% of blacks were punished for earning bad grades, only 11% received this treatment, compared with 20–21% of Asians and Latinos.

A similar profile emerges at age 13, at which time 58% of blacks recalled being punished for bad grades and 45% remembered being punished for disobedience often or very often, compared with figures of 40% and 23% among whites. Among Latinos, 49% reported punishment for bad grades and 32% for disobedience, whereas 34% of Asians were punished for bad grades and 23% for disobedience. Compared with whites, moreover, all three minority groups were more likely to report parents who sought to limit the time they spent with friends—15% for the minorities and only 5% for whites.

Even as high school seniors, blacks continued to experience rather stern discipline compared with other groups. Nearly a quarter (23%) said they were punished for disobedience compared with 10% for whites and Asians and 18% for Latinos. Likewise, some 15% were punished for bad grades, compared with 5% of whites, 7% of Asians, and 14% of Latinos. Minority respondents were also more likely to have parents forbid them things when they were displeased. Only 9% of whites said their mothers forbade them things as punishment, and only 14% of white fathers did so. In contrast 15–18% of blacks, Asians, and Latinos reported having mothers who regularly forbade them, and 25% of these groups reported fathers doing so. Whites also tended to have later curfews on week nights and weekends, although intergroup differences were not great.

To derive a general assessment of the discipline respondents experienced while growing up, we again computed a summated ratings scale from the items in table 3.5, which yielded an index ranging from 0 to 56 (α = .702). The bar chart in figure 3.5 shows the mean scale score achieved by each group (see appendix table B4 for the details of index construction). As is immediately evident, all three minority groups displayed a greater proclivity toward parental discipline than whites. Whereas the strictness index was only 12.9 for whites, all minority groups displayed scores of 16 or greater, with blacks leading the way at 17.7, followed by Latinos at 17.0 and Asians at 16.3. According to this scale, then, the style of child rearing employed by African American parents was 37% stricter than that employed by white parents.

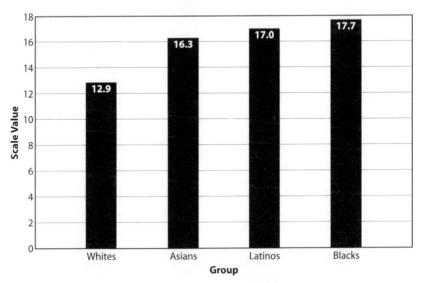

Figure 3.5. Strictness of parental discipline

Use of Shame and Guilt

The last facet of child rearing we consider is the use of shame and guilt by parents, which we assessed using a series of items focused on the senior year. Once again minority parents were more likely than whites to employ shame and guilt to secure compliant behavior, with Asians standing out as the most extreme. Whereas only 22% of whites reported that their mother "acted cold" when displeased, the figure was 32% for Asians and Latinos and 29% for blacks. Likewise, only 23% of whites reported fathers who acted cold as a sign of displeasure, compared with 37% of Asians, 34% of Latinos, and 32% of blacks. In addition to being punished for bad grades, minorities were also made to feel guiltier. Thus 29% of Asian mothers and 31% of Asian fathers were reported to instill feelings of guilt, compared with only 17% of white mothers and 18% of white fathers. In the use of guilt, however, blacks were much more like whites (with figures of 19% for mothers and 18% for fathers), and Latinos were much more like Asians (with 27% reporting guilt-inducing mothers and 25% guilt-inducing fathers).

White respondents also reported more companionate parents than the minority groups: 85% said their mother did "fun things" with them, and 70% said she spent lots of time "just talking" to them. At the other extreme, 65% of Asians said their mothers did fun things with them, and 51% spent a lot of time just talking. Among blacks the respective figures were 70% and 63%, whereas among Latinos they were 78% and 65%. Very similar patterns were observed when respondents were asked about the behavior of their fathers.

TABLE 3.9
Parental reliance on shame and guilt when respondent was a senior in high school

Item	% Answering Agree or Strongly Agree			
	Whites	Asians	Latinos	Blacks
M Acted Cold to R When Displeased	21.8	31.6	32.4	28.6
M Made R Feel Guilty for Poor Grades	17.0	28.9	26.9	19.4
M Did Fun Things with R	84.9	64.8	78.2	69.6
M Spent Lots of Time Just Talking to R	70.3	50.9	65.1	63.2
F Acted Cold to R When Displeased	23.0	36.7	34.0	32.3
F Made R Feel Guilty for Poor Grades	17.9	31.4	24.8	18.3
F Did Fun Things with R	84.1	72.9	80.3	84.2
F Spent Lots of Time Just Talking to R	81.6	65.5	74.7	79.2

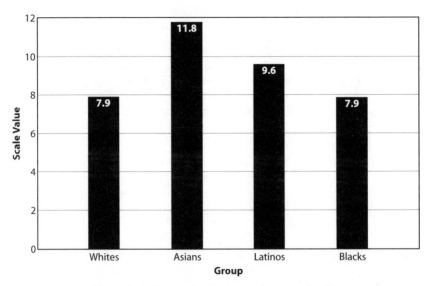

Figure 3.6. Parental reliance on shame and guilt

The summated rating scale for these items yielded an index that ranged from 0 to 32 and proved quite reliable ($\alpha = .702$—see appendix table B4). The bar chart in figure 3.6 clearly documents the great contrast between whites and Asians with respect to the use of shame and guilt in the course of child raising. The Asian scale score of 11.8 was roughly 50% greater than the white score of 7.9. The black score of 7.9 was identical to that of whites, whereas Latinos scored 9.6. Clearly the groups differ on this dimension, with whites and blacks on one extreme and Asians on the other, with Latinos in-between.

Continuities and Contrasts

Our sample of students is obviously highly selected. After all, they have all been admitted into the most elite sector of American higher education. Given this fact, it is not surprising that family backgrounds displayed many continuities across groups. Nearly everyone reported growing up in a household with supportive parents who offered strong emotional support and encouraged academic success. Parents were actively engaged in cultivating respondents' human, cultural, and social capital, and older siblings generally provided strong role models by attending college ahead of them.

Despite these continuities, however, respondents in the four groups differed in many ways with respect to family background. Whites tended to grow up in intact, two-parent households containing few people outside their nuclear families, and we know from the prior chapter that their parents were quite affluent and homogeneously professional in status. White parents read to their young children with great frequency, checked their homework often, and usually helped them with homework. White children were very unlikely to be punished for receiving bad grades, and while they were often rewarded for good grades in primary school, this positive reinforcement tended to disappear as they got older.

White parents tended to favor a companionate style of child rearing in which they involved themselves intensively in the lives of their children. They spent large amounts of time just talking to respondents, doing fun things with them, and getting to know their friends. In child rearing, white parents emphasized autonomy and independence in thought and action and generally employed reason rather than discipline to secure compliant behavior. Punishment was infrequently used, and white parents rarely sought to make their children feel guilty. By high school, the vast majority of white respondents were trusted to stay out late at night.

In contrast, black respondents were much more likely to grow up in a single-parent household. Compared with whites, their homes were much more likely to contain people from outside the nuclear family. From the prior chapter we know that a large fraction of black families were of poor or modest economic circumstances. The vast majority of black mothers were employed full time and not in school. Although a majority of black respondents reported that their parents read to them often or very often in primary school, 40% said they did not. Black parents, however, were more likely than white parents to check and help with homework. They also paid very close attention to the respondents' grades, meeting out rewards for good marks and punishment for bad marks. This tendency to punish and reward did not decline as sharply with age as it did among white parents.

Compared with whites, black parents appeared to favor a more authoritarian style of child rearing. Relatively fewer black parents spent time just talking with their children, knowing their friends, or doing fun things with the respondents while they were growing up, and far more black parents relied on punishment and a withdrawal of affection (acting "cold") for transgressions. Rather than encouraging independence, black parents sought to instill obedience. Black parents were more likely to believe that children shouldn't argue with adults, that parents shouldn't be questioned, and that children should generally give in on arguments. Black parents were relatively unlikely to explain reasons for their decisions, and much more likely to tell respondents they'd understand when they grew up. Although more authoritarian than white parents in their style of child rearing, however, black parents were relatively unlikely to make their children feel guilty.

Asian respondents reported experiences and family circumstances that were very similar to those of whites in some ways, but notably different in others. Like whites, they were very likely to grow up in intact, two-parent families, but owing to their immigrant origins they were more likely than whites to live with nonnuclear family members. Although, like whites, Asian parents were homogeneously affluent and upper middle class, they were the *least likely* to read to their children (less than half did so with any frequency). They were also relatively unlikely to check or help with homework, and they were largely uninvolved in PTA activities. In primary school, however, they were the most likely to put their children in some kind of summer educational program.

The approach of Asian parents to child rearing tended to be authoritarian and was the least companionate of any of the groups. Asian parents rewarded their children for good grades and punished them for bad grades and for disobedience (though not to the same extent as black parents), and they were very unlikely to talk to the respondent or get to know his or her friends. The parent-child relationship among Asians seems to be rather distant and formal, with most parents believing that one shouldn't argue with adults, that parents shouldn't be questioned, and that children should acquiesce in disputes. Asian parents were the most unlikely to "do fun things" with the respondent and were most likely to "make life miserable" for them when they got poor grades. In addition to emphasizing respect and authority, Asian parents were most likely to cultivate a sense of guilt for poor academic performance. Although obedience was clearly a virtue for Asian parents, it was not blind, as a clear majority explained the reasons for their decisions (even if they didn't want them questioned).

Latino parents mixed Asian and black styles of child rearing. Only two-thirds of Latinos remained with both parents through high school, and a larger share than whites lived in homes with nonnuclear family members. Like blacks, Latinos came from a mixed class background, with many having poor parents with limited educations. Only 63% reported that their parents read to them often or very often, and Latino parents were generally less likely than black or white parents to check or help with homework. Latino respondents were quite likely to be rewarded for good grades and punished for bad grades, and child rearing was more authoritarian and less companionate. Compared with white parents, those of Latinos tended not to know or interact with respondents or their friends, and they emphasized obedience and authority rather than independence.

Latinos, however, were relatively likely to pair their demand for obedience with an explanation for decisions. Compared with Asians and blacks, Latinos were less likely to be told they would understand when they grew up, and despite the rather hierarchical relationship with their parents, Latino respondents were very likely to report that their parents did fun things with them.

In sum, respondents in the four racial and ethnic groups grew up under a range of family experiences that blended different household compositions with different approaches to discipline, different emphases on obedience and authority, and different manipulations of reward, punishment, and guilt. These contrasts in the home and family life of whites, Asians, African Americans, and Latinos may or may not influence later academic performance (that will be assessed in later phases of research). Whatever the academic consequences, however, it is clear that white and black parents are positioned at the opposite ends of several continua, and that Asian and Latino parents generally lie in-between, although the patterns of similarities and differences are often quite complex. No doubt some of the differences in child rearing reflect class differences among groups, and still others may reflect differences in neighborhood environment, the topic to which we turn in the next chapter.

CHAPTER 4

NEIGHBORHOOD BACKGROUND

DESPITE THE PASSAGE of the Fair Housing Act in 1968 and more than two decades of civil rights enforcement, when it comes to residence African Americans are still a remarkably segregated people. Indeed, blacks in large urbanized areas experience higher levels of segregation than any other group in the history of the United States—more than ethnic European immigrants early in the twentieth century and more than Asians and Latinos today. In a subset of large metropolitan areas that house nearly 40% of all African Americans, the segregation of blacks is so intense and occurs on so many geographic dimensions simultaneously that Massey and Denton (1989) have labeled it *hypersegregation*. Unlike the situation for other groups, the degree of black segregation does not vary significantly by income (Massey and Fischer 1999).

Residential segregation is important because where one lives strongly determines the opportunities and resources at one's disposal, and hence, substantially influences one's life chances (Brooks-Gunn, Duncan, and Aber 1997). Because of the ongoing reality of racial segregation, blacks are much less able to attain favorable neighborhood circumstances than other racial and ethnic groups, and they experience fewer residential returns with respect to prior achievements in income, education, and occupation (Logan, Alba, McNulty, and Fischer 1996; South and Crowder 1998).

Over the past several decades, black segregation has interacted with broader structural transformations in society to concentrate poverty disproportionately in black communities (Massey and Denton 1993; Massey and Fischer 2000). As the spatial concentration of poverty increases, so does anything that is correlated with poverty—joblessness, dependency, single parenthood, substance abuse, gang violence, crime—creating a social environment that is unusual in the extent of its disadvantage. As a result of racial segregation, therefore, African Americans in general, and middle-class blacks in particular, are more likely to live near poor people and their associated socioeconomic problems, making both the staging of upward mobility and the perpetuation of class status more problematic for them than for other groups (see Patillo-McCoy 1999; Morenoff and Sampson 1997). In any study of achievement involving African Americans, therefore, it important to measure, understand, and control for differences in the neighborhood background.

Early Neighborhood Circumstances

At around age 6, children begin to spend an increasing fraction of their time outside the confines of home and family. In addition to spending more time at school and in other institutional settings (e.g., day care or after-school programs), they increasingly explore the social and material world of their neighborhoods. To assess the character of the local environment into which respondents delved at age 6, we asked them to the estimate the racial/ethnic composition of their neighborhood and to report on signs of social disorder and violence within it. We defined "neighborhood" for respondents as a three-block radius around their home. Table 4.1 summarizes the neighborhood characteristics that respondents reported they had known as primary school students.

As can be seen in the first panel of the table, the racial/ethnic composition of the neighborhood at age 6 varied quite markedly across groups, which is not surprising given the trends and patterns of residential segregation just described. As primary-school students, white respondents tended to live in homogenous, overwhelmingly white neighborhoods that contained a smattering of other groups. The average white respondent estimated that at age 6 he or she lived in a neighborhood that was 87% white, 4% Asian, 5% black, and 3% Latino. African Americans, in contrast, lived in a residential environment inhabited primarily by other

TABLE 4.1
Composition and character of neighborhood where respondent
was in primary school

	Whites	Asians	Latinos	Blacks
Estimated Racial/Ethnic Composition				
% White	86.6	59.2	57.5	35.3
% Asian	3.8	26.8	4.4	2.5
% Black	5.1	5.8	8.0	53.3
% Latino	3.1	5.9	27.8	6.0
% Ever Witnessing Social Disorder				
Homeless People	11.5	19.9	30.3	30.4
Prostitutes	1.3	1.4	3.4	8.2
Gang Members	4.3	12.0	19.2	25.0
Drug Paraphernalia	3.1	4.4	11.9	22.7
Selling of Drugs	1.6	2.0	7.0	18.3
Public Drunkenness	20.5	23.6	35.6	43.3
% Ever Witnessing Violence				
Physical Violence	13.0	21.2	29.9	36.6
Gunshots	6.2	7.1	16.2	27.2

blacks; on average their neighborhood was 53% black, 35% white, and just 3% Asian and 6% Latino.

Although neither Asians nor Latinos reported the same degree of exposure to white neighbors as whites did, they were not nearly as isolated as blacks. Whereas the average black respondent lived in a majority-black neighborhood during primary school, the average Latino lived in one that was just 28% Latino, and the average Asian lived in one that was only 27% Asian. Thus, both groups lived in areas where whites constituted the majority (59% and 58%, respectively). In terms of exposure to whites, therefore, we see a clear continuum, going from whites themselves through Asians and Latinos to blacks. Although whites, as the majority, are usually not thought of as "segregated," they are actually the most racially isolated of all groups (that is, they are less likely to come into contact with members of other groups). Among minorities, blacks are by far the most isolated, followed by Latinos and Asians.

Patterns and processes of segregation not only produce different rates of intergroup exposure, they also yield neighborhood settings characterized by very different levels of social disorder and violence. In the NLSF questionnaire, we asked respondents whether they remembered *ever* witnessing homelessness, prostitution, gang activity, drug trading, and public intoxication in their neighborhood as 6-year old children. Although these behaviors may not represent serious crimes, they suggest a broader pattern of public insecurity and a lack of social control (Wilson 1983; Skogan 1990).

In general, as young children, whites and Asians tend to inhabit neighborhoods with relatively few signs of social disorganization. For white respondents, fewer than 5% recalled ever seeing prostitutes, gang members, drug paraphernalia, or drug selling in their neighborhoods at age 6, and only 12% remembered ever seeing homeless people. The only visible sign of disorder was public intoxication. About a fifth of white respondents (20.5%) recalled public drunkenness in their neighborhood at age 6. Asians displayed a similar profile of exposure to signs of neighborhood disorder. Fewer than 5% of respondents ever witnessed prostitutes, drug paraphernalia, or drug selling, although 12% said they recalled seeing gang members. The principal signs of neighborhood disorder facing Asians were homelessness (20% reported seeing homeless in their neighborhoods). In other words, most Asians and whites appear to have spent their early childhood in efficacious environments characterized by a high degree of order and trust.

In contrast, substantial numbers of black and Latino respondents reported being exposed to various forms of social disorder at a rather young age. Nearly a third of both groups (30%) recalled seeing homeless people around their neighborhoods as 6-year-olds, and 20–25% witnessed gang activities. Blacks were relatively likely to recall drug activity and public intoxication in their local communities: 23% remembered seeing drug paraphernalia in the neighborhood, 18% witnessed the selling of illegal drugs, and 43% recalled incidents of public drunkenness. The corresponding figures for Latinos were 12%, 7%, and 36%.

Not surprisingly, this differential exposure to drug activity is associated with different rates of exposure to neighborhood crime and violence. Whereas 37% of African Americans witnessed physical violence in their neighborhood as primary-school students and 27% recalled hearing gunshots, among whites only 13% recalled violence and just 6% remembered gunshots. Asians and Latinos fell between these two extremes, with the former tending to report conditions similar to those in white neighborhoods and the latter recalling conditions that were more like those in black neighborhoods.

The Early Adolescent Environment

The neighborhood in which a child spends early adolescence is likely to be particularly important in the formation of his or her character, as between the ages of 13 and 16 young people experiment with different roles and identities, trying out different lifestyles and imitating adult behaviors they see around them (Erikson 1975). In terms of race and ethnicity, the data in table 4.2 suggest that adolescent whites continue to experience very low rates of exposure to other racial and ethnic groups. As in primary school, the typical white middle-school student lived in a neighborhood that was 86% white. Within white neighborhoods Asians averaged just 4% of the population, blacks 5%, and Latinos 3%. Thus, the opportunities for direct contact with minority groups were quite limited.

Between primary and middle school, in contrast, the neighborhoods inhabited by Asian, Latino, and black respondents all shifted toward greater integration and exposure to whites. As they moved from the primary to middle school, the percentage of whites in the neighborhood inhabited by the typical Asian went from 59% to 67%. For Latinos the shift was from 58% to 62%, and for blacks, from 35% to 43%. Despite this movement toward neighborhood diversity, the rank ordering of groups with respect to racial isolation remained the same: blacks continued to be the most residentially isolated of the minority groups, living in neighborhoods that averaged 43% black. Latinos followed, reporting neighborhoods that averaged 22% Latino. Asians were the least isolated, living in neighborhoods that were only 19% Asian, on average.

In middle school we also observe the same rank ordering of groups in terms of exposure to social disorder in neighborhoods. As before, the res-

TABLE 4.2
Composition and character of neighborhood where respondent
was in middle school

	Whites	Asians	Latinos	Blacks
Estimated Racial/Ethnic Composition				
% White	86.4	66.9	62.1	42.8
% Asian	4.3	19.2	5.4	3.4
% Black	4.5	5.4	7.1	45.8
% Latino	3.1	5.8	22.2	5.9
% Ever Witnessing Social Disorder				
Homeless People	12.0	19.6	33.2	32.0
Prostitutes	1.8	4.3	9.2	13.0
Gang Members	10.7	21.6	30.4	34.8
Drug Paraphernalia	9.8	13.4	22.9	33.6
Selling of Drugs	6.2	7.7	20.9	31.2
Public Drunkenness	33.7	37.6	49.9	50.9
% Ever Witnessing Violence				
Physical Violence	26.2	33.2	42.9	49.1
Gunshots	9.0	9.7	22.2	35.9

idential circumstances of Latinos and blacks generally contrast unfavorably with those faced by whites and Asians. Whereas around a third of blacks and Latinos recalled seeing homeless people in their neighborhoods in middle school, the corresponding figure was only 12% for whites and 20% for Asians. Likewise, 13% of blacks and 9% of Latinos witnessed prostitution, compared with only 2% of whites and 4% of Asians. As before, a substantial fraction of black respondents (roughly a third) reported seeing gang activity, drug paraphernalia, and the selling of drugs as middle-school students. Among Latinos a third reported witnessing gang activity, and 21–23% reported seeing drug paraphernalia and drug selling. About half of Latinos and blacks reported public drunkenness in their neighborhoods, compared with around a third of whites and Asians.

As at age 6, these contrasts with respect to gang and drug activity were associated with contrasting exposure to actual violence. Whereas only 26% of whites and 33% of Asians remembered witnessing an act of physical violence in their neighborhoods around age 13, the figures were 43% for Latinos and 49% for African Americans. Likewise, only 9% or 10% of whites and Asians recalled hearing gunshots, compared with 22% for Latinos and 36% for blacks. As black and Latino respondents aged, therefore, they were progressively exposed to much greater violence and social disorder.

Neighborhoods in Late Adolescence

Table 4.3 completes the analysis by describing the neighborhood characteristics experienced by respondents when they were in high school. As at earlier points in the life cycle, whites inhabited a very homogeneous social environment in which other whites constituted 86% of their neighbors, compared with just 5% Asian, 5% black, and 3% Latino. Thus, the typical white freshmen entering an elite academic institution in the fall of 1999 was likely to have spent his or her entire life within a social environment inhabited overwhelmingly by other whites. Most freshmen of European origin thus come to college with little or no direct experience interacting socially with minorities.

For minority respondents, the degree of exposure to majority-group members as high school students once again varied substantially across groups. Whereas the average neighborhood inhabited by Asians and Lati-

TABLE 4.3
Composition and character of neighborhood where respondent
was a senior in high school

	Whites	Asians	Latinos	Blacks
Estimated Racial/Ethnic Composition				
% White	85.5	67.3	63.1	43.3
% Asian	4.6	18.7	6.0	3.8
% Black	5.1	5.3	7.3	44.6
% Latino	3.1	6.2	19.8	6.0
% Ever Witnessing Social Disorder				
Homeless People	13.0	13.6	26.0	28.2
Prostitutes	1.7	4.2	10.1	14.8
Gang Members	12.0	20.9	32.1	35.0
Drug Paraphernalia	14.0	14.0	23.7	35.0
Selling of Drugs	9.7	8.9	22.1	34.2
Use of Drugs	17.9	14.6	26.7	39.0
Public Drunkenness	41.8	39.5	50.2	54.4
Graffiti on Businesses	30.6	37.1	49.0	48.5
Graffiti on Homes	15.9	21.8	30.7	28.1
% Ever Witnessing Violence				
Physical Violence	22.8	24.8	33.3	41.9
Gunshots	8.8	7.0	18.6	36.0
Stabbing	0.3	1.3	5.1	6.7
Shooting	0.4	1.5	3.9	8.4
Mugging	3.0	5.6	9.5	13.1

nos contained a majority of white residents (67% and 63%, respectively), blacks continued to inhabit residential settings where whites were a distinct minority (43%), although by senior high school their neighborhoods had come to house a roughly equal number of blacks and whites (the percentage of blacks was 45%).

Racial and ethnic differentials in the degree of exposure to social disorder are also similar to those observed in middle school: about a third of all black respondents recalled seeing homeless people, gang members, drug paraphernalia, and drug use in their neighborhoods as high school students, whereas 39% reported the open use of drugs and 54% witnessed public intoxication. Similarly, about a third of Latinos remembered seeing gang members and around a quarter recalled homelessness, drug paraphernalia, drug selling, and drug use, while 50% reported drunkenness. In contrast, the percentage of whites and Asians witnessing these sorts of behaviors generally ranged from 10% to 20%, with the exception of drunkenness, which was around 40%.

In addition to the questions asked earlier, we also asked respondents about graffiti they observed on homes and businesses as high school students. Although graffiti in principle harms no one, the presence of "tags" on structures, particularly if they are gang-related, sends a strong signal to everyone that the public sphere is uncontrolled and insecure (Skogan 1990). Whereas 31% of whites and 37% of Asians recalled graffiti on businesses, only 16% and 22%, respectively, remembered seeing such markings on homes. In contrast, 49% of blacks and Latinos reported graffiti on businesses around 30% reported graffiti on homes, providing a strong symbolic statement about the level of disorder in their neighborhoods.

Segregation and Social Disorder

The foregoing tables basically describe the "average neighborhood" inhabited by white, Asian, Latino, and black respondents at different points while growing up. For whites and Asians, this "average" accurately represents circumstances experienced by the vast majority of group members. Among Asian and white respondents, there is very little variation from person to person or time to time in the racial composition or social character of the neighborhoods they inhabited at younger ages. Virtually all whites and Asians experienced the same sorts of neighborhoods at ages 6, 13, and 18. Because of segregation, however, the same cannot be said of black and Latinos.

For blacks, especially, the characteristics of the "average neighborhood" are likely to be experienced by relatively few respondents. Because of segregation, the "average" black neighborhood is actually a composite of traits from two radically different sorts of residential environments. On the one hand, some African Americans will have succeeded in overcoming discriminatory barriers to settle in predominantly white neighborhoods that replicate the characteristics routinely experienced by whites and Asians. On the other hand, other African Americans will for one reason or another have remained segregated in racially isolated neighborhoods characterized by high concentrations of poverty and social problems. To the extent that blacks are split between these two extremes, the average will represent the actual neighborhood circumstances of no one.

Although earlier we asserted that levels of black segregation stood apart from those experienced by all other racial and ethnic groups, in reality the situation is more complex because a significant share of Latinos—notably those from the Caribbean—are partially of African ancestry and are perceived and treated as "black" in U.S. society (see Waters 1999). Darker skin color among Latinos is thus associated with a higher degree of discrimination in housing markets (Yinger 1995) and a higher degree of residential segregation across neighborhoods (Massey and Bitterman 1985; Denton and Massey 1989). Because the elite academic institutions we sampled tend to be located in the Northeast, and because Latinos from the Northeast are disproportionately Caribbean (e.g., Puerto Ricans, Cubans, Dominicans), a significant share of the Latinos in our sample are "black" according to U.S. sensibilities and thus are likely to have grown up in segregated neighborhoods.

Table 4.4 examines how members of each group were distributed across neighborhoods, classified by minority percentage. For our purposes, we combine blacks and Latinos to define the "minority" population and then compute the share of people in different sorts of neighborhoods when they were in high school. As can be seen, for whites and Asians the resulting distributions do not yield any new information beyond that already gleaned from the averages in table 4.3. As high school students, the vast majority of whites and Asians (94% of the former and 90% of the latter) indeed lived in neighborhoods that were overwhelmingly white (containing 30% or fewer minority members).

TABLE 4.4
Detailed racial/ethnic composition of neighborhood where
respondent was a senior in high school

	Whites	Asians	Latinos	Blacks
% *Black or Latino*				
0–30	93.6	89.3	69.9	41.5
31–50	4.2	7.0	8.3	11.0
51–70	1.3	2.9	4.5	9.8
>70	0.9	0.9	17.2	36.8

The distributions of Latinos and blacks, in contrast, are decidedly bi-modal. Although 70% of Latinos reported living in a predominantly white neighborhood, 22% lived in a neighborhood where a majority of inhabitants were black or Latino, and 17% inhabited a neighborhood where more than 70% were minority members. For blacks, the bimodal nature of the distribution was even more pronounced. Whereas 42% of African Americans lived in an area that was 30% minority or less, 37% lived in a neighborhood that was more than 70% minority, and nearly half (47%) lived in a neighborhood where minority members constituted a majority of all residents.

To examine more accurately the range of residential environments experienced by black and Latino respondents in their high school years, we classified neighborhoods into one of three categories based on racial/ethnic composition. We defined *integrated neighborhoods* as those where blacks and Latinos together constituted less than 30% of the population; *mixed neighborhoods* as those from 30% to 69% black or Latino; and *segregated neighborhoods* as those where blacks and Latinos together represented 70% or more of all inhabitants. We sorted African American and Latino respondents into one of these three neighborhood types as high school students and found that about half of all black and Latino respondents lived in an integrated setting during high school. Roughly 30% lived in a segregated neighborhood, and another 20% lived in a racially mixed setting.

To assess how residential experiences vary by degree of segregation, we pooled blacks and Latinos together and sorted them into integrated, mixed, and segregated neighborhoods. We then computed measures of social disorder and violence. The results of this exercise are presented in table 4.5. As can be seen, the Latino and black respondents who inhabited integrated neighborhoods (roughly 70% of the former and 40% of the latter) experienced a residential environment that was virtually identical to that experienced by whites and Asians—one characterized by low levels of exposure to social disorder and physical violence. No more than 15% of blacks and Latinos living in integrated neighborhoods reported seeing graffiti on homes, prostitution, homelessness, drug paraphernalia, gang members, or drug selling in their neighborhood, and just 19% reported actual drug use. Although 38% of those living in integrated neighborhoods recalled public drunkenness and 33% reported graffiti on businesses, these figures were statistically indistinguishable from those reported by white and Asian respondents.

Exposure to violent acts was even rarer for blacks and Latinos living in integrated surroundings than for whites and Asians generally. Although 20% recalled witnessing some kind of physical violence during high school, this figure was actually lower (though not significantly so) than

TABLE 4.5
Composition and character of neighborhood when respondent was a senior in high school

			Latinos and Blacks by Neighborhood Composition		
	Whites	Asians	Integrated[a]	Mixed	Segregated[b]
% Ever Witnessing Social Disorder					
Homeless People	13.0	13.6	12.6	33.1	49.8
Prostitutes	1.7	4.2	2.9	17.8	26.3
Gang Members	12.0	20.9	14.6	50.3	57.3
Drug Paraphernalia	14.0	14.0	12.8	41.1	51.8
Selling of Drugs	9.7	8.9	11.8	35.9	53.0
Use of Drugs	17.9	14.6	18.5	41.8	53.1
Public Drunkenness	41.8	39.5	37.8	57.0	75.7
Graffiti on Businesses	30.6	37.1	32.7	59.3	71.5
Graffiti on Homes	15.9	21.8	14.5	42.3	48.4
% Ever Witnessing Violence					
Physical Violence	22.8	22.4	20.9	50.8	59.4
Gunshots	8.8	7.0	6.8	36.7	58.2
Stabbing	0.3	1.3	1.8	8.5	11.7
Shooting	0.4	1.5	1.3	8.4	13.4
Mugging	3.0	5.6	4.3	13.3	22.7

[a]If blacks plus Latinos are less than 30%.
[b]If blacks plus Latinos are greater than or equal to 70%.

the 22% of whites and 21% of Asians who recalled seeing violence. More-over, just 9% of blacks and Latinos in integrated areas could recall hearing gunshots, 2% witnessed a stabbing, 2% witnessed a shooting, and 5% ever saw a mugging. In other words, those minority members who came of age in integrated surroundings experienced the same safe, secure residential environment universally enjoyed by whites and Asians.

In contrast, blacks and Latinos who grew up in segregated neighborhoods experienced very different residential circumstances. Absolute majorities (50%+) of blacks and Latinos who inhabited segregated neighborhoods reported witnessing gang members, drug paraphernalia, drug selling, and drug use, and just under half recalled seeing homeless people and graffiti on homes, while 76% saw public drunkenness and 71% reported graffiti on businesses. More than a quarter (26%) recalled seeing prostitutes in their neighborhoods.

These indicators of social disorder are very strongly associated with rates of actual violence. Compared with blacks and Latinos in integrated neighborhoods, those in segregated neighborhoods were exposed to three times more physical violence (59% recalled witnessing it), eight times more gun play (58% recalled hearing gunshots), and five times more mugging (23% had witnessed one). Although even in segregated neighborhoods relatively small percentages of respondents ever witnessed a stabbing (12%) or an actual shooting (13%), the risks were many times those experienced in integrated neighborhoods (where the respective percentages were 1–2%). The relatively small number of black and Latino respondents who lived in mixed neighborhoods (around 20% of the latter and 13% of the former) generally experienced residential circumstances that were in-between those faced by their counterparts in integrated and segregated neighborhoods.

Even though the residential segregation of African Americans and Latinos does not vary greatly by socioeconomic status, it may still be the case that those who *do* achieve integration are of higher average status. Table 4.6 thus considers the socioeconomic and demographic traits of blacks and Latinos living within integrated, mixed, and segregated neighborhoods as high school students. We see a clear negative gradient in terms of socioeconomic status as we move from integrated to segregated residential circumstances. Whereas 81% of those from integrated neighborhoods had a parent who had graduated from college, the percentage fell to 65% for those from mixed neighborhoods and 52% for those from segregated neighborhoods. Likewise, roughly half of the respondents who came from an integrated setting (48%) had a parent with an advanced degree, compared with just a third in mixed neighborhoods (32%) and a quarter in segregated neighborhoods (24%). As one moves from integrated to mixed to segregated neighborhoods, the percentage of households with incomes over $100,000 falls from 41% to 20% to 14%; the median income drops from $54,700 to $29,100 to just $25,000; and the value of the home goes from $227,000 to $107,000 to $102,000. At the other extreme, the percentage of families ever receiving welfare rises from 9% to 16% to 24%.

We also observe clear, though less extreme, differentials with respect to demographic characteristics by level of segregation. As might be expected, the sex ratio is most imbalanced among respondents from segregated neighborhoods, only 35% of whom were male. Although the relative number of males rose to 41% among those from integrated neighborhoods (which approached the Asian figure of 44%), it still remained substantially below the white figure of 47%. The percentage of respondents from single-parent families also fell sharply as one moved from segregated (46%) to mixed (45%) to integrated (28%) neighborhoods, but once again it never equaled the figures typical of Asians and whites.

A very high proportion of students from mixed neighborhoods report

TABLE 4.6
Characteristics of blacks and Latinos living in integrated and segregated neighborhoods, compared with whites and Asians

	Whites	Asians	Latinos and Blacks by Neighborhood Composition		
			Integrated[a]	Mixed	Segregated[b]
Demographic Traits					
% Male	47.1	44.5	40.5	42.7	35.2
% Single Parent Household	16.5	11.1	27.9	45.3	45.5
% Mixed Race	5.9	8.5	17.6	68.6	17.5
Skin Color (1 = very light, 10 = very dark)	1.6	3.2	3.2	4.2	4.6
% Mother or Father Born Abroad	12.7	94.4	50.6	48.7	40.8
Socioeconomic Traits					
% Mother or Father a College Graduate	88.9	82.1	80.7	65.4	52.4
% Mother or Father with Advanced Degree	63.0	56.2	47.7	31.5	24.2
% Household Ever on Welfare	4.4	8.5	9.2	16.0	23.5
% Respondent Applied for Financial Aid	63.1	68.3	79.5	90.2	90.5
% Parents Own Home	94.7	85.7	86.4	68.9	70.9
Household Income $100,000+	51.0	42.1	54.7	29.1	25.0
Median Household Income (in $000s)	87.5	62.5	41.3	20.2	13.6
Value of Home (in $000s)	289	298	227	107	102

[a]If blacks plus Latinos are less than 30%.
[b]If blacks plus Latinos are greater than or equal to 70%.

racially mixed origins. Whereas 18% of blacks and Latinos from integrated and segregated neighborhoods said they were racially mixed, the figure was 69% in racially mixed areas. As part of the survey methodology, interviewers also rated the skin color of respondents on a scale from 1 (very light) to 10 (very dark). Given the higher prevalence of racially mixed backgrounds among those from integrated neighborhoods, it is perhaps not surprising that the skin color of those in integrated neighborhoods also tended to be lighter. Whereas minority members in integrated neighborhoods averaged 3.2 on the 10-point scale, the figure was 4.2 among those in mixed and 4.6 among those in segregated areas. Foreign origins were also more likely among those living in integrated neighborhoods: 51% among minorities in integrated neighborhoods compared with 41% among those in segregated neighborhoods.

The Consequences of Residential Segregation

It is thus quite clear that the residential experience of freshmen entering selective colleges and universities in the fall of 1999 was structured by the degree of neighborhood segregation they experienced while growing up. Throughout their lives, white freshmen occupied racially homogenous, overwhelmingly white, and decidedly advantaged neighborhood environments. Whether one considers the residential circumstances that prevailed during primary, middle, or high school, white respondents lived in areas that were at least 85% white and contained few racial and ethnic minorities. Within these neighborhoods, they were unlikely to be exposed to any kind of social disorder or violence, and there was little variation between respondents: nearly all whites had the same neighborhood profile.

Although as primary school students Asians tended to live in neighborhoods that contained a significant percentage of Asians, as they aged their families moved toward areas characterized by greater integration and more exposure to whites, so that by high school the typical Asian lived in a neighborhood that was nearly three-quarters white and just 19% Asian. Beyond this modest difference in racial composition, however, the residential environments experienced by whites and Asians were remarkably similar: members of both groups reported very low levels of exposure to social disorder or neighborhood violence, and, like whites, the residential background of Asians varied little from person to person.

Latinos and blacks, in contrast, grew up under circumstances that were considerably more segregated and disadvantaged, on average. Compared with the other groups, they tended to grow up in neighborhoods that contained considerably more of their own group and far fewer whites. They also experienced greater exposure to social disorder and violence, at least on average. Yet as we have shown, averages can be deceiving, for the degree of neighborhood segregation experienced by Latinos and blacks varied substantially from person to person.

Roughly 70% of Latino and 40% of black freshmen came from integrated neighborhoods in which minorities constituted less than 30% of the total population. Within these residential settings, neighborhood conditions were virtually identical to those observed for whites and Asians, with very low levels of exposure to crime, violence, and social disorder. At the same time, however, a relatively large number of Latinos and blacks (30% of the former and 60% of the latter) came from racially mixed or segregated neighborhoods characterized by much higher levels of violence and social disorder, and a significant fraction of each group (17% of the former and 37% of the latter) came from neighborhoods characterized by a very high degree of racial isolation. Within these segregated minority settings, sizeable majorities of respondents were exposed to multiple manifestations of disorder and violence.

As in the last chapter, we sought to create overall indices of exposure to disorder and violence that could be used to summarize the nature of the social environment that different group members experienced while growing up. Whereas the earlier scales simply added together scores across multiple items, weighting each item equally, in this case we sought to create a scale that assigned different magnitudes to different items to reflect the fact that the different transgressions we listed varied considerably in their severity (from graffiti to shootings).

The procedure we used to develop the scale is summarized in appendix tables B5 and B6. We began as before, by summing up the frequency with which respondents reported different manifestations of neighborhood disorder and violence at ages 6, 13, and 18. At age 6, respondents simply indicated whether or not they recalled seeing various examples of disorder and violence. We coded every "yes" answer as 1 and every "no" as 0. At ages 13 and 18, respondents estimated the relative frequency with which they witnessed these transgressions: never, rarely, sometimes, often, or very often, which we coded from 0 to 4. At age 18 we also asked about the frequency of stabbings, shootings, and muggings, also coded 0 to 4. We then added the ratings at ages 6, 13, and 18 to create two summated rating scales: one for disorder that ranged from 0 to 60 and one for violence that ranged from 0 to 48.

Although both scales were highly reliable (disorder $\alpha = .901$ and violence $\alpha = 898$), they were misleading in that they weighted each transgression equally. To factor in the severity of the different manifestations of disorder and violence, we used the Sellin-Wolfgang Crime Severity Index to weight each item (see Sellin and Wolfgang 1964). Specifically, we took the Sellin-Wolfgang ratings developed and calibrated on the National Survey of Crime Severity (Wolfgang et al. 1985) and matched each transgression listed on the NLSF with the nearest transgression measured using the national survey. We then assigned the associated scale value to the item.

For example, offense number 110 on the National Survey of Crime Severity reads "a person is drunk in public" and has a severity score of 0.2. We matched this description to "witnessed public drunkenness" on the NLSF questionnaire and gave it a weight of 0.2. At the other extreme, offense number 23 states: "A person intentionally shoots a victim with a gun. The victim requires hospitalization." We matched this offense, which has a severity score of 24.8, with the NLSF item "witnessed shootings"

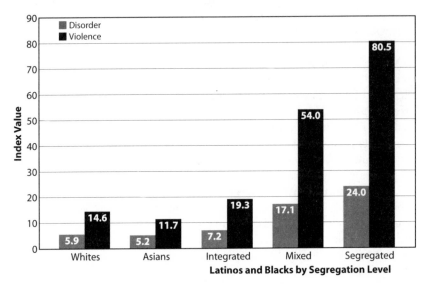

Figure 4.1. Indices of exposure to neighborhood disorder and violence

and gave it an associated weight of 24.8. (The maximum score on the severity scale was 71.1: "A person plants a bomb in a public building. The bomb explodes and 20 people are killed.")

Proceeding in this fashion item by item, we assigned to each indicator of disorder or violence a severity value associated with the closest analogue from the National Survey of Crime Severity. We then multiplied each scale score by the reported frequencies and summed across ages and items to create new, severity-weighted indices of disorder and violence. The index of exposure to neighborhood disorder had a range of 0 to 107 ($\alpha = .780$), and the index of exposure to neighborhood violence had a range of 0 to 567.1 ($\alpha = .779$). Mean index values are presented for whites and Asians and for blacks and Latinos by segregation in the bar chart of figure 4.1.

As can be seen, whites and Asians both experienced a relatively low exposure to neighborhood social disorder while growing up, with respective index values of 5.9 and 5.2 on the 104-point scale. On average, Latinos and African Americans were more exposed to social disorder (with mean values of 11.1 and 16.8, respectively—data not shown); but their exposure varied markedly by level of neighborhood segregation. Those growing up within integrated neighborhoods had a cumulative exposure index of only 7.2, just 22% above that experienced by whites. In contrast, those growing up in segregated neighborhoods had an exposure index of 24—

four times greater than that of whites and three times greater than that experienced by blacks and Latinos in integrated neighborhoods. The inhabitants of racially mixed neighborhoods experienced an exposure to disorder that was more than twice that of integrated areas (17.1).

The contrast in experience by neighborhood is even more pronounced in the case of actual violence. Blacks and Latinos growing up within integrated neighborhoods experienced a cumulative exposure to violence of 19.3 on our index, about 32% higher than the index of 14.6 experienced by whites (that for Asians was even lower at 11.7). But those coming of age within segregated neighborhoods achieved a cumulative index of 80.5, more than five times greater than that of whites; and the index value of 54 observed for blacks and Latinos growing up in mixed neighborhoods was nearly four times as great.

As in the last chapter, the startling contrast is not between advantaged whites and disadvantaged minorities, but between the relative homogeneity of the white and Asian residential experience and the remarkable heterogeneity of black and Latino experiences. This finding has profound implications for the nature of intergroup relations among students in America's elite colleges and universities. Once again, whites and Asians come from homogeneous, privileged backgrounds; yet in college they encounter populations of blacks and Latinos bifurcated into two very different categories. One group of minority students grew up under residential conditions similar to their own. Black and Latino students coming of age within integrated settings experienced considerable interaction with whites within a residential environment that was secure and controlled, yielding a stable, nonthreatening environment within which to develop and learn.

However, another group of minority students came from transitional or segregated neighborhoods characterized not only by a high degree of racial isolation, but by remarkably high rates of violence social disorder. These students must have adopted, at least in part, values, behaviors, and cultural styles required to survive a threatening, insecure, and rather hazardous environment. As Anderson (1990, 1999) has documented, these traits are widely misunderstood outside of the context in which they evolve, creating great potential for confusion, miscommunication, and misinterpretation of motives and intents across groups, not only between whites and Asians, on the one hand, and blacks and Latinos, on the other, but also among blacks and Latinos themselves—between those who had the advantage of growing up in secure, integrated settings and those who did not.

The fact that some respondents adapt as children and adolescents to life in an insecure and often hostile environment also carries serious implications for their learning styles and abilities. Prolonged exposure to disorder and violence leads to elevated levels of adrenaline and other hormones within the bloodstream, which may in turn diminish attention span, reduce the ability to concentrate, and lower the threshold of frustration (LeDoux 1986). By exposing children to disorder and violence from an early age, segregation may cause relatively permanent physiological changes in the brain that undermine normal cognitive functioning; reduce the ability to absorb, process, and retain information; and thus ultimately lower the chances for success in college.

CHAPTER 5

PRIOR EDUCATIONAL EXPERIENCES

ALTHOUGH SCHOOL comes after home and neighborhood in the order experienced while growing up, it is probably a more important ecological setting for determining social and economic outcomes—maybe even more important than the family. Not only is school where young people receive formal instruction in reading, writing, and arithmetic; it is also the venue in which in which they develop friendships, interact with peers, acquire values, and are socialized into the ways of human interaction (Coleman 1961; Coleman, Hoffer, and Kilgore 1982). In terms of sheer time spent, moreover, school dwarfs other childhood and adolescent settings.

For these reasons (as well as the obvious connection between school quality and educational success), it is crucially important to know and understand the educational settings in which the different groups grew up and matured. As before, we focus on three phases of the life course—childhood, early adolescence, and late adolescence—and consider the kind of school attended (public or private), its racial/ethnic composition, and the level of social disorder and violence encountered within it. Since college freshmen are likely to have particularly vivid memories of their high school years, we focus in some detail on this period.

The Primary School Setting

A child's first encounter with formal education comes at around age 5 or 6 when he or she enters kindergarten or grade school. Perhaps the most fundamental distinction among schools is their auspices—whether public or private—and for the latter, whether the school is religious or secular in orientation. As table 5.1 shows, the large majority of freshmen attending the nation's elite colleges and universities began their educational careers in public schools. Among whites and Asians, roughly three-quarters were enrolled in a public elementary school. Among those in private schools, Asians displayed a relatively even distribution between secular and parochial institutions (13% religious and 11% secular), whereas whites were skewed more toward religious institutions (16% compared with 11% secular).

TABLE 5.1
Composition and character of respondent's primary school

	Whites	Asians	Latinos	Blacks
Kind of School Attended				
% Public	72.2	75.1	62.9	70.3
% Private Religious	16.4	12.9	25.0	17.6
% Private Nonreligious	11.2	11.3	11.4	11.9
Estimated Racial/Ethnic Composition				
% White	80.8	58.4	57.2	44.9
% Asian	5.1	25.6	5.7	4.2
% Black	8.0	6.7	8.2	41.9
% Latino	4.4	6.8	26.3	5.9
% Ever Witnessing Social Disorder				
Students Cutting Classes	10.2	13.5	14.4	18.2
Students Cutting School	13.2	15.2	18.5	20.2
Vandalism of Property	49.6	47.3	46.3	50.3
Theft of Property	36.3	39.7	34.7	38.6
Students Using Alcohol	1.1	1.0	1.9	1.9
Students Using Illegal Drugs	0.6	0.9	1.5	2.1
Verbal Abuse of Teacher	31.4	25.6	26.5	39.4
% Ever Witnessing Violence				
Students Fighting	67.8	61.5	68.3	71.1
Violence Directed at Teacher	7.8	6.5	10.3	11.7
Students with Knives	7.0	5.8	8.7	10.1
Students with Guns	0.3	0.6	0.5	1.6

Given that Latinos are overwhelmingly Catholic and that the Catholic Church maintains a well-developed system of parochial schools in many large cities, it is not surprising that 36% of Latino primary students reported going to a private grade school, and that religious schools outnumbered secular schools by a 2–1 margin. Parochial school systems are particularly well-developed in large urbanized areas of the Northeast, places that also house substantial African American populations. For middle-class black parents who are dissatisfied with public education, Catholic schools offer a reasonably priced alternative. Although 70% of black respondents attended a public elementary school, 18% went to parochial schools and another 12% attended private secular institutions.

The second panel of table 5.1 shows the racial/ethnic composition of the elementary schools attended by our respondents. In general, the ethnic composition of the schools attended by whites, Asians, and Latinos followed the composition of the neighborhoods where they lived. White respondents, for example, estimated that their neighborhood was 87%

white at age 6 and that their grade school was 81% white. Asians, for their part, attended schools that were 58% white, and Latinos went to schools that were 57% white, figures that were nearly identical to the white percentages in their neighborhoods (59% and 58%, respectively).

Black respondents, in contrast, attended grade schools that were significantly more integrated, on average, than their neighborhoods. Whereas the average black respondent lived in a neighborhood that was only 35% white and 53% black, he or she attended a school that was 45% white and 42% black. In general, then, black parents, at least those with children who end up in top colleges and universities, endeavor to send their children to schools, often private, that are significantly more diverse than the neighborhoods in which they live.

The third panel of table 5.1 considers the extent to which social disorder characterized the respondent's primary school environment, while the fourth panel considers the degree of exposure to violence within schools. At the grade school level at least, intergroup differences do not appear to have been large; but as was the case with neighborhoods, whites and Asians generally faced less disorder than Latinos or blacks. Whereas 10% of whites and 14% of Asians recalled seeing students cutting classes in primary school, the figure was 18% for blacks. A similar contrast emerged with respect to skipping school entirely: 13% and 15% of whites and Asians, respectively, recalled such behavior compared with 19% for Latinos and 20% for African Americans. The verbal abuse of teachers also varied across groups, going from 26% among Latinos and Asians to 31% for whites to 39% for blacks. Although very few students in any group recollected physical violence directed at teachers, the percentage was 6–8% for whites and Asians but 10–12% for Latinos and blacks. There were few meaningful differences between groups, however, in the extent of fighting, theft, or vandalism encountered within elementary schools, and only a small fraction of any group recalled other students using alcohol, drugs, knives, or guns.

The Middle School Environment

Respondents generally reported similar conditions for the schools they attended as young adolescents. We uncovered few shifts in racial/ethnic composition as students moved from primary to middle school. According to table 5.2, the share of blacks attending a public school increased somewhat to 75%, roughly matching that of whites, and the percentage of Asians and Latinos in public education also rose slightly, to 77% among the former and 69% among the latter; but these small shifts toward public instruction did not entail significant changes in the diversity

TABLE 5.2
Composition and character of respondent's middle school

	Whites	Asians	Latinos	Blacks
Kind of School Attended				
% Public	73.0	77.3	68.7	74.6
% Private Religious	14.4	10.9	19.3	12.9
% Private Nonreligious	12.5	11.7	12.0	12.4
Estimated Racial/Ethnic Composition				
% White	73.9	56.7	56.3	43.9
% Asian	7.0	20.5	7.2	6.4
% Black	10.9	10.0	11.2	39.2
% Latino	6.4	10.1	23.2	7.4
% Witnessing Disorder Often/Very Often				
Students Cutting Classes	11.5	22.8	23.8	33.7
Students Cutting School	8.0	17.1	16.9	27.1
Students Tardy for Class	37.7	42.5	41.0	50.5
Vandalism of Property	11.5	17.3	19.4	23.3
Theft of Property	5.4	10.1	12.1	17.9
Students Using Alcohol	3.0	5.8	7.1	7.8
Students Using Illegal Drugs	1.3	3.9	5.7	10.1
Verbal Abuse of Teacher	6.5	7.5	9.5	19.3
% Witnessing Violence Often/Very Often				
Students Fighting	10.2	10.8	14.3	25.6
Violence Directed at Teacher	0.6	1.0	2.1	4.5
Students with Knives	0.5	1.6	4.0	7.1
Students with Guns	0.3	0.1	0.8	1.4
Robbery of Students	1.7	4.9	5.8	9.8

of the student body. Whites continued to attend schools that were overwhelmingly white (74%), while Asians and Latinos went to more mixed but still predominantly white schools (57% white for Asians and 56% for Latinos). As before, blacks attended schools with the largest share of minorities: 39% black, 7% Latino, and 6% Asian compared with 44% white.

Despite these continuities with respect to composition, the aging of students as they moved into middle school was accompanied by significant changes in the level of reported violence and social disorder. As one might expect, entry into early adolescence was linked to a significant increase in disruptive behavior. Whereas table 5.1 only reported the percentage of students who *ever* witnessed various examples of social disorder, table 5.2 shows the percentage who recalled them as occurring often or very often. Even using this more stringent threshold, the percentages in the table are generally greater. Whereas only 18% of black respondents recalled students *ever* cutting classes in primary school, for example, 34% reported that such behavior occurred often or very often in middle school (compared with figures of 12% for whites and Asians, 22% for Asians, and 23% for Latinos).

As in primary school, exposure to social disorder generally increased as one moved from whites through Asians and Latinos to blacks. Whereas only 8% of whites witnessed students cutting school often or very often, the percentage was 17% for Asians and Latinos and 27% for African Americans. Likewise, some 38% of whites and roughly 42% Asians and Latinos witnessed tardiness often or very often, compared with 51% of blacks. Moreover, whereas 12% of whites and 17% of Asians reported vandalism occurring often or very often, the frequency was 19% for Latinos and 23% for blacks. Exposure to theft in the middle school also increased from the 5% of whites who witnessed it often or very often, through the 10% of Asians and 12% of Latinos, to the 18% of African Americans. Finally, whereas only 6–8% of whites and Asians saw teachers verbally abused often or very often, 10% of Latinos and 19% of blacks did so.

In middle school, we also begin to see the emergence of substance abuse as a significant social problem, and accompanying it, rising levels of violence. Some 8% and 10% of black respondents reported seeing students take drugs and consume alcohol on school grounds often or very often, compared with under 3% of whites. Fighting was seen often or very often by 26% of black respondents and 14% of Latinos, but only 10–11% of whites and Asians. Likewise, robbery occurred often or very often in 10% of the middle schools attended by black respondents, but only 2% of those attended by whites, 5% of those attended by Asians, and 6% of those attended by Latinos. Although possession of knives and guns and violence directed at teachers were once again very infrequent across all groups, the levels reported by blacks were generally several times those reported by whites.

Life in High School

In moving from middle school to high school, we continue to observe relatively few changes in the kind of school attended or its racial/ethnic composition. The percentage of Asians, Latinos, and blacks in public schools rose slightly and the share going to parochial schools fell, but the composition of the student body remained fairly constant. As before, the principal changes were in the degree of disorder experienced within school. Table 5.3 reveals, for example, that by high school tardiness was endemic to all groups, with 60% to 70% of all respondents witnessing it often or very often regardless of race or ethnicity. Absenteeism also seems to have become a relatively common occurrence in high school, although the rate was greater for Latinos and blacks than for whites. Whereas 41% of whites and 50% of Asians and Latinos reported their fellow high school students to cut classes often or very often, the percentage was 63% for blacks. Moreover, whereas half of all blacks (52%) witnessed other students cutting school often or very often, only 40% of Asians and Latinos and 30% of whites did so.

Vandalism and theft were about twice as likely to occur in schools attended by black respondents as in those attended by whites. Whereas 18%

TABLE 5.3
Composition and character of respondent's high school

	Whites	Asians	Latinos	Blacks
Kind of School Attended				
% Public	71.6	75.3	66.4	70.3
% Private Religious	13.5	10.8	20.0	14.7
% Private Nonreligious	14.8	13.7	13.5	14.9
Estimated Racial/Ethnic Composition				
% White	70.0	55.1	53.6	43.8
% Asian	8.6	20.5	9.6	8.0
% Black	11.8	10.8	11.5	36.5
% Latino	7.4	10.6	20.9	8.6
% Witnessing Disorder Often/Very Often				
Students Cutting Classes	40.7	50.5	50.0	62.7
Students Cutting School	29.8	39.8	39.7	52.3
Students Tardy for Class	63.3	70.8	69.7	72.4
Vandalism of Property	9.8	15.1	14.3	18.3
Theft of Property	8.0	10.5	11.4	17.2
Graffiti on School Property	10.8	13.2	16.5	22.1
Students Using Alcohol	12.8	13.2	18.0	17.5
Students Using Illegal Drugs	10.0	9.2	16.3	18.9
Verbal Abuse of Teacher	5.1	7.1	9.2	18.5
% Witnessing Violence Often/Very Often				
Students Fighting	5.8	5.7	9.4	15.5
Violence Directed at Teacher	0.5	0.3	0.9	4.6
Students with Knives	1.5	1.6	3.4	6.3
Students with Guns	0.0	0.2	0.9	2.4
Robbery of Students	2.1	4.8	7.2	8.7
Gang Activities	1.8	3.1	8.1	9.7
% Schools Containing				
Uniformed Security Officers	47.6	53.9	56.5	68.3
Metal Detectors at Entrance	2.7	2.8	3.7	8.7

of blacks saw vandalism occurring often or very often and 17% saw theft with this frequency, the respective figures for whites were 10% and 8%. In addition, only 11–13% of whites and Asians reported seeing graffiti on school property often or very often; but 17–22% of Latinos and blacks did so. Consumption of drugs and alcohol was witnessed often or very often by 18–19% of blacks, 16–18% of Latinos, 9–13% of Asians, and 10–13% of whites.

As the students aged, aggressive and violent behavior likewise became more frequent within schools, especially those attended by Latinos and blacks. Whereas just 5% of whites and 7% of Asians reported seeing teachers verbally abused by students often or very often, the figure was 9% for Latinos and 19% for blacks. Fighting among students was likewise seen often or very often by 6% of white and Asian students, compared with 9% of Latinos and 16% of blacks. Reflecting these differentials with respect to violence, fewer than half of the high schools attended by whites contained uniformed security officers, compared with two-thirds of those attended by blacks (with figures 54% for Asians and 57% for Latinos). Moreover, in around 9% of the schools attended by blacks and 7% of those attended by Latinos, students were robbed often or very often, compared with just 5% of those attended by Asians and 2% of those attended by whites. Gang activities followed a similar pattern, but once again few students of any group recalled seeing knives, guns, or violence toward teachers, although the percentage witnessing such things was always greater for blacks than for whites and Asians.

Our analysis thus detects consistent differences in the educational environments experienced by different group members while growing up. Whites and Asians generally attended predominantly white schools, some three quarters of which were public; and within these institutions they were exposed to little violence and low levels of social disorder. In contrast, Latinos and especially blacks attended schools with much higher minority percentages (but which were more integrated than their neighborhoods), and only 60–70% of the institutions were public. Within the schools attended by Latinos and especially blacks, we observed much higher rates of exposure to disorder and violence. Intergroup differentials can be traced back to the earliest years of primary school, and the contrast between whites and Asians, on the one hand, and Latinos and blacks, on the other, grew sharper as students progressed from grade school to middle school to high school.

As in the prior chapter, however, the foregoing averages obscure more than they reveal for blacks and Latinos. As before, black and Latino freshmen really consist of two very different groups: those who attended integrated schools and those who did not. Table 5.4 reclassifies respondents' high schools by the estimated percentage of minority group members

TABLE 5.4
Detailed racial/ethnic composition of respondent's high school

	Whites	Asians	Latinos	Blacks
% Black/Hispanic				
0–30	80.8	77.1	64.1	41.1
31–50	13.5	16.8	13.5	22.6
51–70	4.9	5.0	8.0	11.5
>70	0.8	1.0	14.5	24.8

(blacks plus Hispanics) they contained. Once again the average indicators reported above accurately represent circumstances for whites and Asians but not blacks and Latinos. Whereas more than three quarters of whites and Asians *did* attend schools that were predominantly white, only 64% of Latinos and 41% of blacks did so. At the same time, 15% of Latinos and 25% of blacks attended segregated institutions that were more than 70% minority.

To examine differences in the social environment prevalent in integrated versus segregated schools, we classified institutions attended by Latinos and blacks into three groups: those that were integrated (less than 30% minority), those that were racially mixed (30–69% minority), and those that were segregated (at least 70% minority). In table 5.5 we contrast indicators of violence and social disorder for whites directly with those computed for blacks and Latinos by degree of school segregation. As can be seen, more than three quarters of all segregated high schools were public, whereas the figure only reached 61% for integrated schools. Of the nearly 40% of schools that were in the private sector, about half were parochial and half were secular.

It thus appears that one means by which black and Latino parents overcome neighborhood segregation to achieve integration for their children is by sending them to racially diverse private schools. Indeed, 22% of all black respondents whose families resided in a segregated neighborhood during high school attended an integrated educational institution, and another 28% went to a racially mixed school. In contrast, only a small minority of students whose families lived in integrated neighborhoods attended segregated schools. Of black respondents who lived in an integrated neighborhood during high school, only 8% attended a segregated school. Minority families thus appear to value integration and are apparently willing to make sacrifices (by paying private school tuition) to achieve it.

Considering how violence and social disorder vary from integrated to segregated schools, it is not hard to see why minority parents value integration. In general, segregated, and even racially mixed, schools are char-

TABLE 5.5
Composition and character of respondent's high school by level of segregation

	Whites	Asians	Latinos and Blacks by School Composition		
			Integrated[a]	Mixed	Segregated[b]
Kind of School Attended					
% Public	73.0	77.3	60.8	85.3	77.3
% Private Religious	14.4	10.9	19.4	10.7	16.3
% Private Nonreligious	12.5	11.7	19.7	4.0	6.4
% Witnessing Disorder Often/Very Often					
Students Cutting Classes	40.7	50.5	46.7	64.0	67.0
Students Cutting School	29.8	39.8	34.9	55.5	57.7
Students Tardy for Class	63.3	70.8	64.1	78.7	75.9
Vandalism of School Property	9.8	15.1	9.2	19.2	28.4
Theft of Property	8.0	10.5	9.0	16.4	23.1
Graffiti on School Property	10.8	13.2	7.8	27.6	33.6
Students Using Alcohol	12.8	13.2	18.1	18.1	16.5
Students Using Illegal Drugs	10.0	9.2	14.2	22.3	18.6
Verbal Abuse of Teacher	5.1	7.1	6.2	17.5	25.9
% Witnessing Violence Often/Very Often					
Students Fighting	5.8	5.7	4.9	17.5	22.5
Violence Directed at Teacher	0.5	0.3	0.6	4.6	5.0
Students with Knives	1.5	1.6	1.7	6.1	10.3
Students with Guns	0.0	0.2	1.1	1.4	3.3
Robbery of Students	2.1	4.8	5.6	8.9	11.8
Gang Activities	1.8	3.1	2.9	11.3	19.4
% Schools Containing					
Uniformed Security Officers	47.6	53.9	49.9	70.5	79.1
Metal Detectors at Entrance	2.7	2.8	1.3	7.4	15.7

[a]If blacks plus Latinos are less than 30%.
[b]If blacks plus Latinos are greater than or equal to 70%.

acterized by much higher levels of violence and social disorder than integrated schools. Indeed, the latter generally replicate the salubrious social conditions enjoyed by white and Asian students. Within integrated high schools, for example, 39% of blacks and Latinos reported that students cut classes often or very often, and 28% said that students skipped school with this frequency (see table 5.5). These percentages are virtually identical to those reported for whites (40% and 30%, respectively). In contrast, 70% of the blacks and Latinos who went to segregated high schools reported that cutting classes occurred often or very often, and 60% reported that students skipped school with this frequency.

The percentage of black and Latino respondents who reported that other students were late to class also varied by segregation, rising from 61% in integrated schools to 78% in segregated schools (compared with 63% in the schools attended by whites). Seeing students tardy or absent from class and skipping school obviously exposes students to negative role models, suggesting that segregated schools tend to support adolescent peer cultures that offer less support for schoolwork and academic achievement.

Segregated schools are also characterized by relatively high rates of social disorder, which can undermine concentration and focus emotional energies away from learning. Whereas only 9% of blacks and Latinos in integrated schools witnessed vandalism and 7% witnessed theft of property often or very often (roughly the same frequencies as for whites), the percentage rose substantially for those in mixed and segregated schools. In mixed schools, 17% of blacks and Latinos witnessed vandalism this often and 14% witnessed theft with this frequency, whereas in segregated neighborhoods, respective figures were 30% and 25%. Likewise, only 8% of blacks and Latinos in integrated institutions observed graffiti on school property often or very often, compared with 22% of those in mixed schools and 32% of those in segregated schools. The witnessing of drug use often or very often nearly doubled, from 9% among students in integrated schools to 16% among those that were segregated, while the verbal abuse of teachers increased by a factor of six or seven, going from 4% in integrated schools to 27% in segregated educational institutions.

The foregoing indicators of social disorder were accompanied by high rates of actual violence. Whereas only 3% of minorities attending integrated high schools recalled seeing students fight often or very often, the frequency was 25% in segregated schools. In segregated schools, moreover, 9% of blacks and Latinos recalled students being robbed often or very often, compared with just 3% in integrated institutions. Reflecting the more dangerous conditions in segregated schools, security precautions were more visible. Whereas 81% of segregated schools had uniformed security officers and 15% had metal detectors at the entrance, the respective figures were 42% and 2% in integrated schools.

Blacks and Latinos attending integrated schools thus experienced rather benign school environments that were comparable to those experienced by their white and Asian counterparts. Not only did blacks and Latinos within integrated institutions experience very different social environments from their fellows in segregated institutions, they also tended to come from qualitatively different socioeconomic and demographic backgrounds. As table 5.6 indicates, the sex ratio among respondents from integrated schools was considerably higher than among those from seg-

TABLE 5.6
Characteristics of blacks and Latinos attending integrated and segregated schools

| | Whites | Asians | Latinos and Blacks by School Composition | | |
			Integrated	Mixed	Segregated
Demographic Traits					
% Male	47.1	44.5	40.7	39.4	36.3
% Single Parent Household	16.5	11.1	29.5	37.9	49.4
% Mixed Race	5.9	8.5	27.7	23.2	10.3
Skin Color (0–10 Scale)	1.6	3.2	3.3	4.1	4.6
% Mother or Father Born Abroad	12.3	94.4	49.9	44.9	45.4
Socioeconomic Traits					
% Mother or Father a College Graduate	88.9	82.1	79.0	65.8	53.9
% Mother or Father with Advanced Degree	63.0	56.2	44.9	34.8	26.5
% Household Ever on Welfare	4.4	8.5	9.7	16.2	23.7
% R Applied for Financial Aid	63.1	68.3	79.5	89.2	90.1
% Parents Own Home	94.7	85.7	81.3	76.4	75.9
Household Income $100,000+	51.0	42.1	38.0	23.5	16.3
Median Household Income (in $000s)	87.5	62.5	62.5	42.5	42.5
Value of Home (in $000s)	289	298	205	145	115

regated schools (41% male compared with 36% male). Students attending integrated schools were also much less likely than those from mixed and segregated schools to have originated in a single-parent family. As one moves from integrated to mixed to segregated schools, moreover, the percentage of mixed racial origins declines and skin color generally darkens.

Minority students within integrated schools tended to come from a more privileged class background. Whereas 79% of those attending an integrated high school had a parent with a college degree and 45% had a parent with an advanced degree, the respective figures were just 54% and 27% among those from segregated neighborhoods. Likewise the share of respondents with household incomes over $100,000 fell from 38% in integrated schools to 16% in segregated institutions, while the average home value fell from $205,000 to $115,000. Clearly, Latino and black families sending their children to integrated rather than segregated schools were better educated, had higher incomes, possessed greater wealth, and came from more stable, two-parent families.

Segregation and School Quality

The social experience of education among our respondents thus appears to be strongly conditioned by school segregation. What remains to be seen is whether or not segregation in schools translates into measurable differences in quality of education. The most basic way to assess school quality is to ask whether or not certain academic and extracurricular resources were even available. This information is reported in table 5.7 for Latinos and blacks by level of school segregation, with figures for whites and Asians shown for comparison.

Naturally, the most important resources in any school are academic, and fortunately we detect relatively few differences between groups and schools with respect to the academic resources. Virtually all respondents—regardless of school segregation—had access to a library, computers, guidance counselors, and regular visits from college recruiters. The only apparent differential occurred with respect to the availability of foreign language labs. Whereas 59% of Latinos and blacks attending integrated

TABLE 5.7
Educational and extracurricular resources available at respondent's high school by level of segregation

			Latinos and Blacks by School Composition		
	Whites	Asians	Integrated	Mixed	Segregated
Academic Resources					
Library	99.8%	99.9%	99.4%	99.9%	98.7%
Foreign Language Lab	51.5	52.8	59.1	57.1	43.7
Computers for Student Use	99.3	98.0	99.5	98.0	99.3
Nonteaching Guidance Counselor	95.4	97.9	96.1	96.4	95.1
School Psychologist	59.9	57.2	59.3	58.4	60.6
Visits from College Recruiters	97.6	97.4	97.6	94.7	93.9
Extracurricular Resources					
Radio/TV studio	47.8	47.3	48.4	47.9	36.5
Drama Theater	91.1	92.5	89.5	87.5	78.6
Band Rehearsal Room	95.8	96.8	95.7	95.3	88.6
Sports Resources					
Swimming Pool	38.3	53.4	48.1	43.4	41.2
Tennis Courts	77.5	86.1	79.6	75.3	64.0
Running Track	86.5	90.6	83.1	86.9	78.1
Indoor Gym	98.5	98.6	98.4	97.1	93.6
Weight Room	96.8	97.4	97.2	93.5	90.9

schools had access to a foreign language lab, the percentage fell to 57% in mixed schools and just 44% in segregated schools.

Although they may not be central to a good education, extracurricular activities comprise an important part of the high school experience. The next panel in the table examines the degree of access to certain "luxury" amenities, such as a radio or television studio, a theater, and a band or orchestra rehearsal room. As can be seen, the great majority of students again reported access to a theater and music rehearsal facilities regardless of race or ethnicity. Nonetheless, access to these extracurricular resources did vary by school segregation. Whereas 89–93% of whites, Asians, and minorities in integrated schools had access to a theater, the percentage fell to 79% for blacks and Latinos in segregated institutions. Although less than half of any group had access to a television or radio studio within their high school (48% for whites, 47% for Asians, and 48% for minorities in integrated schools), the percentage was just 37% for blacks and Latinos attending segregated schools.

Sports facilities are a key component of any physical education program, and virtually all respondents (90% or more) reported access to an indoor gym and weight room in high school. Although access to a running track was somewhat lower (in the 79–90% range), there were no clear differences in access among minorities by level of segregation. The strongest differentials occurred with respect to swimming pools and tennis courts. The percentage of blacks and Latinos attending a school with a tennis court was 80% in integrated institutions (a little higher than for whites) but only 64% in segregated schools. The percentage of blacks and Latinos with access to a swimming pool likewise fell from 48% to 41% as one moved from integrated to segregated educational settings.

In general, however, there do not appear to be strong differentials in access to academic or extracurricular resources between groups or among institutions. Compared with others, blacks and Latinos in segregated schools are somewhat less likely to have access to a school psychologist, a foreign language lab, a theater, and certain "luxury" facilities such as swimming pools, tennis courts, and media studios; but access to the educational basics—libraries, computers, guidance counselors, recruiters, gymnasiums—did not really vary much across groups or settings.

Mere access to resources does not guarantee quality, of course, so in addition to reporting on the existence of amenities, we also asked respondents to rate their quality. The top panel of table 5.8 shows the percentage of students who rated different features of their high school's infrastructure as "excellent." As can be seen, as one shifts attention from mere access to quality of educational resources, stronger intergroup differentials emerge. Perhaps the most basic resource is the school building itself. As Kozol (1991) has shown, U.S. schools are plagued by a variety of "sav-

TABLE 5.8

Quality of educational and extracurricular resources available at
respondent's high school by level of segregation

| | % Rating Resources as Excellent | | | | |
| | | | Latinos and Blacks by School Composition | | |
	Whites	Asians	Integrated	Mixed	Segregated
Infrastructure					
School Building	32.1	29.6	44.2	25.1	12.8
Classrooms	22.7	24.7	37.7	17.5	7.7
Audiovisual Equipment	31.8	32.6	38.7	22.4	15.7
Library	31.2	25.5	39.4	21.4	13.9
Computers	47.0	39.2	57.3	39.7	26.7
Teachers					
Teacher Interest	51.2	45.9	51.0	35.2	37.2
Teacher Preparedness	50.2	42.5	49.2	34.2	32.9
Strictness of Discipline	19.8	16.1	25.1	21.9	24.8
Fairness of Discipline	16.5	15.0	15.8	11.2	15.4
Overall Quality					
Self-Rating of School	47.2	41.1	52.2	31.4	20.8
Public Reputation of School	65.2	66.9	72.8	51.6	42.2
School Spirit	31.1	28.4	33.9	37.9	39.5

age inequalities" that compel some children to learn under harrowing
conditions characterized by deteriorating buildings with poor lighting,
overcrowded classrooms, dilapidated furnishings, inferior libraries, and
outdated audiovisual and computing equipment.

As table 5.8 shows, the quality of the school building varies quite sharply
by degree of racial/ethnic segregation. Whereas some 44% of Latinos and
blacks in integrated high schools rated the quality of the physical structure
as excellent (a figure that was even greater than the 30–32% reported by
whites and Asians), significantly fewer of those attending racially mixed
schools (only 25%) rated the building as excellent, and among those in segregated schools the percentage dropped to a mere 13%!

The quality of classrooms and the tools within them also fell off markedly
as one moved from integrated to mixed to segregated schools. In every
case, the percentage rating a resource as excellent was greater for blacks
and Latinos in integrated schools than for either whites or Asians or for
blacks and Latinos in mixed and segregated schools. Although 38% of
minorities within integrated high schools rated their classrooms as excellent, only 8% of those in segregated schools did so. The excellence rating

likewise fell from integrated to segregated settings for audiovisual equipment (from 39% to 16%), libraries (from 39% to 14%), and computers (from 57% to 27%). Although we did not detect strong differences in the degree of *access* to academic resources, therefore, we do find rather substantial differences in the apparent *quality* of those resources by school segregation.

Schools are more than just buildings and equipment, of course, and probably the most important educational resource is teachers. We therefore asked respondents to assess teacher quality on several dimensions, and these data are presented in the second panel of table 5.8. With respect to teacher interest, we see the same pattern of decline from integrated to segregated schools: 51% of Latinos and blacks in integrated schools rated teacher interest as excellent, a percentage that compares favorably with the 51% among whites and the 46% among Asians. In racially mixed and segregated schools, however, the percentage dropped into the range of 35–37%. Teacher preparedness fell off even more sharply, declining from 49% excellent within integrated schools to 33% in those that were segregated. In terms of the strictness and fairness of discipline, we did not find strong differentials by degree of school segregation.

The bottom panel shows respondent ratings of the overall quality and reputation of the school. Once again, blacks and Latinos attending integrated institutions rated their schools as excellent with a higher frequency (52%) than either whites and Asians (47% and 41%, respectively). These respondents also thought that the general public regarded their school highly: nearly three-quarters (73%) of blacks and Latinos within integrated high schools felt the public would rate their institution as excellent, compared with two-thirds of whites and Asians. In contrast, only 20% of blacks and Latinos in segregated institutions rated their schools as excellent, and only 42% felt the public would do so. Despite these perceived differences in quality, however, our respondents did not report systematic differences in "school spirit."

Differences in Academic Achievement

The quality of educational resources available in the respondent's high school thus appears to vary substantially from student to student depending on group and level of segregation. On the one hand are whites, Asians, and blacks and Latinos in integrated schools. These freshmen entered the nation's elite colleges and universities with a relatively privileged educational background. Throughout their lives, they attended institutions that provided safe, secure, and ordered environments for learning. Their schools had all the educational resources one could want, and these resources were generally of high quality. On the other hand are blacks and Latinos who attended racially mixed and segregated schools. In contrast to other students, they came of age in educational settings characterized by relatively high levels of violence and social disorder and infrastructures and teaching of decidedly lower quality.

Given this pattern, we might expect students from different groups to display few differences in the *number* of courses taken, but that the *quality* of the education received might differ by race and ethnicity. Table 5.9 considers first the quantity of schooling by calculating the average years of course work reported by respondents in different academic subjects. As expected, the groups display rather small differences in the number of years of course work taken in different subjects. The average freshman

TABLE 5.9
Years of high school coursework taken by respondents in
different high school subjects

	Whites	Asians	Latinos	Blacks
Mathematics and Sciences				
Calculus	0.68	0.67	0.64	0.76
Biology	1.26	1.40	1.22	1.26
Chemistry	1.22	1.32	1.11	1.08
Physics	0.95	1.07	0.88	0.76
Geology or Earth Sciences	0.32	0.25	0.35	0.37
Computer Sciences	0.41	0.45	0.50	0.54
Social Sciences				
U.S. History	1.19	1.16	1.17	1.14
World History	1.11	1.08	1.03	1.00
Economics	0.34	0.45	0.38	0.39
Politics or Civics	0.61	0.58	0.61	0.65
Sociology	0.11	0.07	0.10	0.13
Psychology	0.20	0.23	0.26	0.22
Humanities				
English	1.99	1.99	1.99	1.98
Foreign Language	1.97	1.98	1.93	1.93
Music	0.84	0.81	0.65	0.79
Drama	0.28	0.19	0.26	0.36
Art	0.67	0.54	0.73	0.58
Life Skills				
Typing	0.32	0.23	0.38	0.55
Metal or Wood Shop	0.29	0.30	0.39	0.50
Home Economics	0.80	0.82	0.79	0.78
Health	0.98	1.18	0.86	0.75
Sex Education	0.30	0.31	0.48	0.33

came to college with around 0.70 years of calculus, 1.3 years of biology, a little over a year of chemistry, a year of physics, 0.3 years of geology, and half a year of computing. On average, blacks and Latinos reported slightly less chemistry and physics than whites and Asians, but the differences were not great.

With respect the social sciences, intergroup differences were likewise small. On average, students reported entering college with 1.2 years of U.S. history, 1.1 years of world history, 0.3–0.4 years of economics, 0.6 years of civics, and 0.2 years of psychology, plus a minuscule amount of sociology. We encountered even less variation with respect to humanities courses, with all groups reporting about 2 years of English, 2 years of a foreign language, just under a year of music, and 0.6–0.7 years of art. In terms of life skills, blacks were somewhat more likely than others to have taken typing and metal or wood shop, and slightly less likely to have taken health; but in general, the distributions of high school course work are quite similar for whites, Asians, Latinos, and blacks.

Table 5.10 considers the grade-point average earned by respondents in selected subjects (on a 0–4 scale) as well as the perceived difficulty of those subjects (on a 0–10 scale). Although the differences are not large, black respondents generally report lower grades as high school students. The average grade point across all subjects was 3.53 for African Americans, which is very good to be sure, but less than the 3.77 reported by

TABLE 5.10
Grades and difficulty reported by respondents in different high school subjects

	Whites	Asians	Latinos	Blacks
Reported Grades (4-point scale)				
English	3.81	3.82	3.73	3.61
History	3.80	3.82	3.78	3.56
Math	3.67	3.81	3.51	3.33
Natural Sciences	3.75	3.81	3.64	3.48
Social Sciences	3.86	3.89	3.74	3.62
Foreign Languages	3.72	3.83	3.78	3.59
Average	3.77	3.83	3.70	3.53
Reported Difficulty (10-point scale)				
English	4.44	4.99	4.43	3.84
History	4.31	4.79	4.24	3.96
Math	5.00	4.99	5.57	5.55
Natural Sciences	4.70	4.99	4.99	4.84
Social Sciences	3.76	3.99	3.94	3.46
Foreign Languages	4.57	4.25	3.80	4.08
Average	4.46	4.67	4.49	4.29

whites, the 3.83 reported by Asians, and the 3.70 reported by Latinos. Grade point averages for African Americans were notably lower in math (3.3, compared with 3.7 for whites and 3.8 for Asians) and the natural sciences (3.5, compared with around 3.9 for whites and Asians).

Paradoxically, even though black freshmen report *lower* grade point averages in their high school courses than either whites or Asians, they simultaneously reported having had *less difficulty* in them. Whereas the mean difficulty rating was 4.46 for whites, 4.67 for Asians, and 4.49 for Latinos, it was only 4.29 for blacks. Only in the natural sciences did African Americans report more difficulty than whites or Asians.

Thus, whereas African Americans and Latinos gave their teachers and schools lower quality ratings than did whites or Asians, and whereas they generally reported their classes to be easier than did other groups, they nonetheless reported earning lower grades. Whether good minority students were simply bored by having to endure lower-quality classes and consequently earned lower marks than other groups or whether they actually learned less than other groups is a question we cannot answer here. If the latter is true, however, we would expect to detect differences in academic performance as students progress through college.

One final indicator of the quality of high school education is less ambiguous: whether or not respondents took Advanced Placement (AP) courses (table 5.11). As discussed earlier, AP courses are special classes offered in many high schools to prepare students for standardized examinations that allow them to "place out" of certain college courses. Here the relatively modest intergroup differences noted earlier widen considerably. As a rule, Asians display the highest rates of participation in AP courses, followed in order by whites, Latinos, and blacks. One particularly important AP course, calculus, exemplifies the pattern well. Whereas 76% of Asians reported AP credit in calculus, the percentage was 53% for whites, 43% for Latinos, and just 34% for blacks.

These intergroup differences are replicated in the natural sciences, although they generally are not quite as large as for calculus. At one extreme we again find Asians, 46% of whom took AP biology, 37% of whom took AP chemistry, and 33% of whom took AP physics. At the other extreme are blacks, only 26% of whom reported AP course work in biology, 12% in chemistry, and just 9% in physics. As with AP calculus, whites and Latinos fell in-between.

Whereas Asians stand out for their high level of participation in mathematics and science courses, they are much closer to whites in the social sciences and humanities, while Latinos and blacks continue to lag considerably behind. Whereas 58% of Asians and 44% of whites reported taking an AP course in U.S. history, only 32% of Latinos and 30% of blacks did so; and whereas 22–23% of whites and Asians took an AP

TABLE 5.11
Percentage of respondents who took Advanced Placement courses
in different subjects

	Whites	Asians	Latinos	Blacks
Mathematics and Sciences				
Calculus	53.4	75.7	42.6	34.3
Biology	27.6	45.7	24.3	25.8
Chemistry	19.4	37.0	16.0	12.2
Physics	19.3	32.9	18.3	9.0
Social Sciences				
U.S. History	43.6	58.6	32.1	29.8
World History	22.3	23.2	12.9	7.7
Economics	8.4	18.5	8.8	5.8
Politics or Civics	18.2	25.7	16.9	12.9
Humanities				
English	59.4	69.6	51.0	48.1
Foreign Language	29.2	37.3	39.0	17.9

course in world history, the figure was just 13% for Latinos and 8% for blacks. Likewise, 59% whites and 60% of Asians reported AP courses in English, compared with 51% of Latinos and only around 48% of blacks. The highest rate of AP placement in foreign languages (39%) was reported by Latinos, most likely reflecting their background in Spanish. Some 29% of whites and 37% of Asians reported AP coursework in a foreign language, compared with only 18% of blacks.

Although we hypothesized that the lower rates of participation in AP courses by blacks and Latinos might reflect the fact that segregated schools were less likely to offer AP curricula, this was not the case. When we computed the AP percentages based on school segregation, we found no consistent differential in AP work between integrated, mixed, and segregated institutions. It thus seems that the intergroup differentials stem either from intentional avoidance of AP courses by minorities or from their differential tracking out of AP courses by school authorities. Whatever the case, it is clear that, on average, Latinos and blacks arrive on college campuses with significantly less college-level preparation, especially in mathematics and the natural sciences.

Toward the Starting Line

In addition to evidence of intergroup differences with respect to family and neighborhood background uncovered in prior chapters, we can now

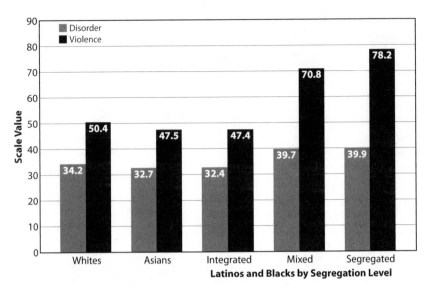

Figure 5.1. Indices of exposure to school disorder and violence

add another layer of difference centered on schooling; and as before, the differences work to undermine the prospects for college success among Latinos and blacks compared with whites and Asians. In addition to coming from less stable and more socioeconomically disadvantaged families and neighobrhoods, students from the former groups are also, on average, more likely to have experienced social disorder, violence, and lower-quality instruction within their schools, especially if they attended racially segregated institutions.

In the same way that we created global indices to measure violence and disorder in neighborhoods, we also developed indices to assess respondents' exposure to disorder and violence within schools. As before, we constructed summated rating scales that weighted instances of exposure to disorder and violence according to their score on the National Survey of Crime Severity. The resulting index of school disorder had a range of 0 to 105.7 and a reliability coefficient of 0.828, and the index of school violence had a range of 0 to 290 and a reliability of .801 (see appendix tables B7 and B8 for details). These indices, which indicate the extent to which respondents were exposed to disorder and violence within their schools while growing up, are summarized in the bar chart in figure 5.1.

In terms of exposure to disorder, whites, Asians, and blacks and Latinos attending integrated schools displayed similar index values (34.2, 32.7, and 32.4, respectively). In contrast, Latinos and African Americans within mixed and segregated schools displayed indices that were about 15% higher compared with whites. As with neighborhoods, moreover, the contrasts were greatest when violence was considered. The violence index of 78.2 in segregated schools is 55% greater than that of whites, which is itself higher than the index of around 47 achieved in Asian and integrated schools (mixed schools are also high at 70.8).

Even though blacks and Latinos report comparable access to most educational resources, the average quality of the resources appears to be lower. To a considerable degree, this inequality is structured by school segregation, as can be seen in figure 5.2, which presents summary indices we constructed to measure the quality of school infrastructure and teaching (the methodology is summarized in appendix table B9). As can be seen, the quality of infrastructure within integrated schools is actually greater than that experienced by whites or Asians, but the infrastructure in segregated institutions is much lower (12.0 in segregated schools compared with 15.3 in integrated schools, $\alpha = .759$). Similarly, the quality of teaching within integrated schools is roughly comparable to that experienced by whites and Asians, whereas teaching quality in segregated schools is lower, although the differential is not as great as with infrastructure (9.1 compared with 9.8, $\alpha = .702$).

As a group, blacks and Latinos earned lower high school grades than either whites or Asians, and they were much less likely to take Advanced

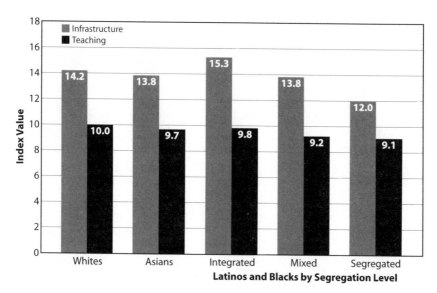

Figure 5.2. Indices of school quality

Placement courses, particularly in math and science. If higher education can be conceptualized as a race, then, the evidence adduced to this point suggests that the various groups begin at rather different starting lines, and that among blacks and Latinos, those attending integrated rather than segregated schools had a considerable head start.

CHAPTER 6

THE SOCIAL WORLD

OF HIGH SCHOOL

A S CHILDREN GROW older, parents and teachers usually feel their relative power ebb, only to be replaced by the rising influence of peers (Rich 1998). The process of peer socialization starts as soon as the child leaves home and begins to interact with other children of the same age—in day care, preschool, or kindergarten. Sensitivity to the opinions of peers gradually increases through primary school and becomes paramount in adolescence. The emergence of a distinctive adolescent peer culture—one that is simultaneously distinct from that of childhood and separate from the world of adults—is a hallmark of modern industrial societies, and beginning with the pioneering work of Coleman (1961), researchers have sought to examine the link between the social world of peers and academic achievement. Two prominent theories that have been advanced to explain minority underachievement are based explicitly on peer mechanisms: oppositional culture and stereotype vulnerability.

The theory of oppositional culture argues that black students underachieve for fear of acting "too white" in front of black peers, whereas the theory of stereotype threat argues that black students fail to perform for fear of appearing intellectually inferior in front of white peers. What students *believe* that their peers think is thus crucial in determining the prospects for success in higher education. In particular, students who think their peers do not value education, do not condone studying, and do not support doing well in school are at heightened risk of succumbing to underachievement by adopting an oppositional stance. Those who lack confidence in their own abilities and fear that they will appear to be less intelligent than others may succumb to stereotype threat. In evaluating these risks, therefore, it is essential to know who a person's friends are, how he or she thinks peers view academic success, how secure respondents are in their abilities, and how sensitive they are to the views of others.

High School Peers and What They Thought

In dealing with issues of race and academic performance, a fundamental issue concerns the racial/ethnic composition of the peer group. Our questionnaire focused on proximate peer effects and thus asked freshmen to consider their ten best friends in high school and to report on whether or not they were black, white, Asian, of Latino. These data are summarized for the various racial and ethnic groups in the top panel of table 6.1. Given what we already know about patterns of neighborhood and school segregation, the results are hardly surprising. The high school friends of white students were overwhelmingly white (8.1 out of 10 friends), and to

TABLE 6.1
Race/ethnicity and attitudes/behavior toward schooling/social life among respondent's ten closest friends

	Whites	Asians	Latinos	Blacks
Race/Ethnicity of 10 Closest Friends				
% White	8.1	4.4	5.5	2.2
% Asian	0.8	4.4	1.0	0.6
% Latino	0.4	0.5	2.4	0.5
% Black	0.5	0.5	0.8	6.1
% of Friends Saying Very Important				
Academics				
Attend Classes Regularly	52.5	48.8	50.7	49.3
Study Hard	35.1	41.0	35.0	38.9
Get Good Grades	52.3	59.0	55.4	63.4
Finish High School	95.6	94.0	92.5	95.5
Go to College	87.2	85.8	79.4	79.8
Social Life				
Be Popular and Well Liked	18.4	13.6	23.9	25.1
Party and Get Wild	16.7	8.7	24.9	17.0
Have Steady Boy/Girlfriend	2.3	2.0	4.9	6.8
Play Sports	27.8	15.4	25.6	24.1
Community Involvement				
Participate in Religion	4.3	4.7	3.9	10.9
Volunteer in Community	6.0	8.3	7.8	11.1
Hold a Steady Job	5.0	3.6	8.4	12.2
% of Friends Saying Uncool/Somewhat Uncool				
In Classroom				
Ask Challenging Questions	13.0	16.5	17.6	15.7
Volunteer Information	12.6	14.6	14.8	14.7
Answer Teachers' Questions	7.5	8.3	10.9	7.8
At Home				
Study Outside of Class	12.9	16.5	21.1	11.8
Help Others with Homework	2.6	1.8	2.9	4.9
Solve Problems Creatively	5.0	5.4	6.1	5.2

the extent that white freshmen had any nonwhite high school friends at all, they were mostly Asian (0.8), with trivial numbers being Latino (0.4) or black (0.5).

In contrast, the ten high school friends mentioned by African American freshmen were predominantly black (6.1), with only a third as many whites (2.2) and tiny numbers of Asians (0.6) and Latinos (0.5). The peer groups reported by Asians and Latinos were more mixed. Both minority groups reported significant numbers of white friends (4.4 for Asians and 5.5 for Latinos), but Asians were more likely to report ingroup friendships than Latinos. Whereas Asians named an average of 4.4 Asian friends, Latinos reported only 2.4 Latino friends. Both groups, however, reported a tiny number of black friends (0.5 for Asians and 0.8 for Latinos).

These configurations of intergroup friendships follow more or less axiomatically from the patterns of school and neighborhood segregation discussed earlier and simply confirm what we already knew: that white freshmen at elite schools come from racially isolated backgrounds that do not expose them to people of different races and ethnicities; that back freshmen are the next most racially isolated group; and that Asians and Latinos tend to grow up under the most diverse circumstances. Probably more important than race or ethnicity per se, however, are the values and beliefs held by one's peers, for these will be central in determining the social pressures for or against certain kinds of attitudes and behaviors.

Our baseline questionnaire thus asked each respondent to report what his or her friends thought about various academic, social, and community issues. The second panel of table 6.1 shows the percentage of respondents saying that their friends rated various *academic* activities as "important or very important." There is little in these data to suggest much intergroup variation in the degree of peer support for school achievement. Nearly all respondents believed that their friends strongly endorsed finishing high school (with 93–96% rating it as important or very important), and a slightly lower fraction felt the same about going to college (79–87%). Within high school, about half of all groups (49–53%) felt that their friends viewed "attending classes regularly" as important or very important.

There were larger intergroup differences with respect to studying and getting good grades, but it was whites rather than minorities who had friends that valued these behaviors less. Whereas 35% of whites reported having friends who thought that studying hard was important or very important, and 52% had friends who felt the same about getting good grades, the respective figures for blacks were 39% and 63%; for Latinos they were 35% and 55%; and for Asians 41% and 59%. Although the peer culture of all groups clearly and consistently recognized the value of finishing high school and attending college, therefore, the peers of white respondents seemed to adopt a somewhat more casual attitude toward academic work than others.

We found relatively minor differences between groups in terms of peer attitudes toward social life. In general, the high school friends of freshmen entering elite institutions did not think it was particularly important to be popular, to be ready "to party," to have a steady romantic interest, or to play sports. Of all these behaviors, respondents attached the most importance to sports: 28% of whites and 24% of blacks said that their friends rated sports as important or very important; but these were the maximum percentages reported for any group in any category. Although intergroup differences were modest, they were consistent in suggesting that white and Asian peer groups attach less importance to social life than those of blacks and Hispanics.

Our respondents' high school peers attached even less importance to community participation, whether measured in terms of religious involvement, community volunteering, or labor-force participation. The highest percentage rating an activity as important or very important was only 12%, and this was for black peers considering the importance of holding a job. To the extent that respondents attached any importance whatsoever to community involvement, however, the groups once again followed a clear progression. White peers generally attached the least importance to community participation, followed in order by those of Asians, Latinos, and African Americans.

In general, then, we find little evidence among our respondents of exposure to an adolescent peer culture that systematically devalued academic work and education, at least among freshmen entering elite colleges and universities in the fall of 1999. Nor do we detect any evidence of a prevailing mindset that privileged social activities over schoolwork, or emphasized participation in the community to the detriment of academic pursuits. To the extent that we found any devaluation of study habits at all, it was among whites, not minorities.

Acknowledging that academic achievement is important, however, is quite different from valuing it as something fashionable, desirable, or good. Drawing on adolescent vernacular, we therefore asked respondents how "cool" their friends thought various behaviors were. In a more directed effort to detect a peer culture hostile to academic achievement, the bottom panel of table 6.1 reports the percentage answering "uncool or somewhat uncool" to selected questions about academic endeavors. Once again there are few differences between groups and little evidence of a negative social valence being attached to school-related work. Only 13–18% of respondents reported having friends who thought that asking challenging questions or volunteering information in class was uncool, and only 7–11% said their friends thought answering teachers' questions was uncool. The highest fractions were reported for friends who thought that studying outside of class was uncool, but here the range was only 13–21%. Only very small percentages of any group reported having friends who thought that helping others with homework or solving problems using new and original ideas lacked social coolness.

Among a teenager's range of friends and acquaintances, the most influential single person is likely to be his or her best friend. Most young people at some point in their lives cultivate a friendship that stands above others with respect to time spent together, number of conversations held, and personal knowledge shared. Such a "best friend" is likely to play a particularly important role as a confidante, counselor, and sounding board for life's important issues. Our survey thus asked respondents to imagine their best friend and to report on his or her attitudes and behaviors with respect to various social and academic characteristics. Table 6.2 gives the percentage of respondents from each group who stated that the trait under consideration was "very true" of their best friend.

The top panel of the table focuses on academics. The best friends of all group members evinced similar levels of interest in education: 53–59% said it was "very true" of their best friend that he or she was "interested in school"; and nearly all best friends planned to go to college, although the percentage was somewhat higher for whites and Asians (95–97%) compared with blacks and Latinos (86–89%). Sharper intergroup differentials emerged with respect to other academic behaviors, however. Whereas 63%

TABLE 6.2
Percentage of respondents who said certain traits and behaviors
were "very true" of their best friend

	% Saying "Very True" of Best Friend			
	Whites	Asians	Latinos	Blacks
Academics				
Got Good Grades	63.2	62.8	57.8	55.5
Interested in School	58.3	56.4	53.4	58.6
Studied Hard	50.6	51.5	44.8	43.9
Read a Lot	32.8	28.5	29.1	28.5
Attended Classes Regularly	74.3	70.5	66.9	63.9
Planned to Go to College	95.1	97.0	88.6	86.1
Friends				
Popular with Others	68.2	55.1	66.5	68.0
Played Sports	48.7	33.8	45.0	40.4
Watched a Lot of TV	19.6	22.1	22.7	28.5
Drank Alcohol	30.5	17.4	26.1	12.1
Took Drugs	10.6	6.4	12.9	6.8

of Asians and whites said that it was "very true" of their best friend that he or she got good grades, the percentage was only 58% for Latinos and 56% for blacks. Likewise, whereas nearly three quarters of whites and Asians said it was very true that their best friend attended classes regularly, the percentage fell to 67% among Latinos and 64% among blacks. A similar progression emerged with respect to studying hard: the percentage saying it was very true that their best friend studied hard went from 52% among Asians and 51% among whites to 45% among Latinos and 44% among blacks. Finally, whereas a third of whites said it was very true that their best friend read a lot, only 29% of blacks did so. In this case, however, Asians and Latinos displayed the same percentage as blacks.

The second panel of the table considers various social traits of the best friend. Whereas around two-thirds of whites, blacks, and Latinos said it was very true that their best friend was popular, the percentage fell to 55% for Asians. Whites were most likely to have a best friend who played sports (49%), with the percentage falling to 45% among Latinos, 40% among blacks, and 34% among Asians. Blacks were least likely to have best friends who drank alcohol or took drugs, and whites were most likely: whereas 31% of whites said it was very true of their best friend that he or she drank alcohol and 11% said that he or she took drugs, among blacks the respective percentages were only 12% and 7%. With respect to both of these risk-taking behaviors, the best friends of Latinos looked similar to those of whites, and those of Asians mimicked those of blacks. Blacks, however, stood out in having best friends who watched a lot of television: whereas 29% of blacks said watching a lot of television was very true of their best friend, the share was around 23% for Latinos, 22% for Asians, and 20% for whites.

So far, the data paint a fairly consistent picture in which the peers of all racial/ethnic groups strongly endorse academic values and behaviors, show relatively little concern for social life or community involvement, and display little negative valuation of pro-educational behavior. These orientations hold true whether one considers friends in general or the respondent's best friend in particular. In general, intergroup differences are modest, but those that we *do* observe suggest that Asian peers display the strongest orientation toward academics, followed in order by whites, Latinos, and blacks. In contrast, the peers of whites are most concerned with social life, followed in order by those of Latinos, blacks, and Asians.

As before, however, overall patterns of variation between groups may be deceptive because of widespread differences in the degree of school and neighborhood segregation. Table 6.3 thus classifies blacks and Latinos by degree of segregation they experienced in high school and repeats the earlier analysis of the respondent's ten best friends and their orientations toward academic, social, and community life. Naturally, the racial/ethnic composition of the respondent's friendship network varies directly with school segregation: blacks and Latinos attending integrated schools reported an average of 5.6 out of 10 friends being white and 0.9 being Asian; those in segregated schools reported only 1 white friend and 0.3 Asian friends. Among blacks and Latinos in racially mixed schools, a majority were nonwhite: 3.9 black and 1.5 Latino.

TABLE 6.3

Race/ethnicity and attitudes/behavior toward schooling/social life among respondent's ten closest friends by ethnicity and degree of school segregation

			Blacks and Latinos by School Composition		
	Whites	Asians	Integrated	Mixed	Segregated
Race/Ethnicity of 10 Closest Friends					
White	8.1	4.4	5.6	3.2	1.0
Asian	0.8	4.4	0.9	0.9	0.3
Latino	0.4	0.5	0.8	1.5	2.9
Black	0.5	0.5	2.2	3.9	5.5
% of Friends Saying Very Important					
Academics					
Attend Classes Regularly	52.5	48.8	53.5	42.9	52.0
Study Hard	35.1	41.0	39.6	33.6	35.6
Get Good Grades	52.3	59.0	58.3	58.4	63.3
Finish High School	95.6	94.0	94.2	94.4	93.0
Go to College	87.2	85.8	84.7	73.8	75.9
Social Life					
Be Popular and Well Liked	18.4	13.6	24.6	24.8	24.7
Party and Get Wild	16.7	8.7	22.0	18.7	22.1
Have Steady Boy/Girlfriend	2.3	2.0	4.2	6.2	9.1
Play Sports	27.8	15.4	26.0	25.1	22.0
Community Involvement					
Participate in Religion	4.3	4.7	5.2	8.2	11.1
Volunteer in Community	6.0	8.3	7.7	9.2	13.5
Hold a Steady Job	5.0	3.6	8.3	11.1	13.6
% of Friends Saying Uncool/Somewhat Uncool					
In Classroom					
Ask Challenging Questions	13.0	16.5	15.9	18.1	16.4
Volunteer Information	12.6	14.6	12.0	16.2	19.2
Answer Teachers' Questions	7.5	8.3	7.8	10.6	11.3
At Home					
Study Outside of Class	12.9	16.5	16.2	14.7	20.0
Help Others with Homework	2.6	1.8	2.9	3.7	6.4
Solve Problems Creatively	5.0	5.4	4.6	5.5	8.4

The attitudes and values of friends varied significantly by school segregation. Curiously, the percentage with friends who viewed attending classes as very important was highest in integrated and segregated schools (54% and 52%, respectively) and lowest in racially mixed settings (only 43%). A similar pattern prevailed with respect to peers' attitudes toward studying, with 40% of those in integrated schools saying that peers rated it very important, but only 34% of those in racially mixed schools, compared with 37% in segregated schools. The percentage of respondents reporting peers who rated getting good grades as very important actually *increased* from integrated to mixed to segregated schools (going from 58% in the former two categories to 63% in the latter). We thought that these patterns might reflect the greater frequency of private schools among segregated institutions, but considering public and private schools separately yielded similar patterns.

Although nearly all friends rated finishing high school as very important, the percentage with friends who thought that going to college was very important declined significantly as segregation increased. Whereas 85% of peers in integrated schools viewed college attendance as very important, the percentage dropped to 74% in mixed schools and 76% in segregated schools. Attitudes and behaviors toward social life did not differ very much by school segregation, but community involvement, though still small, tended to increase from integrated to segregated settings. Whereas the percentage of friends who thought it was very important to participate in religious activities was 5% in integrated settings, it was 8% in racially mixed schools and 11% in segregated institutions. Likewise, the percentage of friends who rated volunteering in the community as very important went from 8% in integrated schools to 14% in those that were segregated; and the share of friends who thought that holding a steady job was very important went from 8% to 14%.

When the data on the "coolness" of various activities are broken down by school segregation, we see a few indications of an oppositional peer culture in segregated schools, as hypothesized by Ogbu, Fordham, and others. Whereas 19% of blacks and Latinos in segregated schools felt their friends would find it uncool to volunteer information and 11% would find it uncool to answer teachers' questions, the respective figures for respondents in integrated schools were only 12% and 8%. Likewise, whereas 16% of those in integrated schools said their friends would find studying outside of class to be uncool, the figure was 20% for blacks and Hispanics in segregated schools. Small declines in coolness from integrated to segregated settings were also observed for helping others with homework (from 6% to 3%) and solving problems creatively (8% to 5%), although such antiacademic values were far from the prevailing values within any school.

Table 6.4 examines the attitudes and behaviors of the respondents' best

TABLE 6.4.

Attitudes and behaviors of respondent's best friend
by ethnicity and degree of school segregation

	% Saying "Very True" of Best Friend				
			Blacks and Latinos by School Composition		
	Whites	Asians	Integrated	Mixed	Segregated
Academics					
Got Good Grades	63.2	62.8	57.7	54.9	56.7
Interested in School	58.3	56.4	55.6	55.5	57.2
Studied Hard	50.6	51.5	48.3	43.2	36.9
Read a Lot	32.8	28.5	31.0	27.8	25.1
Attended Classes Regularly	74.3	70.5	70.4	62.2	58.7
Planned to Go to College	95.1	97.0	89.0	86.0	85.4
Social Life					
Popular with Others	68.2	55.1	69.8	61.7	69.1
Played Sports	48.7	33.8	46.7	44.0	31.8
Watched a Lot of TV	19.6	22.1	21.8	28.4	30.1
Drank Alcohol	30.5	17.4	22.3	15.2	15.7
Took Drugs	10.6	6.4	10.7	11.2	6.2

friends by degree of school segregation. With a few notable exceptions, the academic traits of best friends do not shift much as school segregation changes, which is not surprising given the likely self-selection of friendship dyads based on common traits and interests. There are no clear patterns by level of segregation with respect to best friends getting good grades, being interested in school, or planning to attend college. However, the percentage of Latinos and blacks who said it was very true that their best friend studied hard fell from 48% in segregated schools to 37% in integrated schools while the percentage who said the best friend read a lot went from 31% to 25%. Likewise, the percentage saying it was very true that their best friend attended classes regularly went from 70% in integrated schools to 62% in mixed to 59% in segregated schools.

In terms of social life, blacks and Latinos reported best friends with a similar degree of social popularity regardless of segregation, but the percentage saying it was very true that their best friend played sports declined steadily with growing racial isolation. Some 47% of those attending integrated schools said it was very true that their best friend played sports (about the same percentage as among whites), but this figure declined to 44% in mixed neighborhoods and 32% in segregated neighborhoods. Likewise, the best friend's reported usage of drugs and alcohol declined from integrated to segregated schools, and in all cases levels were lower than among whites in general. Only in terms of television watching did best friends in racially mixed and segregated schools compare unfavorably with those in integrated schools. Whereas 22% of students in integrated institutions said that it was very true that their best friend watched a lot of television, the figure was 28% in mixed schools and 30% in segregated schools.

In general, then, freshmen entering elite institutions in the fall of 1999 seem to have emerged from a high school social milieu in which academic success was prized, where social life and community participation were secondary concerns, and where studying hard, getting good grades, attending classes, and doing well in school did not carry a significant social stigma. Intergroup differences were relatively modest. Those minorities attending integrated schools generally reported social milieus that were identical to those experienced by whites.

How Students Feel about Themselves

The influence of peers depends partially on how a person sees himself or herself: as a leader or follower, athlete or scholar, popular social figure or pathetic nerd. It also depends on the degree to which people have confidence in themselves and their own views—on their feelings of self-esteem and self-efficacy. Students who feel secure in who they are, who generally hold themselves in high esteem, and who feel empowered to succeed in the world are probably less susceptible to peer pressure than those who lack these tokens of confidence.

Table 6.5 explores how members of different racial/ethnic groups define themselves socially and conceive of their relationship with others. The top panel shows the percentage who said that various traits and characteristics were "very true" of themselves. Black respondents appear to be the most confident of their overall popularity: 54% said it was very true that they were socially popular. Latinos were not far behind at 53%, whereas the percentage for whites stood at 46%. Asians trailed well behind at 30%. Asians were also least confident of their athletic prowess (only 20% said they were a good athlete, compared with 37% of Latinos and blacks and 40% of whites), and they also lacked faith in their leadership potential (where just 31% said they were class leaders, compared with 46% among blacks and 41% among whites and Latinos). Perhaps more surprising is that Asians were also least likely to see themselves as good students. Although three-quarters of Asians said it was very true that they were good students, the figure was 83% for Latinos, 80% for blacks, and 84% for whites.

TABLE 6.5
Respondent's self-definition and self-perceptions by race/ethnicity

	Whites	Asians	Latinos	Blacks
Self-Definition[a]				
Socially Popular	46.2	29.5	52.7	54.3
Good Athlete	40.4	19.6	36.8	37.4
Good Student	84.2	75.4	83.4	79.7
Class Leader	40.7	30.8	40.5	45.5
Troublemaker	1.5	1.9	2.5	2.4
Class Clown	4.3	3.1	4.5	5.4
Politically Active	13.3	11.2	15.7	20.6
Self-Perception[b]				
Thought/Acted Like Others	53.6	54.2	49.8	40.1
Hung Out Where Others Went	66.8	68.1	71.8	61.8
Felt Comfortable with Others	94.0	92.8	91.0	90.5
Valued Same Things as Others	58.7	61.0	64.0	51.7

[a]Percentage saying the description is very true of himself or herself.
[b]Percentage agreeing with the statement about himself or herself.

Very small percentages of any group defined themselves as class clowns, and an even smaller share self-identified as troublemakers. These facts are important because Fordham and Ogbu (1986) describe how minority students often seek to evade "the burden of acting white" by cutting up, acting out, or joking around to deflect attention. We certainly see little evidence of such behavior among the black and Latino freshmen in our sample. Nor do any of the groups appear to be very active politically. No more than a fifth of all respondents said it was very true that they were politically active, with the percentage ranging from a low of 11% among Asians to a high of 21% among blacks. The figures were 13% for whites and 16% for Latinos.

The bottom panel of table 6.5 considers how respondents saw themselves socially relative to others. Here we begin to detect a certain feeling among our respondents that they saw themselves as *not* like their peers, especially the black freshmen. Whereas 54% of whites and Asians agreed that they "acted and thought like most people of my age," only 40% of blacks did so. Although the discrepancies were not quite as large, blacks were also least likely to agree that they "hung out where most people of my age go" or "valued the same thing as other students." Only 52% of black students agreed with the latter statement, compared with 58% of whites, 61% of Asians, and 64% of Latinos. Some 62% of blacks felt they hung out in the same place as others, compared with 72% of Latinos, 67% of whites, and 68% of Asians.

Thus we detect an interesting paradox: whereas Asians are least confident in their social popularity, athleticism, leadership qualities, and even their academic performance, they were most likely to say they thought like, acted like, and valued the same things as their peers. In contrast, blacks were the most confident in their social popularity, and highly confident in their leadership skills, athletic abilities, and academic performance, but they were least likely to say that they thought or acted like others, valued the same things, or hung out in the same places as their peers. White and Latino perceptions of themselves and their positions vis-à-vis others were more congruent, expressing strong confidence in their social, academic, and academic abilities and believing themselves to be quite like others of their age. Despite these contrasts, however, all groups appeared to feel quite comfortable with others, with the percentage in agreement ranging narrowly from 90% to 94%.

In addition to respondents' perceptions of themselves as social beings, we asked them to evaluate their self-esteem and self-efficacy using a set of standard scale items, which are presented in table 6.6. In general, respondents did not seem to be burdened by a lack of self-esteem. More than 90% of all respondents agreed that they were of equal worth to others, had many good qualities, and did things as well as other people did. In addition, 79% to 90% agreed that they took a positive attitude toward themselves and were satisfied with who they were. Intergroup differences were small, and certainly there is no hint that Latinos or blacks possess less self-esteem than others. If any group betrays a lack of self-esteem, it is Asians.

Feelings of self-esteem can be measured in the positive or the negative, but practically no respondents were willing to agree that they were failures or had little to be proud of. Larger percentages were willing to endorse the statement that "I wish I could have more respect for myself" and "I feel useless at times." Once again, however, it was Asians who showed the strongest inclination to agree with these negative statements, not Latinos or blacks. Whereas 37% of Asians said they felt useless at times and 24% said they could respect themselves more, only 20% of blacks agreed with the former statement and 16% with the latter. The respective percentages for whites were 24% (feeling useless) and 19% (respecting themselves more), whereas for Latinos they were 26% and 21%.

Given the foregoing data, it is no surprise that black freshmen were the *least likely* to agree that "at times I think I'm no good." Only 10% of black respondents agreed with this statement, compared with 21% of Asians, 13% of whites, and 17% of Latinos. Thus, whereas all groups generally express a rather high degree of self-esteem, Asians are most prone to self-doubts and blacks the least. Yet self-esteem is only one potential determinant of a person's susceptibility to peer influence. Another

TABLE 6.6
Respondent's self-esteem, self-efficacy, and academic confidence
by race/ethnicity

	Whites	Asians	Latinos	Blacks
Feeling of Self-Esteem[a]				
Positive				
I am of Equal Worth to Others	97.4	95.9	97.3	96.5
I Have Many Good Qualities	98.9	97.0	98.2	98.7
Do Things as Well as Others	94.8	90.8	95.2	95.6
Positive Attitude Toward Self	88.1	78.9	90.2	90.6
Satisfied with Self	88.2	78.7	89.3	88.4
Negative				
I Feel That I Am a Failure	1.1	3.8	2.7	1.4
Not Much to Be Proud of	2.1	2.8	3.5	3.6
Wish Could Respect Self More	19.1	24.3	21.3	15.5
Feel Useless at Times	24.2	36.5	25.9	20.2
Sometimes Think I'm No Good	13.4	21.0	17.2	10.0
Feelings of Self-Efficacy[a]				
Positive				
Almost Certain Plans Work	82.7	74.4	85.5	85.7
If Work Hard Will Do Well	97.9	96.4	98.1	97.6
Negative				
No Control Over Life	3.5	8.3	5.0	4.5
Luck More Important than Work	1.8	4.1	2.9	2.2
Stopped When Try to Get Ahead	2.1	3.2	3.8	6.7
Feel Left Out of Things	12.2	15.6	14.7	14.3
Academic Confidence[b]				
Finish One Year of College	97.5	96.9	94.8	96.4
Finish Two Years of College	92.9	94.0	91.7	94.4
Graduate from College	85.8	88.0	84.1	91.7
Go to Grad/Prof School	25.4	43.6	39.2	50.4
Complete Grad/Prof School	21.8	39.1	35.3	49.8

[a]Percentage agreeing with statement.
[b]Percentage certain of outcome.

is self-efficacy: the belief that one's actions and intentions substantially determine one's fate. These data are presented in the second panel of table 6.6.

As before, all groups feel a rather high degree of personal empowerment. Over 96% of respondents in all groups believed that if they worked hard they would do well, and at least three quarters were "almost certain" that when they made plans, they would work out. Likewise, only small percentages agreed that they had no control over their lives, that luck was more important than hard work, and that "every time I try to get ahead something or somebody stops me." Consistent with these sentiments, fewer than 16% of the respondents in any group felt left out of things going on around them. To the extent that there were any salient patterns by group, it was once again *Asians* who displayed the least proclivity toward self-efficacy, not Latinos or blacks, who generally compared quite favorably with whites.

Given these self-described feelings of esteem and efficacy, one would expect that freshmen had a great deal of confidence in their prospects for academic success, even though they had just entered the most elite segment of American higher education. This is indeed the case. We asked respondents to rate the chances of completing various educational milestones on a 1–10 scale. The ratings were so high that the only variance we observed was in the percentage of respondents who selected a rating of 10, indicating *complete* certainty of success. The outcomes we considered were finishing the first year of college, finishing the second year, graduating from college, attending a graduate or professional school, and completing a graduate or professional degree.

There is little variance among group members in their certainty of completing at least one year of college: 95–98% were completely certain of making it this far. There was likewise little variation between groups in the certainty of completing a second year. As one moves through college and onto graduate or professional school, however, an interesting differential emerges: blacks are *most certain* of academic success while whites are least certain. Although the vast majority of respondents were completely certain that they would graduate from college, the figure was 92% for blacks but only 86% for whites (Latinos stood at 84% and Asians stood at 88%). Not only were blacks more certain that they would finish college, they were also quite sure that they would attend a graduate or professional school and complete an advanced degree. In fact, the percentage of blacks who expressed total certainty in finishing a graduate or professional degree (50%) was more than twice that for whites (22%) and well above that for Asians (39%) and Latinos (35%).

Of all freshmen entering elite institutions of higher education, therefore, blacks have the highest self-described levels of esteem, efficacy, and confidence in academic success. Asians have detectably lower levels of self-esteem and self-efficacy but nonetheless express great confidence in their prospects for success. Whites have high feelings of self-esteem and self-efficacy, but less confidence in academic success, while Latinos are most consistent in simultaneously expressing a high degree of self-esteem, self-efficacy, and confidence of success.

These intergroup differentials are precisely opposite those of high school achievement and generally inconsistent with measured differentials in home, school, and neighborhood environments, where blacks fared worse, on average, than other groups. The lack of association between prior academic performance and expressed self-esteem is a well-established phenomenon for minority groups such as African Americans, who historically were subject to subordination and discrimination on the basis of race rather than accomplishment. In general, poor performance does not lower self-esteem when it can be attributed to an external cause, such as racism, rather than an internal cause, such as lack of ability. Crocker and Major (1989) refer to the uncertainty about whether events happen because of prejudice or because one deserves them as "attributional ambiguity" (see also Major and Crocker 1993; Crocker and Quinn 1998). In this case, ambiguity protects the self-esteem of stigmatized groups because it provides a ready external attribution for negative outcomes.

Ogbu and Fordham's hypothesis that black students fail to perform academically in order to avoid the burden of acting white grew out of their ethnographic work in segregated, inner-city schools, and we might therefore expect the self-conceptions of minority students to vary depending on whether fellow students are mostly white or predominantly black. Table 6.7 thus considers self-definitions and self-perceptions of Latinos and blacks in integrated, mixed, and segregated schools. If black students

TABLE 6.7
Respondent's self-definition and self-perception by degree of school segregation

	Whites	Asians	Blacks and Latinos by School Composition		
			Integrated	Mixed	Segregated
Self-Definition					
Socially Popular	46.2	29.5	56.4	50.4	50.9
Good Athlete	40.4	19.9	38.7	37.4	33.0
Good Student	84.2	75.4	81.3	79.2	85.5
Class Leader	40.7	30.8	40.5	40.1	52.4
Troublemaker	1.5	1.9	1.9	2.4	3.7
Class Clown	4.3	3.1	4.4	4.9	6.2
Politically Active	13.3	11.2	16.4	17.9	22.4
Self-Perception					
Thought/Acted Like Others	53.6	54.2	48.9	43.2	38.8
Hung Out Where Others Went	66.8	68.1	71.1	61.7	64.5
Felt Comfortable with Others	94.0	92.8	92.8	91.1	85.7
Valued Same Things as Others	58.7	61.0	66.1	54.6	43.9

in segregated schools are indeed more sensitive to the burden of acting white, then we would expect the percentage seeing themselves as troublemakers, class clowns, and political activists to increase as we move from integration to segregation (thus deflecting attention away from academic interests and achievements), and the percentage seeing themselves as like their peers to fall.

In general, the data seem to follow the expected pattern. As the percentage of blacks and Latinos who see themselves as good students increases from integration (81%) to segregation (86%), so do the share who see themselves as troublemakers (2–4%), class clowns (4–6%), and political activists (16–22%). Although consistent with expectations, however, the differentials are rather small. More support for the idea that high-achieving minorities see themselves as ill-fitting socially comes from questions on self-perceptions. Whereas 66% of blacks and Latinos attending integrated schools agreed that they "valued the same things as others," only 44% of those in segregated schools did so. The percentage who felt they thought and acted like others likewise fell from 49% to 39% moving from integrated to segregated settings, and the share saying they hung out where others went fell from 71% to 65%. The percentage of blacks and Hispanics who said they felt comfortable with others dropped from 93% to 86%.

In table 6.8 we examine self-evaluations of esteem, efficacy, and confidence by level of school segregation. In general, the feelings of self-esteem expressed by Latinos and blacks do not vary systematically by level of segregation and are universally high: minorities in all settings endorse positive feelings and reject negative feelings of self-esteem in nearly identical numbers. Likewise, there are few differences in feelings of self-efficacy. The only significant difference concerns feelings of being left out of things: whereas only 13% of blacks and Latinos within integrated institutions said they felt left out (about the same percentage as among whites), the share agreeing rose to 17% in mixed schools and 20% in those that were segregated.

The last panel of table 6.8 considers the data on academic self-confidence by degree of school segregation. This analysis only deepens the paradox described earlier, where blacks expressed greater certainty than other groups finishing college and going on to earn a graduate or professional degree, despite lower self-reported grades, preparation, and educational quality in high school. Not only are blacks and Latinos surer than other groups of graduating from college and earning an advanced degree, the percentage expressing complete certainty in doing so rises as one moves from integrated to segregated schools. Whereas the percentage saying they were totally certain of going to graduate or professional school was 42% within integrated schools, it rose to 46% in mixed schools and

TABLE 6.8

Respondents' self-esteem, self-efficacy, and academic confidence
by degree of school segregation

			Blacks and Latinos by School Composition		
	Whites	Asians	Integrated	Mixed	Segregated
Feelings of Self-Esteem					
Positive					
I am of Equal Worth to Others	97.4	95.9	97.4	96.2	96.7
I Have Many Good Qualities	98.9	97.0	98.4	98.0	99.1
Do Things as Well as Others	94.8	90.8	95.5	95.7	94.8
Positive Attitude toward Self	88.1	78.9	90.2	90.3	90.9
Satisfied with Self	88.2	78.7	89.2	87.7	89.8
Negative					
I Feel That I Am a Failure	1.1	3.8	1.4	2.7	2.8
Not Much to Be Proud of	2.1	2.8	2.6	5.5	3.2
Wish Could Respect Self More	19.1	24.3	19.5	17.6	17.1
Feel Useless at Times	24.2	36.5	24.7	20.3	23.2
Sometimes Think I'm No Good	13.4	21.0	15.6	11.8	11.5
Feelings of Self-Efficacy					
Positive					
Almost Certain Plans Work	82.7	74.4	85.6	86.9	83.5
If Work Hard Will Do Well	97.9	96.4	97.7	98.3	97.6
Negative					
No Control Over Life	3.5	8.3	4.2	4.2	6.6
Luck More Important than Work	1.8	4.1	2.9	1.1	3.7
Stopped When Try to Get Ahead	2.1	3.2	6.0	3.1	6.6
Feel Left Out of Things	12.5	15.6	13.2	15.0	16.9
Complete Academic Confidence					
Finish One Year of College	97.5	96.9	96.1	94.2	96.2
Finish Two Years of College	92.9	94.0	93.9	90.7	94.1
Graduate from College	85.8	88.0	86.9	86.4	92.0
Go to Grad/Prof School	25.4	43.6	41.5	46.0	50.1
Complete Grad/Prof School	21.8	39.1	39.0	41.9	51.1

reached 50% in segregated institutions. Likewise the share certain of finishing a graduate or professional degree rose from 39% to 51% moving
from integrated to segregated schools. Again this pattern most likely reflects attributional ambiguity, whereby students in segregated schools are
more likely to attribute lack of achievement to lack of opportunity rather
than lack of ability.

Sensitivity to Peer Pressure

Whether or not minority students are susceptible to social pressure also depends on the degree to which they are sensitive to the views of others. We thus asked respondents to express how self-conscious they were about how whites', blacks', Asians', and Latinos' perceptions of themselves, using a scale of 0 (not conscious at all) to 10 (extremely sensitive). These ratings are presented in the top panel of table 6.9. In general, whites were nearly equally as sensitive to the opinions of other whites as to those of minorities. Whereas the average sensitivity of whites to the views of other whites was 2.6, their sensitivity to the views of Asians was 1.3, compared with ratings of 1.4 for Latinos and 1.8 for blacks. Asians and Latinos also expressed relatively a relatively high degree of sensitivity to ingroup opinions. Asians rated their sensitivity to the views of other Asian students at 3.1, whereas Latinos put their sensitivity to the views of other Latinos at 2.3. Whereas whites were relatively unconcerned with the opinions of outgroups, however, Asians and Latinos were almost as sensitive to the feelings of whites as of their own ingroups. Asians rated their sensitivity to whites at 2.7, and Latinos put theirs at 2.2. Blacks shared roughly the same level of sensitivity to white opinion (2.5) but were significantly more sensitive to the views of other blacks. With a rating of 3.7, their ingroup sensitivity score exceeded that of all other groups, as one might expect given Ogbu and Fordham's (1986) reasoning.

Thus, to the extent that their same-race peers hold views antagonistic

TABLE 6.9
Respondents' behavior toward and sensitivity to opinions
of others by race/ethnicity

	Whites	Asians	Latinos	Blacks
Sensitivity to Views of Others				
Of White Students	2.6	2.7	2.2	2.5
Of Asian Students	1.3	3.1	1.5	1.3
Of Latino Students	1.4	1.4	2.3	1.4
Of Black Students	1.8	1.7	1.7	3.7
Of Teachers	4.8	5.4	5.0	5.5
Behavior with Respect to Peers				
Did Not Report Good Grades	12.7	21.5	11.9	12.9
Acted Less Intelligent	4.3	9.4	5.8	6.5
Worried about Being Nerd	1.2	1.7	0.8	1.2
Tried to Be More Likeable	6.2	8.0	5.7	2.8
Worried What Others Thought	17.9	20.6	14.3	11.9

to studying hard, getting good grades, and succeeding in school, our black respondents will be quite sensitive to them, more so than other groups, suggesting significant potential for the burden of acting white to undermine performance. The last line of the top panel suggests that black students might also be more susceptible to stereotype vulnerability, as their estimated sensitivity to teachers' opinions is also the highest of any group. Whereas whites' sensitivity to teachers averaged only 4.8, among blacks it was 5.5, compared with 5.4 for Asians and 5.0 for Latinos.

The second panel seeks to determine whether respondents changed their behavior in any way to seem less intelligent than they really were, to appear less academically accomplished, or whether they worried about being perceived as a "nerd" or "brainiac." Among all groups, Asians seemed to alter their behavior most consistently in anticipation of their peers' negative reaction. Some 22% said they did not report getting good grades to their friends, 9% said they acted less intelligent than they really were, and 8% said they sought to be more likeable. At the other extreme were whites: only 13% did not report good grades, 4% acted less intelligent, and 6% tried to be more likeable.

Compared with Asians, blacks did not seem to alter their behavior very much at all. Although 13% said they did not report good grades to their friends (about the same as whites but less than Asians), only 6% said they acted less intelligent and 3% said they tried to be more likeable. Latinos displayed a similar profile, except that a slightly higher fraction tried to be more likeable. Although practically no one in any group worried about being perceived as a "nerd," Asians were more worried about what others thought (21%), followed by whites (18%), Latinos (14%), and African Americans (12%). When we broke the data on sensitivity down by level of school segregation, we did not find many differences among blacks and Latinos attending integrated, mixed, and segregated high schools (data not shown).

Vulnerabilities

In general, the data developed in this chapter auger well for the success of freshmen entering elite institutions of higher education in the fall of 1999, regardless of race or ethnicity. As high school students, they inhabited a social world in which hard work, good grades, and academic prowess were valued, and in which social life and community participation assumed secondary importance to education. We found little evidence that taking school seriously was negatively valued by peers or that academic success was significantly stigmatized. To the extent that we detected any favoring of social over academic pursuits, it was not among minorities but

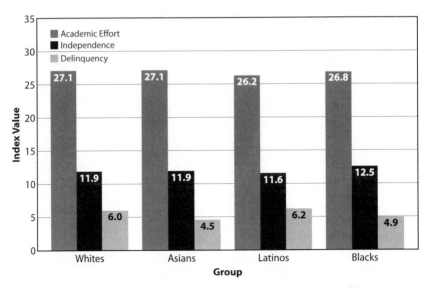

Figure 6.1. Indices measuring peer support for academic effort,
intellectual independence, and delinquency

among whites, who were most concerned with social life, followed in
order by blacks, Latinos, and Asians.

The degree to which this academically supportive milieu held true for
all racial and ethnic groups is suggested by the data depicted in figure 6.1,
which presents summary indices of peer support for academic effort, intellectual independence, and delinquency. As before, these were created as
summated ratings scales that coded the extent of agreement to sets of
items pertaining to each subject and then added up the assigned values
across items to create the scale (see appendix table B10 for details).

The scale of peer support for academic effort contained items dealing
with the degree to which friends thought it was cool to study outside of
class, get good grades, plan to go to college; how important they thought
it was to attend classes, study hard, get good grades, and go to college;
and the extent to which their best friend was interested in school, got good
grades, studied hard, attended class, planned to attend college, and read
a lot. The result index had a reliability coefficient of .819. As can be seen,
differences between groups on this index were truly marginal, with mean
levels varying from a low of 26.2 for Latinos to a high of 27.1 for whites
and Asians.

The index of support for academic independence was based on five items
that asked the respondent how cool their friends thought it was to ask challenging questions, volunteer information, and answer questions in class, as

well as to help others with homework and solve problems using new ideas. This index was also highly reliable ($\alpha = .814$) and varied little between groups, with mean values ranging narrowly from 11.6 to 12.5.

There was somewhat more variance in the index of support for delinquency, which was based on five items that assessed how important their friends thought it was to party and get wild, how many of them got drunk and used drugs, and the frequency with which their best friend got drunk and took drugs. Its reliability coefficient was .825. In general, whites and Latinos reported coming from a social milieu in which such actions were supported more than did Asians or blacks. Whereas the average support for delinquency stood at 6.0 for whites and 6.2 for Latinos, it was only 4.9 for blacks and 4.5 for Asians.

For the most part, the high school peer environment was associated with a high degree of self-esteem, self-efficacy, and self-confidence, with only modest differences across groups. Blacks generally reported the highest levels of self-esteem, efficacy, and confidence. Asians had detectably lower levels of self-esteem and self-efficacy but reported considerable confidence in their prospects for academic success. Whites evinced high levels of self-esteem and self-efficacy but expressed less confidence in their prospects for academic success. Latinos consistently reported relatively high degrees of esteem, efficacy, and confidence of success.

A closer look at the data reveals a dark lining to this otherwise silver cloud, however. Although intergroup differences were modest, they did follow a clear pattern: the friends and best friends of blacks were consistently least oriented toward academic success, followed in order by Latinos, whites, and Asians. Moreover, within segregated schools, the modest orientation of Hispanics and blacks away from academic work was accentuated, and scholarly success seemed to carry more stigma. Latinos and African Americans in integrated schools, in contrast, reported social milieus that were indistinguishable from those of whites.

Another cause for concern stems from the fact that minorities' expressed self-confidence in graduating from college and attending graduate school *rose* as one moved from integrated to segregated school settings, despite the fact that the same respondents consistently rated the quality of teachers, infrastructure, and education to be markedly lower in segregated than integrated schools, and segregated schools evinced by far the highest levels of violence and social disorder. Although blacks were most confident of their prospects for success in higher education, they also reported the lowest grades, the least preparation in mathematics and sciences, and the fewest Advanced Placement courses. Among at least some minority students, therefore, we observe something of a disconnect between prior academic preparation and assessments of the prospects for success in college.

In addition to the psychological vulnerabilities of stereotype threat and racelessness, therefore, we might add another potential pitfall: overconfidence. Our respondents are entering the most selective colleges and universities in the country. In doing so, they are moving from a school environment in which they stood out as academic stars, well above the vast majority of their peers in accomplishment and intelligence, to a new environment in which *all their fellow students* will be highly accomplished and of equal or greater intelligence. For the first time in their lives, many students will find that they are not the smartest, best prepared, or most accomplished. The level of knowledge assumed by their instructors will be a quantum leap above that assumed by their high school teachers, the competition will be tougher, and expectations for work and proficiency will be markedly higher.

For these reasons, moving from high school to college is a difficult adjustment for all but the most exceptional students, and the psychological problems accompanying this move are likely to be exacerbated among those whose initial confidence is most out-of-keeping with their prior preparation. The data collected in the baseline survey permit us to identify such students. Through a judicious cross-tabulation of reported self-confidence and indicators of prior academic success and preparation, we can identify a subset of black and Latino students whose confidence seems most out-of-keeping with their actual level of college preparation, people at greatest risk of experiencing psychological trauma in encountering the realities of academic life in very selective institutions.

We selected those black respondents who said they were completely certain they would graduate from college and distributed them by the quality of their high school, the number of Advanced Placement courses taken, and grade point earned. We found that 12% of all African American freshmen were totally sure of graduating from college but came from a school that they rated as only fair or poor in quality. Likewise, 16% were completely sure they would graduate from college and yet had taken *no* Advanced Placement courses, and 17% were certain of graduating yet had earned a grade point average under 3.0 in high school. Among Latinos, 12% were completely certain of graduating from college yet said they came from a school that was fair or poor in quality, 9% were sure of graduating yet had taken no Advanced Placement courses, and 31% were completely confident of graduating from college but had earned a grade point average under 3.0. Considering everything, the share of blacks whose confidence in college success seems to be most inconsistent with prior performance is 12–17%, and for Latinos the percentage is at least 10% and perhaps as high as 31%. These people are most at risk of experiencing emotional shock, disappointment, and depression in response to their encounter with college-level work.

Our survey data can also be used to identify the subset of minority students most at risk of underperformance because of stereotype threat. By cross-tabulating sensitivity to the opinions of white peers with reported feelings of self-esteem and self-efficacy, we should be able to get at the issue. Respondents who simultaneously report themselves as being sensitive to the opinions of whites and express doubts that they are good students would seem to be at greatest risk of stereotype threat. The share of respondents who simultaneously reported themselves as being very sensitive to the opinions of whites (a sensitivity score of 7+) and reported that it was "not true" or only "somewhat true" that they were good students was very small—only around 2.2% of all black and Latino students. Likewise, the percentage who were sensitive to whites (rating of 7+) and also wished they could have more self-respect was only 5% of both blacks and Latinos.

Stereotype threat might also involve fears of poor performance in front of teachers, who tend to be white themselves or are seen to represent the values and norms of the white establishment (Fordham 1996). The share who reported themselves as being very sensitive to the opinion of teachers (a rating of 7 or higher) and who also said that it was not true or somewhat true that they were good students was slightly larger: about 8% of blacks and 6% of Latinos. Around 8% of both blacks and Latinos simultaneously said they were very sensitive to the views of teachers and wished they could have more self-respect. Thus the relative number of respondents who would appear to be at serious risk of stereotype vulnerability is around 2–3% of black and Latino students if we base our assessment on sensitivity to white peers, and around 8% if we base it on sensitivity to the opinions of teachers.

Ogbu and Fordham refer to the psychological burden of racelessness, the feeling that by doing well in school and achieving academic distinction, one is acting "white" rather than "black," and thus being put in the position of having to deny one's racial identity (to become "raceless") in order to succeed in school. Those who are at greatest risk of succumbing to this psychological pressure are those that are sensitive to the opinions of other black students and believe them to hold views that are unsupportive of educational achievement. The share of respondents who simultaneously said they were very sensitive to the opinions of co-ethnics (with a sensitivity rating of 7+) and believed their friends viewed studying hard as being of little or no importance was 3% for blacks and 2% for Latinos. Roughly the same percentages simultaneously were sensitive to the views of black students and believed them to view studying as somewhat or very uncool. If we expand the latter category to include those who rated studying as neutral (that is, all those who did not explicitly state that studying was cool or very cool), the percentage rises to 11% for blacks and 6% for Hispanics.

Thus, in terms of potential for undermining the psychological motivation for success in higher education, the most serious threat seems to be overconfidence. Somewhere between 10% and 20% of Latinos and blacks appear to exhibit a serious discrepancy between their scholarly preparation and their certainty in graduating from college. The next most important threat in terms of the number of people at risk is stereotype vulnerability, which is a serious concern of some 2–8% of blacks and Latinos. Not far behind is the threat of racelessness, which seems to be a serious risk for 2–3% of minority students, and perhaps as many as 11%.

Obviously these characterizations are very rough and inexact, and to the extent that students experience threats to academic achievement from these psychological sources, they probably operate on a continuum rather than a dichotomy. Nonetheless, the good news is that the large majority of blacks and Latinos entering elite colleges and universities in the fall of 1999 would not seem to be at serious risk of stereotype vulnerability, racelessness, or overconfidence. The bad news is that the potential numbers of minority students who *are* at risk are large enough to have significant effects on overall rates of graduation and achievement. Fortunately, this issue need not remain in the realm of idle speculation, for the NLSF will follow those we have identified as being at significant risk or not at risk and follow them as they progress from one educational milestone to another. By identifying persons most at risk of these psychosocial processes *before* academic outcomes are recorded, we will be in a strong position to test and evaluate the corresponding theories.

CHAPTER 7

RACIAL IDENTITY AND ATTITUDES

S OCIETAL MESSAGES about the presumed superiority or inferiority of various racial or ethnic groups influence our perceptions, both of ourselves and of others (Fiske and Taylor 1991). As such, racial attitudes are crucial to the development of self-identity, especially for minority group members. As the dominant group in society, European-origin whites often reach adulthood without ever considering their own racial identity. For them, being white is just "normal" (Tatum 1997). Whites are more likely to see themselves as individuals, a view that is consistent with dominant American ideologies of individualism and meritocracy, and, hence, more conducive to academic success (Kluegel and Smith 1986; Hochschild 1995).

For African Americans, Latinos, and Asians, however, the experience being a member of a distinct racial or ethnic minority is not "normal" at all. Asking "Who am I?" requires grappling with fundamental questions about what it means to be African American, Latino, or Asian in twenty-first-century America. The process of identity construction begins early in life and continues into adulthood. It requires young minority members to confront the negative stereotypes that still pervade society, to resist internalizing the negative self-perceptions that they imply, and to assert confidently a positive ethnic definition of oneself (Tatum 1997).

What we learn from society about racial and ethnic groups becomes a fundamental part of our perceptions of how "people like me" are perceived by others, and what kind of treatment one can expect to receive as a result (Operario and Fiske 2001; Fiske et al. 2002). The racial attitudes and perceptions that students bring with them to college help to define the general racial climate on campus, influencing the degree to which groups defined by society as "other" feel comfortable enough to enjoy the full range of experiences that college has to offer, things as basic as raising one's hand to ask a question in class, approaching a professor for individualized attention, or feeling confident enough to discuss one's performance openly and honestly with a professor. Degree of comfort also determines social behaviors, such as whether to run for student government, whether to seek out diverse friendships, whether to pledge a fraternity or sorority, or simply whether to feel safe walking across campus at night. Doubts about these matters are particularly strong for minority students attending predominantly white colleges and universities (Feagin, Vera, and Imani 1996).

For these reasons, racial attitudes may have potentially important implications for collegiate academic achievement. For minority students, having a healthy and well-developed racial identity contributes to feelings of self-esteem and self-efficacy; and for all students, the ability to resist internalizing negative stereotypes and to have tolerant, inclusive racial attitudes can enrich the college experience and, by extension, improve the quality of academic performance. At the same time, a healthy racial identity and a tolerant racial climate may decrease the chances that minority students behave in ways that are consistent with the development of an oppositional culture (Ogbu 1978; Fordham 1996) or succumb to stereotype vulnerability and its concomitant disidentification with academic achievement (Steele 1992, 1997, 1998, 1999).

These risks play out in different ways for different groups. For black and Latino students, a strong group identity may result in academic underperformance to avoid "acting white" and possible ostracism from peers; but an identity that disregards race entirely may contribute to increased sensitivity to the perception of whites, yielding fears about confirming negative stereotypes that depress academic performance. For Asian students, fear of *not* living up to the "model minority" stereotype of intellectual prowess, dedication, and achievement may produce poor performance as students "choke" under the pressure of high expectations (Cheryan and Bodenhausen 2000).

Racial Identity

Because racial identity is potentially such a critical factor influencing academic performance, we asked black, Latino, and Asian respondents a variety of questions on the issue. First, we asked them to tell us which identity—their American identity, their ingroup identity, or both—was most important to them as they entered college. Responses to this question are summarized by group in the top panel of table 7.1. It is immediately clear that ingroup identity is important to all three groups, though not to the same degree. Black students are most likely to adhere to an single ingroup identity. Nearly one-fifth (18%) identified only as a member of their own group, compared with 12% of Latinos and 4% of Asians. The large majority of respondents in each group—87% percent of Asians, 74% of Latinos, and 70% of blacks—said that their American *and* their ingroup identities were both important. Together, then, roughly 90% of all minority group members said that an ingroup identity was somehow important to them.

The extent to which students believe that what happens to other members of their own group affects them—their sense of sharing a common

TABLE 7.1

Indicators of racial/ethnic identity by group

Indicator	Asians	Latinos	Blacks
Most Important Identity			
Mostly American	9.2%	12.9%	9.7%
American and Ingroup	86.5	73.7	69.5
Mostly Ingroup	4.0	12.3	18.2
Sense of Common Fate			
None or a Little	7.9	17.7	13.3
Some	32.4	38.5	44.8
A Lot	59.3	43.6	41.7
Support for Group-Supporting Behaviors			
% Agreeing That Ingroup Members Should:			
Not Date White Men (Ingroup Women)	3.1	1.0	9.4
Not Date White Women (Ingroup Men)	1.8	1.1	14.4
Not Marry Outside of Group	51.0	52.9	26.7
Have Mainly Ingroup Friends	1.2	2.1	10.6
Live in Mainly Ingroup Neighborhoods	1.9	1.2	7.4
Attend Mainly Ingroup Schools	0.4	0.6	6.3
Have Ingroup Staff in Ingroup Schools	14.0	19.8	49.3
Shop at Ingroup Stores	2.9	4.2	40.1
Vote for Ingroup Candidates	1.3	3.3	8.8
Study Ingroup Languages	34.1	48.8	22.5
Give Children Ingroup Names	10.2	7.7	4.6

fate with their ingroup—may also influence academic performance in important ways, affecting the susceptibility of minority students to either oppositional subcultures or stereotype threat. The second panel of table 7.1 therefore considers the degree of common fate identity expressed by black, Latino, and Asian freshmen. Respondents from all three groups appear to believe that their fate is at least partially bound up with that of their group. For instance, 92% of Asians said that what happens to their group had "some" or "a lot" of effect on what might happen to them individually, as did 87% of blacks and 82% of Latinos.

Although freshmen of all racial and ethnic backgrounds may perceive some degree of common fate identity, however, the strength of the connection varies considerably from group to group. Whereas 59% of Asians said that what happened to others in their group personally affected them a lot, only 44% of Latinos and 42% of blacks did so. Moreover, the effect of a common fate identity on academic performance appears to vary across groups depending on the nature of the stereotypes affecting them—whether negative in the case of blacks or positive in the case of Asians.

In addition to common fate identity, we also asked students to indicate their level of support for various behaviors undertaken to promote racial solidarity, express group pride, strengthen within-group ties, and/or maintain intergroup boundaries. We equate support for these actions as indicating a strong racial identity. The third panel in table 7.1 reports the percentage of respondents who agreed or strongly agreed with statements about the relative desirability of intergroup dating, marriage, friendships, schools, and neighborhoods.

In general, levels of ingroup support are quite low; but blacks stand out as showing the most support for separatist behaviors, a fact that is particularly evident with respect to dating and intermarriage. Nine percent of black respondents said that black women should not date black men, and 14% said that black men should not date black women. In contrast, just 1% of Latinos agreed that Latino men and women should not date whites. Likewise, only 3% of Asians thought that Asian women should not date white men, and 2% agreed that Asian men should not date white women. Consistent with these views, 28% of African Americans agreed that blacks should not marry outside the group, compared with 8% of Asians and 4% of Latinos.

In addition to romantic relationships, blacks are also more likely support racial exclusivity in other areas of social life. Thus 11% of African Americans agreed that blacks should mainly have ingroup friends, compared with 2% of Latinos and just 1% of Asians. Similarly, 7% of blacks agreed with the desirability of living in predominantly black neighborhoods, 6% endorsed attending predominantly black schools, and 9% thought that blacks should vote for black candidates. Among Asians and Latinos, the corresponding ingroup percentages never exceeded 3% in any category. In addition, nearly half of all black respondents agreed that ingroup schools should have ingroup teachers and administrators; but only 20% of Latinos and 14% of Asians did so. The greatest intergroup differentials were observed with respect to shopping behavior. Whereas 40% of African American respondents agreed that blacks should shop at black-owned stores, only 4% of Latinos agreed that Latinos should patronize Latino stores, and just 3% of Asians said the same about Asian-owned establishments.

Two exceptions to this pattern of greater support for separatism among blacks are noteworthy. First, Latinos and Asians are more likely than blacks to support studying ingroup languages. Nearly half of all Latinos (49%) agreed that Latinos should study Spanish, and 34% of Asians supported the learning of an Asian language, compared with only 23% of black respondents who supported studying an African language. Second, Latinos and Asians were two to three times more likely than blacks to support giving children indigenous names, most likely reflecting a desire on the part of second- and third-generation immigrants to preserve the culture of their parents and grandparents.

Results to this point suggest that African American, Latino, and Asian freshmen entering elite colleges and universities in the fall of 1999 had rather well-developed racial identities. The vast majority placed at least some importance on their status as an ingroup member. When we cross-tabulated group identity (American, ingroup, or both) by degree of common fate identity and relative support for various group-supporting behaviors, we found that minority students whose core identity was simply "American" had weaker ingroup sentiments and attachments than those whose most important identity was the ingroup alone (tabulation not shown). At the same time, minority students endorsing exclusive ingroup identity tended to express the strongest sense of common fate and were most likely to support behaviors to enhance group solidarity and maintain intergroup boundaries.

As in prior chapters, we considered the effect of segregation by looking at identity indicators endorsed by Latinos and African Americans separately for those in integrated, mixed, and segregated neighborhoods (see table 7.2). In general, we expected that minority students living under segregated circumstances would express stronger ingroup identities and offer more support for ingroup endogamy than those living under conditions of relative integration.

As hypothesized, adherence to American and compound identities declines as one moves from integrated to mixed to segregated neighborhoods, while support for an exclusively minority identity increases. Whereas 12% of blacks and Latinos in integrated neighborhoods identified themselves exclusively as ingroup members, for example, the percentage was 20% among those in segregated neighborhoods. Likewise, acknowledgment of a common fate identity increased as segregation rose. The percentage agreeing that what happened to their group affected them "a lot" rose from 37% in integrated neighborhoods to 50% in segregated neighborhoods.

Consistent with these patterns, the proportion supporting various endogamous behaviors also rose from integrated to segregated neighborhoods. The percentage agreeing that ingroup women should not date white men went from 3% to 9%, the share agreeing that ingroup men should not date white women went from 5% to 12%, and the percentage agreeing that one should not marry outside one's group rose from 12% to 24%. Support for shopping at ingroup stores likewise rose from 14% to 34% moving from integrated to segregated neighborhoods, and the share agreeing that one should vote for ingroup candidates rose from 4% to 9%.

TABLE 7.2

Indicators of identity for Latinos and African Americans by level of
neighborhood segregation in high school

Indicator	Integrated	Mixed	Segregated
Most Important Identity			
Mostly American	12.7%	11.2%	8.9%
American and Ingroup	78.3	70.3	69.4
Mostly Ingroup	12.3	16.2	20.1
Sense of Common Fate			
None or a Little	17.5	13.9	13.0
Some	45.6	37.2	37.0
A Lot	36.5	48.5	50.0
Support for Group-Supporting Behaviors			
% Agreeing That Ingroup Members Should:			
Not Date White Men (Ingroup Women)	3.1	5.8	8.5
Not Date White Women (Ingroup Men)	4.8	9.2	12.0
Not Marry Outside of Group	12.0	14.9	24.1
Have Mainly Ingroup Friends	4.9	9.0	7.1
Live in Mainly Ingroup Neighborhoods	2.3	5.2	7.4
Attend Mainly Ingroup Schools	2.0	4.8	5.1
Have Ingroup Staff in Ingroup Schools	30.8	38.7	38.4
Shop at Ingroup Stores	13.8	25.9	34.4
Vote for Ingroup Candidates	4.2	7.1	8.7
Study Ingroup Languages	35.2	31.9	39.2
Give Children Ingroup Names	5.7	7.2	6.4

Social Distance

The relative social distance between groups—how near or far away one
feels toward a particular race or ethnicity—is an important aspect of identity and attitudes. The NLSF therefore asked respondents to estimate how
close they felt to whites, blacks, Latinos, and Asians "in terms of your
ideas and feelings about things." Responses ranged from 0 (very distant)
to 10 (very close). Mean closeness ratings for all origin and target-group
pairings are reported in table 7.3 and graphed in figure 7.1. Considering
the closeness ratings for each group in general (the last line in each panel),
we see that no group feels what might be called "extreme outgroup distance." The lowest closeness rating for an outgroup was 4.35 (for blacks'
perceived closeness to Asians).

Nonetheless there is systematic variation across groups in how various
target outgroups are perceived. As one might expect, respondents feel
closest to members of their own racial/ethnic groups. Ingroup feelings are

TABLE 7.3
Perceived closeness to different target groups on a scale
of 0 (very distant) to 10 (very close) by race/ethnicity

Target Group	Whites	Asians	Latinos	Blacks
Whites				
Middle Class	7.46	6.48	6.47	5.25
Rich	6.11	5.19	5.18	3.49
Poor	4.95	4.20	4.65	3.81
Professionals	6.89	6.04	6.05	4.75
Business Owners	6.20	4.95	5.22	3.54
Young Women	7.45	6.44	6.72	4.99
Young Men	6.88	5.8	6.10	4.28
Group in General	7.48	6.52	6.69	4.95
Asians				
Middle Class	6.40	7.10	5.66	4.85
Rich	5.38	5.92	4.75	3.49
Poor	4.14	4.80	4.14	3.68
Professionals	6.38	6.48	5.71	4.66
Business Owners	5.38	5.70	4.75	3.86
Young Women	5.89	7.07	5.47	4.54
Young Men	5.33	6.50	4.88	3.97
Affirmative Action Beneficiaries	4.11	4.50	4.90	5.24
Group in General	5.44	7.38	4.98	4.35
Latinos				
Middle Class	6.16	5.60	6.90	5.73
Rich	5.25	4.63	5.65	4.16
Poor	4.00	3.79	5.38	4.73
Professionals	6.15	5.43	6.45	5.34
Business Owners	5.30	4.59	5.63	4.66
Young Women	5.54	5.13	6.86	5.77
Young Men	4.93	4.64	6.33	5.20
Affirmative Action Beneficiaries	4.19	4.40	5.93	6.31
Group in General	4.71	4.76	6.96	5.47
Blacks				
Middle Class	6.60	5.77	6.05	7.55
Rich	5.60	4.81	4.93	5.47
Poor	4.20	3.83	4.40	5.94
Professionals	6.45	5.62	5.85	6.87
Business Owners	6.63	4.66	4.91	6.28
Young Women	5.90	5.27	5.72	7.61
Young Men	5.36	4.78	5.16	7.07
Affirmative Action Beneficiaries	4.29	4.41	5.48	7.08
Group in General	5.16	4.91	5.31	7.42

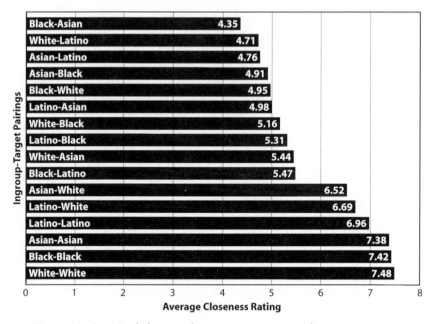

Figure 7.1. Perceived closeness between own group and target outgroups

strongest for whites (7.48), followed by blacks (7.42), Asians (7.38), and Latinos (6.96). Closely behind the ingroup-ingroup pairings are those linking Asians and Latinos to whites. In other words, after members of their own group, both Latinos and Asians perceive themselves to be closest to whites (with ratings of 6.69 for the former and 6.52 for the latter). Given the makeup of high school peer groups discussed in the last chapter, it hardly surprising that Asians and Latinos feel closer to whites than to other minority outgroups. This pattern reflects the general ordering of groups in U.S. society—socially, economically, and residentially, Asians are closest to whites, followed by Latinos. The perceived closeness of Latinos to whites may also reflect the fact that most people of Hispanic origin consider themselves to be "white" (see Denton and Massey 1989; Massey and Denton 1992).

The next closest pairing is between blacks and Latinos, whose closeness rating of 5.47 was followed closely by that between Latinos and blacks (5.31). These two minorities apparently reciprocate in feeling relatively close to one another. As one might expect, the minority group that whites feel closest to is Asians (5.44), followed by blacks (5.16) and more distantly by Latinos (4.71). Paradoxically, whites feel closer to blacks than vice versa. Blacks' closeness rating with respect to whites is only 4.95.

African Americans feel most distant from Asians, however, with a close-ness rating of only 4.35, the lowest observed. Asians generally return the favor by seeing little closeness between themselves and blacks (4.91) and even less with respect to Latinos (4.76).

The foregoing assessments focus on broad racial/ethnic categories that are unconditioned by other, potentially salient characteristics. Consider-ing a well-defined subset of an outgroup that shares one's own traits might yield greater feelings of closeness, especially when the stereotypic charac-teristics of the outgroup are negative. The inclusion of qualifying charac-teristics in the description of a group is particularly important for whites, who have little sense of racial identity compared with most minority group members. We therefore asked respondents how close they felt to various target groups that were explicitly defined with respect to class and gender as well as race or ethnicity. Responses to the resulting subcate-gories are shown in lines of the four panels contained in table 7.3.

Conditioning perceptions on class and gender introduces considerable variation into the ratings. Perhaps not surprisingly, freshmen from all groups felt closest to targets who were middle class, professional, and fe-male. In large part, these closeness ratings reflect the characteristics of the respondents themselves, who, as we have already seen, are disproportion-ately affluent, professional, and female. These ratings testify to the gen-eral tendency for human beings to feel closest to others they perceive to be like themselves.

This tendency is clearly evident in white perceptions of minority out-groups. Whereas whites rate their closeness to African Americans gener-ally at only 5.16, their perceived closeness to *middle-class* blacks was 6.60 (in contrast, closeness to *poor* blacks was put at 4.20). The perceived closeness to black professionals was also high at 6.45. In similar fashion, the closeness that whites perceived toward Latinos generally was only 4.71, but it was 6.16 for middle-class Latinos. A comparable pattern is observed in considering white perceptions of Asians as a target outgroup.

Interestingly, the specification of middle-class status had no effect on the perception that whites had of other whites. The closeness whites felt to-ward whites in general was 7.48 compared with 7.46 for middle-class whites. The lack of an effect of middle-class status stems from the fact that white respondents perceive their own group as homogenously middle class, not because class has no effect on ingroup perceptions per se. Indeed, the closeness rating that whites gave to poor whites was 4.95, only slightly higher than the ratings they assigned to poor blacks (4.20) and poor Asians (4.14). White respondents felt more removed from poor Latinos than from any other group, with an average closeness rating of just 4.0.

Among the various subcategories listed in table 7.3, Asians felt closest to middle-class Asians (7.10) and farthest away from poor Latinos (3.79) and poor blacks (3.83). Their perceived closeness to poor whites was 4.20. Latinos similarly felt closest to middle-class Latinos (6.90) but distant from the poor of other groups (4.14 for Asians, 4.40 for blacks, and 4.65 for whites). Like other respondents, blacks felt close to the middle class of their own group (7.55) and distant from the poor of Asians (3.68) and whites (3.81). Compared with other groups, however, blacks felt considerably closer to poor Latinos (4.73) and their own poor (5.94); and in a very marked departure from what others perceived, they reserved their greatest feelings of alienation for not for the poor, but for *rich* whites and Asians. Indeed, blacks' perceived closeness to rich whites was just 3.49 (compared with 3.81 for poor whites) and only 3.54 for white business owners. Likewise, their perceived closeness to rich Asians was just 3.49 and only 3.86 for Asian business owners.

Although whites, Asians, and even Latino students entered college feeling alienated from the poor of other groups, and relatively close to the rich in their own and other groups, black students walked onto campus feeling relatively close to poor Latinos and poor blacks, relatively distant from poor whites and Asians, but most alienated from rich whites and Asians. Thus, on top of whatever racial and ethnic distance they may feel, black freshmen appear to harbor considerable class resentment. Even with respect to other blacks, their class animosity stands out. The discrepancy in perceived closeness between middle-class and rich blacks was 2.08 points (7.55 for the former and 5.47 for the latter), whereas the perceived social distance between the middle class and the rich was just 1.35 among whites, 1.18 among Asians, and 1.25 among Latinos. The greater alienation that blacks feel toward class privilege does not bode well in their adjustments to life on the nation's wealthiest college campuses.

Affirmative action continues to be a controversial issue among college students and society at large, so we specifically asked respondents how close they felt to minority group members who had "benefitted from affirmative action." As expected, whites expressed the least closeness to affirmative action beneficiaries (4.11 toward Asians, 4.19 toward Latinos, and 4.29 toward blacks). In contrast, blacks felt great closeness to those benefitting from affirmative action, especially when the target group was black (7.08 for blacks, 5.24 for Asians, and 5.47 for Latinos). The perceived closeness expressed by Asians toward affirmative action beneficiaries resembled that of whites, with ratings in the range of 4.40 to 4.50; and the perceptions of Latinos were similar to those of blacks.

Despite the variation in closeness ratings caused by the addition of qualifying information and gender, the basic patterns of social distance persist. When we broke the closeness ratings down by type of racial identity, however, we found that those minority members who identified mostly as "Americans" felt closest to all types of whites, less close to members of their own group, and most distant from minority outgroups (data not shown). In contrast, those identifying exclusively as ingroup members were most distant from whites and closer to various categories of their ingroup. Those who selected both an American and an ingroup identity generally fell in- between, but this was less true for dual-identified Asians.

Among Latinos and blacks, perceptions of closeness also varied by segregation. Table 7.4 presents closeness ratings separately for integrated, mixed, and segregated neighborhoods. As can be seen, perceived closeness to whites and Asians fell as segregation rose while closeness to blacks and Latinos increased. Blacks and Latinos living in integrated neighborhoods had an average closeness rating of 6.41 with respect to whites and 4.80 with respect to Asians, but those living in segregated neighborhoods evinced closeness ratings of just 4.92 and 4.31, respectively. In contrast, perceived closeness to Latinos increased from 6.15 to 6.38 moving from integrated to segregated neighborhoods, while perceived closeness to blacks went from 5.88 to 7.07.

The class sympathies and antipathies characteristic of African Americans are exacerbated by residential segregation. Whereas blacks and Latinos in integrated neighborhoods rated their closeness to rich whites at 5.02, the rating dropped to just 3.43 among those living in segregated neighborhoods. The respective figures for rich Asians were 4.61 and 3.40. At the same time, perceived closeness to poor Latinos and poor blacks strongly increased as one moved from integrated to segregated settings. Thus, perceived closeness to poor Latinos stood at 4.78 among blacks and Latinos within integrated neighborhoods but 5.41 among those in segregated neighborhoods. Likewise, the residents of integrated neighborhoods gave poor blacks a closeness rating of 4.61, whereas those in segregated neighborhoods rated them much closer at 5.87.

In sum, not only was group identity an important psychological element among freshmen entering elite institutions in the fall of 1999, but perceptions of ingroup identities and intergroup boundaries varied in predictable ways. Whites and Asians generally felt closest to each other and most distant from blacks and Latinos, and these general tendencies were heightened when whites and Asians were explicitly labeled as middle class and blacks and Latinos as poor. American-identified or "raceless" black, Latino, and Asian respondents all felt closer to whites and more distant from their own group than those who identified with their ingroup alone. Among blacks and Latinos, ingroup sympathies and outgroup antipathies were markedly increased by greater residential segregation.

Whites and Asians also tended to perceive a great deal of distance between themselves and blacks who benefitted from affirmative action, as did American-identified blacks, Latinos, and Asians. Such perceptions of distance from "affirmative action beneficiaries" carry important implica-

TABLE 7.4

Perceived closeness felt by Latinos and African Americans to different
target groups on a scale of 0 (very distant) to 10 (very close) by level
of neighborhood segregation

Target Group	Integrated	Mixed	Segregated
Whites			
Middle Class	6.42	5.61	5.02
Rich	5.02	3.82	3.43
Poor	4.37	4.26	3.97
Professionals	5.81	5.03	4.91
Business Owners	4.98	4.00	3.56
Young Women	6.40	5.65	5.02
Young Men	5.72	4.82	4.48
Group in General	6.41	5.57	4.92
Asians			
Middle Class	5.64	5.28	4.54
Rich	4.61	3.87	3.40
Poor	3.79	4.24	3.92
Professionals	5.50	5.08	4.69
Business Owners	4.58	4.18	3.89
Young Women	5.22	5.21	4.48
Young Men	4.65	4.59	3.92
Affirmative Action Beneficiaries	4.88	5.43	5.18
Group in General	4.80	4.85	4.31
Latinos			
Middle Class	6.49	6.36	5.98
Rich	5.34	4.57	4.35
Poor	4.78	5.29	5.41
Professionals	6.08	5.67	5.72
Business Owners	5.28	5.04	4.98
Young Women	6.33	6.24	6.34
Young Men	5.70	5.79	5.89
Affirmative Action Beneficiaries	5.90	6.32	6.38
Group in General	6.15	6.13	6.38
Blacks			
Middle Class	6.65	5.06	6.90
Rich	5.38	5.05	4.96
Poor	4.61	5.65	5.87
Professionals	6.32	6.32	6.45
Business Owners	5.43	5.66	5.85
Young Women	6.33	6.93	7.11
Young Men	5.67	6.37	6.74
Affirmative Action Beneficiaries	5.83	6.56	6.89
Group in General	5.88	6.62	7.07

tions for the general tone of race relations on campus because one stereotype that emerges from the myth of intellectual inferiority is that without affirmative action most black and Latino students would not be admitted (Connerley 2000). To the extent that such beliefs are widespread among white students at elite institutions, they will not only increase tensions between whites and minorities on campus; they will also increase the risk of stereotype threat by raising anxiety among minority students about confirming these negative suspicions.

Group Stereotypes

Perceptions that individuals have about members of various racial and ethnic groups—racial stereotypes—are thought by many to be central in structuring intergroup relations (Allport 1954; Ashmore and Del Boca 1981; Stephan 1985; Jackman 1994). Stereotypical attitudes reflect personal likes and dislikes and beliefs about the "proper" status hierarchy among groups (Blumer 1958; Bobo and Johnson 2000). To gain a better understanding of the stereotypes held by students attending elite institutions, the NLSF asked them to assess the degree to which different target groups exemplified various stereotypical traits. Each respondent was presented with a set of characteristics—poor, lazy, violent, unintelligent, hard to get along with, gives up easily, and discriminates against others—and was asked to rate target groups on the degree to which they exemplified these traits on a 1–7 scale. Mean responses the various in- and outgroup pairings are summarized in table 7.5.

In general, the freshmen were reluctant to admit to holding stereotypical views. Since each item is on a 1–7 scale, a score of 4 generally indicates a neutral response. Most of the ratings fell between 3.7 and 4.3. In only one instance was an outgroup clearly stereotyped in a negative manner: blacks, on average, perceived whites to be quite discriminatory (5.28). Latinos, Asians, and whites themselves also rated whites quite negatively on this trait. In fact, all groups tended to see themselves and each other as likely to discriminate against members of other groups. In general, minority group members had favorable stereotypes of whites, as did whites of themselves.

With the sole exception of Howard University, whites constitute the vast majority of students on all campuses in our sample of academic institutions. As a result, their attitudes will be centrally important in determining the atmosphere in which our minority respondents will interact socially and perform academically. In figure 7.2 we display bar charts to indicate white perceptions of the different groups with respect to stereotypes that are particularly relevant to academic success—namely, laziness, intelligence, and diligence.

TABLE 7.5

Racial stereotyping on a scale of 1 (does not exemplify trait at all) to 7 (strongly exemplifies trait) by race/ethnicity

Target Group and Stereotype	Whites	Asians	Latinos	Blacks
Whites				
Poor	3.24	3.12	3.17	3.02
Lazy	3.70	3.69	3.68	3.87
Violent	3.74	3.61	3.62	4.06
Unintelligent	3.54	3.23	3.40	3.50
Live Off Welfare	2.82	2.78	2.83	3.12
Hard to Get Along with	3.19	3.04	3.16	3.78
Give Up Easily	3.65	3.55	3.52	3.44
Discriminatory	4.57	4.13	4.58	5.28
Asians				
Poor	3.35	3.45	3.43	3.13
Lazy	2.94	2.63	2.64	2.68
Violent	3.12	3.00	2.91	3.03
Unintelligent	3.09	2.77	2.81	2.78
Live Off Welfare	2.52	2.36	2.49	2.50
Hard to Get Along with	3.33	3.18	3.49	3.86
Give Up Easily	2.98	2.64	2.68	2.67
Discriminatory	3.89	4.48	4.01	4.51
Latinos				
Poor	4.70	4.74	4.48	4.78
Lazy	3.83	3.89	3.27	3.52
Violent	4.17	4.22	3.89	4.39
Unintelligent	3.94	3.84	3.58	3.76
Live Off Welfare	3.47	3.82	3.42	3.73
Hard to Get Along with	3.54	3.45	2.91	3.42
Give Up Easily	3.82	3.79	3.38	3.66
Discriminatory	4.25	4.17	3.92	4.23
Blacks				
Poor	4.49	4.56	4.46	4.65
Lazy	3.86	3.88	3.52	3.52
Violent	4.34	4.41	4.25	4.54
Unintelligent	3.83	3.73	3.64	3.37
Live Off Welfare	3.47	3.80	3.68	3.66
Hard to Get Along with	3.46	3.43	3.38	3.30
Give Up Easily	3.69	3.68	3.58	3.59
Discriminatory	4.62	4.47	4.49	4.47

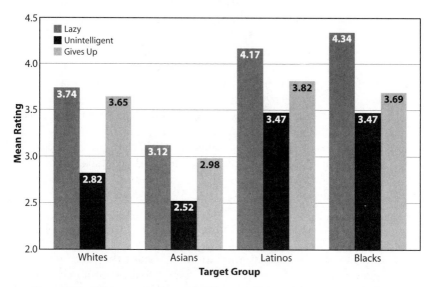

Figure 7.2. White perceptions of different groups with respect to laziness, intelligence, and diligence

With a value of 3.74, whites rate themselves just below the midpoint on the seven-point scale of laziness; and consistent with the stereotype of the "hardworking Asian," they put Asians even lower at 3.12. In contrast, whites assign blacks a score well above the neutral midpoint, giving them a mean value of 4.34. Other groups rate blacks similarly, with Asians giving them a laziness score of 4.41 and Latinos one of 4.25. Indeed, the group that rated blacks as laziest at 4.54 was *blacks themselves* (compared with their rating of whites at 4.06, Asians at 3.03, and Latinos at 4.39) Thus, the stereotype of black laziness seems to have been substantially internalized by African Americans themselves.

Even more crucial in determining vulnerability to stereotype threat is the racist canard that minorities lack intelligence. When asked to rate groups on the degree to which they were unintelligent, whites were quite low at 2.82 and Asians were even lower at 2.52, but Latinos and blacks were each given an average score of 3.47. Although this value lies below the midpoint of neutrality, it is a full point above the score assigned to Asians and 0.65 point above that given to whites. Although not large in absolute terms, these differences suggest that whites do see blacks and Latinos as relatively less intelligent than others—38% less smart than Asians and 25% less intelligent than whites. As with laziness, this negative stereotype appears to have been at least partly internalized by blacks themselves, for they assign blacks an unintelligence score of 3.66 compared with 2.58 for Asians and 3.12 for whites. Blacks only perceive Latinos to be more unintelligent than themselves, giving them an average rating of 3.73.

Finally, we considered stereotypes about diligence by asking whites to evaluate groups with respect to their tendency to give up easily. Once again whites assigned themselves a rating just below the midpoint (3.65) and gave Asians an even lower rating of 2.98. Although Latinos and blacks were likewise given ratings below the midpoint, their averages were considerably higher at 3.82 for Latinos and 3.69 for blacks. Thus whites perceived Latinos to be 28% less diligent than Asians and blacks to be 24% less diligent. In this case, however, blacks did not share the negative stereotyping. Whereas they rated blacks and Latinos roughly equal in terms of the tendency to give up (3.58–3.59), they saw whites and Asians as slightly more like to do so (3.68–3.69).

Although the absolute value of whites' ratings of blacks with respect to laziness, unintelligence, and diligence may not be very large, when expressed relative to ratings assigned to other groups they are quite large and suggestive of a clear hierarchy with respect to traits conducive to academic success: Asians, whites, Latinos, and blacks. The consistency of these perceptions and their apparent endorsement even by blacks suggest the considerable potential for stereotype threat to emerge on American college campuses. Ironically, those at greatest risk appear to be those minority students who are most identified with mainstream American values, for when we tabulated stereotype ratings by identity we found that American-identified blacks and Latinos were more likely than others to stereotype their group as lazy, unintelligent, and easily giving up. Although the differences were not large, we also found self-stereotyping to vary by level of segregation (data not shown), with those living in segregated neighborhoods being more likely to rate blacks and Latinos as lazy, unintelligent, and not diligent. They were also more likely to rate whites as discriminatory.

Beliefs about Racial Inequality

Another important attitudinal dimension is what people believe about the causes of racial inequality: who is responsible, the best way to overcome it, and where the responsibility for combating it lies. As with racial attitudes generally, such beliefs are likely to play a meaningful role in shaping the racial climate on campus. The perception that educated members of racial minority groups have promising futures and will eventually succeed, or that minority group members would do better if they just tried harder, could constitute an additional source of pressure for black and

Latino students already anxious about stereotype threat. At the same time, if blacks and Latinos believe that equally qualified members of their groups consistently lose jobs to whites, they may adopt an oppositional orientation in response to an expectation of unequal treatment despite "playing by the rules." These risks would be exacerbated if white students held beliefs that either blamed minorities for their own disadvantaged status or expected them to assume all responsibilities for overcoming structural discrimination.

The NLSF thus asked respondents about their views on the causes of racial inequality and how best to overcome it. Respondents rated five statements about the relative importance of qualifications, effort, and discrimination in determining group outcomes on a scale of 0 (strong disagreement) to 10 (strong agreement). The results of this exercise are summarized in table 7.6. As one would expect given their status as new college freshmen, members of all groups believed that educated blacks, Latinos, and Asians had promising futures. However, this belief was stronger for some groups than others. It was strongest for Asians, with all groups re-

TABLE 7.6

Beliefs about sources of inequality on a scale of 0 (strongly disagree) to 10 (strongly agree) by race/ethnicity

Target Group and Belief	Whites	Asians	Latinos	Blacks
Asians				
Future Promising for Educated	7.74	7.59	7.67	7.70
Educated Eventually Get Ahead	7.58	7.24	7.31	7.08
Equally Qualified Lose Jobs to Whites	2.53	3.53	2.95	3.69
To Blame for Not Doing Better—				
Should Try Harder	3.56	4.52	4.06	4.46
Beat Discrimination by Being More Qualified	3.22	4.73	4.35	5.92
Latinos				
Future Promising for Educated	6.74	6.63	7.11	6.61
Educated Eventually Get Ahead	6.72	6.50	6.65	5.52
Equally Qualified Lose Jobs to Whites	3.38	4.16	3.75	4.83
To Blame for Not Doing Better—				
Should Try Harder	3.64	4.13	4.01	4.12
Beat Discrimination by Being More Qualified	3.46	4.71	4.77	6.33
Blacks				
Future Promising for Educated	7.15	6.83	6.89	7.25
Educated Eventually Get Ahead	7.04	6.76	6.71	5.82
Equally Qualified Lose Jobs to Whites	3.21	4.08	3.71	4.64
To Blame for Not Doing Better—				
Should Try Harder	3.90	4.19	4.18	4.35
Beat Discrimination by Being More Qualified	3.34	4.55	4.48	6.52

porting mean scores for Asians in the range of 7.6 to 7.7. For blacks and Latinos, in contrast, the scores were in the range of 6.6 to 7.1. That students universally perceive Asians to be in a better position to benefit from educational attainment than blacks or Latinos may indicate the degree to which stereotypes of Asians as intellectually superior and hard-working have been internalized (Tatum 1997).

This response pattern might also indicate an awareness of how discriminatory barriers continue to exist for blacks or Latinos. Although members of all racial groups tended to agree that educated minority members will eventually be accepted and get ahead, blacks were much less likely than others to accept this favorable view of themselves. Whereas the endorsement rating that Asians gave to the view that educated ingroup members would get ahead was 7.24, and the rating that Latinos gave was 6.65, the corresponding rating for blacks was far more pessimistic at 5.82.

Whites were not inclined to believe that equally qualified Asians would lose jobs to whites no matter how hard they tried. White agreement was only 2.53 on the ten-point agree-disagree scale. Whites were somewhat more inclined to acknowledge discrimination against Latinos and blacks, giving them respective ratings on this item of 3.38 and 3.21. Not surprisingly, blacks were most likely to perceive discrimination as a continuing problem. Their agreement rating that equally qualified Asians would consistently lose jobs to whites was 3.69, and for Latinos and blacks it was 4.83 and 4.35, respectively. Although Asians and Latinos fell between these two extremes, it was Asians who perceived greater discrimination in competition with equally qualified whites.

The remaining items suggest that disadvantaged minority groups have mainly themselves to blame for their disadvantaged status: they should "try harder to do better," and the best way to overcome discrimination is "to be more qualified than whites." Once again whites evinced the lowest and blacks the highest levels of agreement on these items, and as before Asians were closer to blacks and Latinos were closer to whites on this dimension. Blacks, for example gave a rating of 6.52 to endorse the view that to beat discrimination they had to be more qualified, while whites gave the same item a rating of just 3.34. Asians stood at 4.55 and Latinos at 4.48. Very similar patterns emerged when Latinos and Asians were considered as target groups. Thus African Americans hold views that are quite consistent with their traditional saying that "you have to work twice as hard to get half as far."

This belief, along with the high degree of confidence in a better future for educated group members, once again points to the ongoing reality of stereotype threat. Although minority students see academic achievement as the key to a promising future, they also realize that overcoming discrimination and living down negative stereotypes will require an ongoing effort and constitute a disproportionate burden. Once again, those most vulnerable to stereotype threat appear to be those who are most invested in a mainstream identity, as we observed a clear tendency for American-identified members of minority groups to agree that their futures are promising and that the educated will eventually get ahead, and to explain group disadvantage in terms of a lack of effort (data not shown).

Latinos and blacks living in integrated settings are likewise more likely to view American society as open to endorse the view that minorities need to be more qualified to beat discrimination. As shown in table 7.7, Latinos and blacks living in integrated neighborhoods gave an agreement rating of 7.80 to the statement that the future was promising for educated Asians, compared with a rating of 7.44 for those in segregated neighborhoods. At the same time, the rating they gave to the idea that Asians had to beat discrimination by being more qualified went from 4.94 in integrated neighborhoods to 5.43 in those that were segregated. A similar pattern is found when Latinos were the target group. However, the tendency to endorse education as the cure for black ills varied less by segregation.

TABLE 7.7

Beliefs about sources of inequality expressed by Latinos and African Americans on a scale of 0 (strongly disagree) to 10 (strongly agree) by level of housing segregation

Target Group and Belief	Integrated	Mixed	Segregated
Asians			
Future Promising for Educated	7.80	7.68	7.44
Educated Eventually Get Ahead	7.30	7.34	6.74
Equally Qualified Lose Jobs to Whites	3.01	3.41	3.89
To Blame for Not Doing Better—			
Should Try Harder	4.03	4.40	4.59
Beat Discrimination by Being More Qualified	4.94	5.22	5.43
Latinos			
Future Promising for Educated	6.98	6.75	6.75
Educated Eventually Get Ahead	6.26	6.13	5.65
Equally Qualified Lose Jobs to Whites	3.99	4.45	4.72
To Blame for Not Doing Better—			
Should Try Harder	3.79	4.22	4.49
Beat Discrimination by Being More Qualified	5.29	5.82	5.76
Blacks			
Future Promising for Educated	7.08	6.97	7.19
Educated Eventually Get Ahead	6.36	6.24	6.10
Equally Qualified Lose Jobs to Whites	3.86	4.38	4.58
To Blame for Not Doing Better—			
Should Try Harder	4.05	4.41	4.55
Beat Discrimination by Being More Qualified	5.16	5.76	5.85

Rather, those living in segregated neighborhoods endorsed the view that equally qualified blacks would lose jobs to whites, with a rating of 4.58, compared with 3.86 in integrated settings. Likewise, the agreement rating for the view that blacks had to beat discrimination by being more qualified went from 5.16 in integrated neighborhoods to 5.85 in segregated areas.

The Campus Racial Climate

In this chapter, we examined the attitudes and identities held by different groups at selective colleges and institutions. The good news is that white, Asian, Latino, and black students generally have positive views of one another. In absolute terms, they perceive themselves to be fairly close with respect to how "they think and feel about things." Moreover, perceived closeness is increased when a target group is given class characteristics similar to those of the respondent's. The bad news is that perceived closeness is substantially decreased when target groups are given stereotypical characteristics such as poverty. Morever, in relative terms we detect a subtle but real tendency to stereotype groups in a manner consistent with racist ideology. African Americans and Latinos, in particular, are more likely to be viewed as having characteristics that are inconsistent with academic success, while the reverse is true for Asians. There is also widely shared rank ordering of groups in terms of traits favorable to academic progress, with Asians on top, followed by whites, Latinos, and blacks. Whites and Asians feel especially distant from blacks and Latinos who "benefit from affirmative action." The perception of blacks and Latinos as "academically underqualified" may be exacerbated by the presence of Asians, who are generally perceived as overqualified.

The overwhelming majority of all minority members claim identities that are dual—involving both an ingroup identity and an American identity. At the same time, a significant fraction of blacks and Latinos reported having either an exclusive American identity or an exclusive ingroup identity, and these differences in racial group attachment had clear effects on other attitudes. In particular, those who identified most strongly as "American"—the identity most consistent with that of whites (Tatum 1997)—display a weaker sense of common fate, are more concerned with how whites perceive them, are less concerned with how they are seen by ingroup members, and tend to reject separatists that maintain racial boundaries. They also have more negative stereotypes about ingroup members, feel closer to whites and more distant from minorities, and are more likely to believe that educated minorities have promising futures and will eventually get ahead.

All of these characteristics are consistent with a "raceless" identity (Fordham 1996; Fordham and Ogbu 1986), and the leading psychological risk for such students is the fear of confirming group stereotypes regarding their intellectual ability. The risk is fairly straightforward for groups stereotyped as intellectually inferior—Latinos and blacks—for whom academic underperformance is the predicted outcome; but for groups stereotyped as highly intelligent, especially diligent, and unusually hard-working, the outcome might be overachievement or psychological breakdown.

Blacks and Latinos identifying solely with an ingroup identity, in contrast, generally have the strongest sense of common fate, are most concerned about the perceptions that ingroup members have of them, are least concerned with how whites view them, and generally support behaviors to maintain racial boundaries. Likewise, having a strong racial identity is associated with greater social distance from whites and an unfavorable view of their discriminatory nature, but greater perceived closeness with ingroup members and more positive stereotypes of them. A strong racial identity increases the belief that qualified minorities lose jobs to whites no matter how hard they try and lessens the belief that educated minorities will eventually get ahead.

For blacks and Latinos with strong ingroup identities, academic underperformance is more likely to occur through the adoption of an oppositional culture, where students internalize negative stereotypes about their group such that excelling in school becomes associated with "acting white." Being so attached to their minority identity, they adopt a stance that opposes mainstream, white America rather than deny their own group. An oppositional stance also protects self-esteem in reaction to the belief that "no matter how hard they try," members of their group cannot expect fair treatment (Fordham and Ogbu 1986).

As in the prior chapter, these data enable us to calculate roughly the share of people who might be vulnerable to oppositional identities or stereotype threat. In general, blacks and Latinos who adopt an exclusively American identity and who at some level buy into the stereotype of their group's intellectual inferiority would seem to be most at risk of succumbing to stereotype threat. Among black respondents to the NLSF, 3.3% were exclusively American-identified and also gave blacks a rating for unintelligence of 5 or greater, and among Latinos the figure was 4.2%. In contrast, those blacks and Latinos who adopt an exclusive ingroup identity but who also accept the notion of minority intellectual inferiority would seem to be most at risk of forming an oppositional identity. Among black respondents, 10.2% were simultaneously ingroup-identified and gave blacks an unintelligence rating of 5 or more, whereas among Latinos the comparable percentage was 5.0%.

These figures suggest the considerable potential for academic underachievement through either a reduction of effort to avoid stereotype threat or the adoption of an oppositional subculture. These processes most likely represent opposing ends of a continuum on which we find a wide range of academic and social outcomes. We will continue to study these students as they make their way through college or university, testing the importance of racial identity and associated racial attitudes on academic outcomes, as well as tracking changes in racial identities as students age and mature.

CHAPTER 8

PATHWAYS TO PREPARATION

THE FOREGOING chapters have documented many differences in the social, economic, and cultural backgrounds of white, Asian, Latino, and African American freshmen entering selective colleges and universities in the fall of 1999. Although these students all entered the gates of America's most elite institutions, the paths by which they did so were varied. Our respondents were raised with divergent parenting styles in different kinds of families, and radically contrasting school and neighborhood environments that offered very different rates of exposure to disorder and violence and contrasting peer cultures. All of the foregoing factors can be expected to bear on the degree to which students are prepared for study at selective institutions of higher education, but heretofore we have not defined exactly what "preparation" entails. In this chapter we specify basic measures of college preparation and consider how they are influenced by prior life experiences.

Dimensions of Preparation

Attending a selective college or university is a total experience. In moving from high school to college everything very suddenly and dramatically changes. Most students leave their parents for the first time. They trade in one set of friends for another. They shift from an academic environment focused on the transmission of information to one focused on the creation of knowledge, and from a setting where they were easily among the top students to one where for the first time in their lives they may struggle to remain in the middle of the pack. Authority figures that stood over them in the past to make sure they attended class, did their homework, and studied hard suddenly vanish and they must motivate themselves. Rather than simply mastering a body of facts, they are asked to think creatively and critically.

To be ready for college, students must therefore prepare themselves in a variety of ways. We conceptualize preparation as involving four basic dimensions: academic, financial, social, and psychological. Table 8.1 presents average values of various indicators selected to tap each of these dimensions, the most basic of which is academic. In the absence of sound academic preparation, other dimensions of college readiness are probably

TABLE 8.1
Dimensions and indicators of preparation for higher education

Dimension and Indicator	Cronbach's Alpha	Whites	Asians	Latinos	Blacks
Academic					
Number of AP Courses Taken		3.01	4.24	2.62	2.03
High School GPA		3.77	3.83	3.70	3.53
Self-Rated Preparation		6.73	6.28	6.15	6.49
Financial					
Share of Cost Paid by Family		0.74	0.68	0.54	0.42
Social					
Susceptibility to Peer Influence	.59	9.82	10.55	9.22	10.38
Social Distance from Minorities	.90	14.18	15.25	11.81	10.69
Social Distance from Whites	.87	8.17	11.23	10.44	15.75
Psychological					
Self-Esteem	.85	32.15	29.78	32.55	33.86
Self-Efficacy	.69	18.96	17.88	18.94	19.04
Self-Confidence	.70	34.57	36.01	35.42	36.65

moot. Our baseline data provide three potential indicators of academic preparation: the number of Advanced Placement courses taken, grade point average earned in high school, and the respondent's own assessment of how well high school prepared him or her for college.

As table 8.1 indicates, intergroup differences in academic preparation are clear but, with the exception of Advanced Placement training, generally modest. On average, Asians took the most Advanced Placement courses (4.24), followed by whites (3.01), Latinos (2.62), and blacks (2.03). On this dimension of academic preparation, then, African Americans are half as well prepared as Asians. The same ordering of groups prevailed with respect to high school grade point averages. Asians led with 3.83, followed by whites at 3.77, Latinos at 3.70, and blacks at 3.53. The order is somewhat different, however, for self-rated preparation. Whites believed they were best prepared (6.73 on a 10-point scale), followed by blacks (6.49), Asians (6.28), and Latinos (6.15).

Given that all our respondents went through a rigorous screening process to get into college in the first place, it is not surprising that academic preparation does not vary that sharply from group to group. Equally unsurprising, given the socioeconomic differentials documented earlier, are the rather large intergroup differences in familial capacity to pay for college. To indicate financial capacity we estimated what percentage of the cost of college would be paid for by the respondent or the respondent's family.

Whereas white students expected to cover an average of around 74% of their college costs through personal or familial resources, the percentage was only 42% for African Americans. To a greater extent than whites, therefore, black students can be expected to be burdened with financial worries. For African Americans on financial aid, dropping a class will involve more than a temporary academic setback—it could mean losing eligibility for a loan or fellowship. The need to work on or off campus will also take time away from studies; and for many students from poor or working-class families, the assumption of debt will represent a serious psychological burden. Asians and Latinos lie between the extremes of blacks and whites, with the former tending toward whites (with 68% of costs met from personal or family resources) and the latter tending toward blacks (with 54% met from these sources).

The next dimension of preparation we consider is social. At college, students must learn to interact with people from a wide array of racial, ethnic, and class backgrounds. At the same time, they must cultivate their autonomy, knowing themselves and their abilities so as to resist social temptations that might threaten their academic progress. We thus sought to measure students' susceptibility to peer influence and the degree to which respondents perceived social distance between themselves and other groups. These data are presented in the third panel of table 8.1.

The index of peer susceptibility was generated by combining a series of questionnaire items that asked respondents about their relationships with other people of the same age, the degree to which they thought and acted like others, hung out with others, felt comfortable and valued the same things as others, whether they worried about being called names, etc. (see appendix table B11 for details about scale construction). The resulting index ranged from 0 to 28 and had a reliability coefficient of .59. All groups clustered around a value of 10. Asians were highest (most susceptible to peer influence) at 10.55, while Latinos were lowest (least susceptible) at 9.22; and blacks and whites lay in-between at 10.38 and 9.82, respectively.

The two social-distance scales reveal clear contrasts between the groups. As might be expected, Latinos and blacks perceive less distance between themselves and minorities than do whites or Asians. The social-distance scales are based on three items: how close the respondent feels to members of the group in general, to female members of that group, and to male group members (see appendix table B11). The index of social distance from minorities was 14.18 for whites and 15.25 for Asians, but only 10.69 for African Americans and 11.81 for Latinos ($\alpha = .90$). With respect to perceptions of distance from whites, in contrast, the index for African Americans was highest. Their distance index value was 15.75, compared with 11.23 for Asians, 10.44 for Latinos, and 8.6 for whites

($\alpha = .87$). Given that whites and Asians see themselves as distant from blacks and Latinos, and that blacks and Latinos see themselves as quite distant from whites, all groups appear to be relatively unprepared for the interracial and interethnic interactions they will experience in college.

The last dimension of preparation we consider is psychological: the degree to which respondents expressed self-esteem, self-confidence, and self-efficacy. The NLSF asked the extent to which students agreed or disagreed with items such as "I feel that I am a person of worth, equal to others" and "I am able to do things as well as most people." Each item was rated on a 5-point scale from strongly disagree to strongly agree (coded 0–4), and responses were summed across ten items to create a summated ratings scale that varied from 0 to 40 with a reliability of .85 (see appendix table B12). All groups displayed a rather high degree of self-esteem, with blacks expressing the highest ratings of all (33.86), followed by Latinos (32.25), whites (32.15), and Asians (29.78).

The scale of self-confidence was built from a set of items that asked respondents to disagree or agree with statements such as "I don't have control over the direction of my life" and "Every time I try to get ahead something stops me." Six such items were coded 0–4 to yield a summated rating scale of self-efficacy that ranged from 0 to 24 and had an alpha of .69. There was even less intergroup variance with respect to this scale, but once again blacks were highest at 19.04, followed by whites at 18.96, Latinos at 18.94, and Asians at 17.88.

Finally, self-confidence was measured using a set of items on which respondents were asked to state on a 0–10 scale how likely it was that they would finish two years of college, graduate from college, go on for education after college, and complete a graduate or professional degree. This scale of academic confidence ranged from 0 to 40 and had a reliability coefficient of 0.70. As seen before, African Americans were most confident in their educational success, with an index value of 36.65, followed by Asians (36.01), Latinos (35.42), and whites (34.57). These three scales provide little evidence that minorities are less psychologically prepared for the rigors of college study than others. Indeed, blacks and Latinos generally report the highest levels of self-confidence, self-efficacy, and self-esteem.

Sources of Preparation

Given the intergroup variation we have documented with respect to demographic characteristics, socioeconomic background, child-rearing practices, school conditions, peer environments, and social attitudes, it would be surprising if such background differences were *not* related in some way to differences in preparation between groups. We thus begin our assessment of how preparation affects achievement by attempting to account for intergroup differences in preparation using the various background measures we have collected. Our basic approach is to regress each measure of preparation on indicators of demographic characteristics, socioeconomic status, parental child-rearing practices, whether the school attended was public or private, and the degree of segregation, quality of education, and peer support it provided. These and all subsequent regressions are estimated using unweighted data.

Academic Preparation

Table 8.2 begins this process by estimating two equations. The first equation (on the left side of the table) shows the effect of group membership on the number Advanced Placement courses taken. As already noted, Asians took the most, followed in descending order by whites, Latinos, and African Americans. The associated coefficients show that these intergroup differences are highly significant. The second equation (on the right side) shows what happens to these group effects once background differences are controlled statistically. As can be seen, the Asian advantage over whites is cut by about half (0.589 to 0.266), and the Latino and black disadvantages are reduced (the Latino effect goes from -0.342 to -0.244 and the black effect goes from -0.905 to -0.685). Although intergroup differences are mitigated, however, they are not eliminated.

As one would expect, the number of advanced courses taken in high school is very strongly predicted by parental education, wealth (as indexed by home value), and to a lesser extent income. The taking of AP courses is also enhanced by the involvement of parents in the cultivation of cultural capital, but interestingly, parental involvement in creating human capital is not associated with the accumulation of AP credits. The reliance of parents on a child-rearing regime of strict discipline strongly lowers preparation along this dimension, whereas the use of shame and guilt modestly increase it.

Other things being equal, students attending private schools earned fewer AP credits than those in public school, as did those attending schools that were either predominantly white or predominantly minority. Thus, students from public, racially mixed schools generally arrived on campus with more AP courses under their belt, possibly as a result of attending charter or magnet schools. As might be expected, AP credits rose with the quality of academic support in high school and with the degree of peer support for academic effort. Although AP credits increase with the level of disorder and violence in the school, they drop sharply as peer support for delinquency rises. Thus, students' preparation in terms of AP

TABLE 8.2
Effect of selected factors on number of Advanced Placement courses taken

Independent Variables	Group Effects		Full Model	
	B	SE	B	SE
Race/Ethnicity				
White	–	–	–	–
Asian	0.589***	0.113	0.266*	0.120
Latino	−0.342***	0.114	−0.244*	0.113
Black	−0.905***	0.110	−0.685***	0.115
Demographic Characteristics				
Respondent Traits				
Male	–	–	0.273***	0.072
Religiosity	–	–	−0.021	0.011
Number of Siblings	–	–	−0.033	0.040
Family Structure				
Two Parents All Ages	–	–	–	–
Two Parents Some Ages	–	–	−0.199*	0.109
Single Parent All Ages	–	–	−0.079	0.143
Immigrant Origins				
Both Parents Natives	–	–	–	–
Foreign Born Parent	–	–	0.284**	0.094
Foreign Born Respondent	–	–	0.009	0.116
Socioeconomic Background				
Household Income				
<$14,999	–	–	–	–
$15,000–$24,999	–	–	0.241	0.192
$25,000–$49,999	–	–	0.194	0.159
$50,000–$74,999	–	–	0.327*	0.165
$75,000+	–	–	0.338*	0.159
Parental Education				
Neither Parent College Grad	–	–	–	–
One Parent College Grad	–	–	0.187*	0.091
Two Parents College Grad	–	–	0.379**	0.121
One Parent Advanced Degree	–	–	0.358***	0.098
Both Parents Advanced Degree	–	–	0.700***	0.120
Home Value				
Value in $100,000	–	–	0.864***	0.164
Poverty Status				
Ever on Welfare	–	–	−0.023	0.115
Parental Child-Rearing Strategies				
Cultivation of Human Capital	–	–	−0.009	0.005
Cultivation of Social Capital	–	–	−0.019	0.012
Cultivation of Cultural Capital	–	–	0.016**	0.005

TABLE 8.2 (cont.)

Independent Variables	Group Effects		Full Model	
	B	SE	B	SE
Parental Child-Rearing Strategies				
Cultivation of Intellectual Independence	–	–	−0.008	0.005
Strictness of Discipline	–	–	−0.019***	0.005
Use of Shame and Guilt	–	–	0.018*	0.007
Kind of School				
Private	–	–	−0.392***	0.090
School Segregation				
<20% Minority	–	–	–	–
20–39% Minority	–	–	0.223*	0.104
40–59% Minority	–	–	0.413**	0.141
60–79% Minority	–	–	−0.064	0.153
>80% Minority	–	–	0.072	0.134
School Quality				
Infrastructure	–	–	−0.029*	0.011
Academic Support	–	–	0.064***	0.016
Disorder/Violence Index (00)	–	–	0.003*	0.001
Peer Environment				
Support for Academic Effort	–	–	0.024**	0.009
Support for Intellectual Independence	–	–	0.000	0.012
Support for Delinquency	–	–	−0.071***	0.012
Intercept	3.248***	0.079	2.464***	0.615
R^2	0.074***		0.149***	
N	3,923		3,133	

$^*p < .05$ $^{**}p < .01$ $^{***}p < .001$

credits is determined basically by parental education, wealth, and child-rearing patterns, along with high school academic and social conditions.

Table 8.3 continues our assessment of academic preparation by focusing on high school grade point average. The group-specific coefficients shown in the left-hand columns indicate that whites and Asians earned essentially the same GPA, while Latinos and African Americans earned GPAs that were significantly lower than those of whites. As in the prior table, these group effects are reduced but not eliminated by the introduction of controls (see the right-hand columns). The Latino-white gap is reduced from −0.075 to −0.044 and the black-white gap is lowered from −0.221 to −0.172.

TABLE 8.3
Effect of selected factors on high school grade point average

Independent Variables	Group Effects		Full Model	
	B	SE	B	SE
Race/Ethnicity				
White	–	–	–	–
Asian	0.011	0.014	0.018	0.019
Latino	−0.075***	0.015	−0.044*	0.018
Black	−0.221***	0.014	−0.172***	0.018
Demographic Characteristics				
Respondent Traits				
Male	–	–	−0.019	0.011
Religiosity	–	–	0.004	0.002
Number of Siblings	–	–	0.015*	0.006
Family Structure				
Two Parents All Ages	–	–	–	–
Two Parents Some Ages	–	–	−0.032*	0.016
Single Parent All Ages	–	–	−0.060**	0.023
Immigrant Origins				
Both Parents Natives	–	–	–	–
Foreign Born Parent	–	–	0.008	0.015
Foreign Born Respondent	–	–	0.004	0.018
Socioeconomic Background				
Household Income				
<$14,999	–	–	–	–
$15,000–$24,999	–	–	0.029	0.031
$25,000–$49,999	–	–	0.069**	0.025
$50,000–$74,999	–	–	0.049	0.026
$75,000+	–	–	0.074**	0.025
Parental Education				
Neither Parent College Grad	–	–	–	–
One Parent College Grad	–	–	0.004	0.015
Two Parents College Grad	–	–	0.030	0.019
One Parent Advanced Degree	–	–	0.019	0.016
Both Parents Advanced Degree	–	–	0.050**	0.019
Home Value				
Value in $100,000	–	–	0.023	0.026
Poverty Status				
Ever on Welfare	–	–	0.016	0.018
Parental Child-Rearing Strategies				
Cultivation of Human Capital	–	–	0.001	0.001
Cultivation of Social Capital	–	–	0.004*	0.002
Cultivation of Cultural Capital	–	–	0.000	0.001

TABLE 8.3 (cont.)

Independent Variables	Group Effects		Full Model	
	B	SE	B	SE
Parental Child-Rearing Strategies				
Cultivation of Intellectual Independence	–	–	−0.001	0.001
Strictness of Discipline	–	–	−0.007***	0.001
Use of Shame and Guilt	–	–	0.001	0.001
Kind of School				
Private	–	–	−0.052***	0.014
School Segregation				
<20% Minority	–	–	–	–
20–39% Minority	–	–	−0.021	0.104
40–59% Minority	–	–	−0.008	0.018
60–79% Minority	–	–	−0.035	0.024
>80% Minority	–	–	0.010	0.025
School Quality				
Infrastructure	–	–	−0.013***	0.002
Academic Support	–	–	0.007**	0.002
Disorder/Violence Index (00)	–	–	0.003*	0.001
Peer Environment				
Support for Academic Effort	–	–	0.004**	0.001
Support for Intellectual Independence	–	–	0.006**	0.002
Support for Delinquency	–	–	−0.012***	0.002
Intercept	3.775***	0.010	3.805***	0.061
R^2	0.081***		0.162***	
N	3,919		3,131	

*$p < .05$ **$p < .01$ ***$p < .001$

Unlike the case of AP credits, however, high school GPA was very weakly related to the socioeconomic or educational background of parents. School segregation also played no significant role in determining grades earned. Although demographic traits bore some relationship to GPA (grades were lower for those from single-parent families and higher for those who were religious and had more siblings), the most important determinants of grades earned were the academic and peer environment the respondent experienced in high school. High school GPA was strongly and positively related to the quality of the academic support received in high school and the degree of peer support for academic effort but was negatively related to the quality of the school's infrastructure, and to peer

TABLE 8.4
Effect of selected factors on perception of how well high school prepared
him or her for college

Independent Variables	Group Effects		Full Model	
	B	SE	B	SE
Race/Ethnicity				
White	–	–	–	–
Asian	−0.395**	0.136	−0.325	0.170
Latino	−0.581***	0.138	−0.064	0.161
Black	−0.374***	0.133	0.074	0.115
Demographic Characteristics				
Respondent Traits				
Male	–	–	0.206*	0.102
Religiosity	–	–	−0.003	0.016
Number of Siblings	–	–	−0.062	0.057
Family Structure				
Two Parents All Ages	–	–	–	–
Two Parents Some Ages	–	–	−0.153	0.139
Single Parent All Ages	–	–	−0.189	0.201
Immigrant Origins				
Both Parents Natives	–	–	–	–
Foreign Born Parent	–	–	0.023	0.135
Foreign Born Respondent	–	–	−0.077	0.164
Socioeconomic Background				
Household Income				
<$14,999	–	–	–	–
$15,000–$24,999	–	–	−0.181	0.274
$25,000–$49,999	–	–	0.017	0.228
$50,000–$74,999	–	–	−0.099	0.236
$75,000+	–	–	0.064	0.229
Parental Education				
Neither Parent College Grad	–	–	–	–
One Parent College Grad	–	–	0.196	0.129
Two Parents College Grad	–	–	0.383*	0.172
One Parent Advanced Degree	–	–	0.326*	0.140
Both Parents Advanced Degree	–	–	0.716***	0.170
Home Value				
Value in $100,000	–	–	−0.087	0.233
Poverty Status				
Ever on Welfare	–	–	−0.159	0.163
Parental Child-Rearing Strategies				
Cultivation of Human Capital	–	–	0.002	0.007
Cultivation of Social Capital	–	–	−0.048**	0.018

TABLE 8.4 (cont.)

Independent Variables	Group Effects		Full Model	
	B	SE	B	SE
Parental Child-Rearing Strategies				
Cultivation of Cultural Capital	–	–	0.010	0.008
Cultivation of Intellectual Independence	–	–	−0.010	0.006
Strictness of Discipline	–	–	−0.034***	0.007
Use of Shame and Guilt	–	–	0.011*	0.010
Kind of School				
Private	–	–	0.181	0.128
School Segregation				
<20% Minority	–	–	–	–
20–39% Minority	–	–	−0.028	0.148
40–59% Minority	–	–	0.000	0.200
60–79% Minority	–	–	−0.004	0.216
>80% Minority	–	–	−0.035	0.190
School Quality				
Infrastructure	–	–	0.188***	0.016
Academic Support	–	–	0.320***	0.022
Disorder/Violence Index (00)	–	–	−0.006***	0.002
Peer Environment				
Support for Academic Effort	–	–	0.022	0.012
Support for Intellectual Independence	–	–	0.034*	0.017
Support for Delinquency	–	–	0.017	0.017
Intercept	6.736***	0.096	1.367***	0.524
R^2	0.004***		0.242	
N	3,726		2,988	

*$p < .05$ **$p < .01$ ***$p < .001$

support for delinquency. GPA was negatively related to peer support for intellectual independence and to strictness of parental discipline. Given the central importance of peer effects, it is not surprising that the degree of involvement of parents in social capital formation was also positively related to a student's high school GPA.

Our respondents' subjective assessments of how well high school prepared them for college are examined in table 8.4. As the left-hand columns indicate, the intergroup differences are highly significant. Whites perceive themselves to be best prepared for college, followed by blacks, Asians, and finally Latinos. In this analysis, however, controlling for background differences eliminates, not just reduces, the intergroup differences. Self-assessed academic preparation is determined largely by parental education and the quality of the physical, academic, and peer environment provided by the school. In general, as the number of degrees held by parents rises and the quality of the educational environment rises, so does perceived preparation for college-level work. Strict parental discipline and high levels of disorder and violence within schools are negatively associated with self-rated preparation.

The foregoing analyses of how background shapes academic preparation generally show that preparation is largely a function of parental education, child-rearing practices, school quality, and peer environments. Although prior chapters have documented substantial intergroup differences with respect to each of these factors, controlling for them statistically does not eliminate intergroup differentials, at least with respect to objective measures such as AP credits and the grades earned in high school. Differences in perceived preparation do disappear once controls are introduced, but remember that these perceptions have been informed with little or no actual experience in college-level courses.

Financial Preparation

Differences between whites, blacks, Latinos, and Asians in the degree of financial capacity to pay for college, documented in table 8.1, are shown in the left-hand columns of table 8.5 to be highly significant. The socioeconomic circumstances of white students generally enable their families to absorb a much higher share of college costs than those of other groups. The share of the cost absorbed by African American students and families, for example, is 33.5 percentage points lower than that absorbed by whites, and for Latinos the share is 22.6 points lower. The percentage of the cost absorbed by Asians or their families is only marginally lower (3.6 points).

As one would expect, variation in the ability to pay for college is most powerfully related to socioeconomic indicators. Financial capacity increases sharply with parental income, education, and home value, and it is significantly lower for students coming from a background of poverty (from families that in the past have been on welfare). Other things being equal, the capacity to cover college costs is reduced by a rising number of siblings (as fixed familial resources are spread over a larger number of recipients), and students who attended public schools generally have less financial capacity than those from private schools, as do students who attended schools that were racially segregated.

Although introducing controls for these and other factors does not eliminate the intergroup differentials in financial capacity, it does reduce

TABLE 8.5
Effect of selected factors on proportion of cost of higher education paid
by respondent's family

Independent Variables	Group Effects		Full Model	
	B	SE	B	SE
Race/Ethnicity				
White	–	–	–	–
Asian	−0.036*	0.017	0.015	0.019
Latino	−0.226***	0.017	−0.073***	0.018
Black	−0.335***	0.016	0.125***	0.018
Demographic Characteristics				
Respondent Traits				
Male	–	–	0.004	0.011
Religiosity	–	–	−0.005**	0.002
Number of Siblings	–	–	−0.029**	0.006
Family Structure				
Two Parents All Ages	–	–	–	–
Two Parents Some Ages	–	–	−0.003	0.016
Single Parent All Ages	–	–	0.011	0.023
Immigrant Origins				
Both Parents Natives	–	–	–	–
Foreign Born Parent	–	–	0.008	0.015
Foreign Born Respondent	–	–	−0.021	0.018
Socioeconomic Background				
Household Income				
<$14,999	–	–	–	–
$15,000–$24,999	–	–	−0.086**	0.031
$25,000–$49,999	–	–	−0.034	0.026
$50,000–$74,999	–	–	0.076**	0.027
$75,000+	–	–	0.181***	0.026
Parental Education				
Neither Parent College Grad	–	–	–	–
One Parent College Grad	–	–	0.040**	0.014
Two Parents College Grad	–	–	0.082***	0.019
One Parent Advanced Degree	–	–	0.073***	0.016
Both Parents Advanced Degree	–	–	0.136***	0.019
Home Value				
Value in $100,000	–	–	−0.286***	0.026
Poverty Status				
Ever on Welfare	–	–	−0.081***	0.018

(continued)

TABLE 8.5 (cont.)

Independent Variables	Group Effects		Full Model	
	B	SE	B	SE
Parental Child-Rearing Strategies				
Cultivation of Human Capital	–	–	0.001	0.001
Cultivation of Social Capital	–	–	−0.003	0.002
Cultivation of Cultural Capital	–	–	0.003**	0.001
Cultivation of Intellectual Independence	–	–	0.000	0.001
Strictness of Discipline	–	–	0.002**	0.001
Use of Shame and Guilt	–	–	−0.002	0.001
Kind of School				
Private	–	–	0.051***	0.014
School Segregation				
<20% Minority	–	–	–	–
20–39% Minority	–	–	−0.055***	0.017
40–59% Minority	–	–	−0.045*	0.022
60–79% Minority	–	–	−0.077**	0.024
>80% Minority	–	–	−0.078***	0.021
School Quality				
Infrastructure	–	–	−0.001	0.002
Academic Support	–	–	−0.008**	0.003
Disorder/Violence Index (00)	–	–	−0.002	0.002
Peer Environment				
Support for Academic Effort	–	–	0.006***	0.001
Support for Intellectual Independence	–	–	−0.003	0.002
Support for Delinquency	–	–	0.006***	0.002
Intercept	0.729***	0.012	0.329***	0.061
R^2	0.137***		0.427***	
N	3,564		2,887	

*$p < .05$ **$p < .01$ ***$p < .001$

them markedly. Our inability to eliminate the differentials entirely probably reflects imperfect measurement of household wealth. Rather than having detailed information about family assets, we only proxy wealth using estimated home value. Were we to have more complete information about family economic background, the remaining group differentials would probably be eliminated. As one would expect, therefore, differences in the capacity to absorb the cost of college are largely a function of objective indicators of family socioeconomic background.

Social Preparation

College is a time of great social as well as academic learning. For many students it represents the first time they experience people from outside the homogenous niche in which they grew up. Although college provides an important venue for the formation of diverse friendships and offers new opportunities for socializing, it also requires students to become self-directed, self-motivated, and autonomous. Hence, the first dimension of social preparation we consider is the degree to which students report themselves to be susceptible to peer influence. Susceptibility to the influence of peers may be good or bad for academic performance, of course, depending on the immediate social environment; but in general, students whose performance depends on their own motivations rather than those of their peers will probably do better.

Table 8.6 reveals that the intergroup differences in peer susceptibility noted earlier are mostly not significant. According to the group-specific coefficients shown in the left-hand columns, no differences in susceptibility can be detected among whites, Asians, or Latinos. Only African Americans stand out. Compared to freshmen from other groups, they are considerably more susceptible to the influence of peers than others, once again underscoring the relevance of theoretical explanations of peer-based explanations for differentials in black academic performance.

As the right-hand columns show, however, once background factors are held constant, the higher degree of black susceptibility disappears. Indeed, once their demographic, economic, parental, and social characteristics are controlled, Asians emerge as the group most sensitive to peer influence, while Latinos appear to be the least likely to be influenced by peer pressure. Remarkably, susceptibility to peer influence is pretty much unrelated to socioeconomic status, being uncorrelated with either income or home value and only modestly related to parental education. Only if students come from a *very* poor background (were on welfare at some point) are they likely to be sensitive to peer influences. Susceptibility to peers is more strongly linked to parental child-rearing practices and to the academic and social environment of high school. Students whose parents were more involved in the cultivation of human and social capital were much less susceptible to peer influences, but those raised by parents who relied on the use of shame and guilt were significantly *more* sensitive to the views of peers. Likewise, students from segregated schools generally reported themselves to be more sensitive to peer opinion (as might be predicted by Ogbu), especially if the schools were also characterized by a high degree of disorder and violence. Fortunately, however, students who reported a high degree of peer support for delinquency were generally *less* sensitive to the views of others. In sum,

TABLE 8.6
Effect of selected factors on susceptibility to peer influence

Independent Variables	Group Effects		Full Model	
	B	SE	B	SE
Race/Ethnicity				
White	–	–	–	–
Asian	0.198	0.206	0.751**	0.278
Latino	−0.208	0.209	−0.671*	0.263
Black	0.569***	0.202	−0.466	0.268
Demographic Characteristics				
Respondent Traits				
Male	–	–	0.368*	0.166
Religiosity	–	–	0.000	0.026
Number of Siblings	–	–	0.049	0.093
Family Structure				
Two Parents All Ages	–	–	–	–
Two Parents Some Ages	–	–	−0.348	0.226
Single Parent All Ages	–	–	−0.575	0.331
Immigrant Origins				
Both Parents Natives	–	–	–	–
Foreign Born Parent	–	–	−0.320	0.219
Foreign Born Respondent	–	–	−0.392	0.268
Socioeconomic Background				
Household Income				
<$14,999	–	–	–	–
$15,000–$24,999	–	–	−0.295	0.444
$25,000–$49,999	–	–	−0.077	0.368
$50,000–$74,999	–	–	0.112	0.382
$75,000+	–	–	−0.229	0.369
Parental Education				
Neither Parent College Grad	–	–	–	–
One Parent College Grad	–	–	−0.107	0.210
Two Parents College Grad	–	–	0.460	0.281
One Parent Advanced Degree	–	–	0.552*	0.227
Both Parents Advanced Degree	–	–	0.534*	0.279
Home Value				
Value in $100,000	–	–	−0.593	0.380
Poverty Status				
Ever on Welfare	–	–	0.690**	0.267
Parental Child-Rearing Strategies				
Cultivation of Human Capital	–	–	0.026*	0.011
Cultivation of Social Capital	–	–	−0.244***	0.029
Cultivation of Cultural Capital	–	–	0.031*	0.013

TABLE 8.6 (cont.)

Independent Variables	Group Effects		Full Model	
	B	SE	B	SE
Parental Child-Rearing Strategies				
Cultivation of Intellectual Independence	–	–	0.001	0.010
Strictness of Discipline	–	–	0.003	0.011
Use of Shame and Guilt	–	–	0.051**	0.017
Kind of School				
Private	–	–	0.317	0.209
School Segregation				
<20% Minority	–	–	–	–
20–39% Minority	–	–	0.389	0.240
40–59% Minority	–	–	0.644*	0.327
60–79% Minority	–	–	0.142	0.354
>80% Minority	–	–	0.771*	0.311
School Quality				
Infrastructure	–	–	−0.035	0.026
Academic Support	–	–	−0.138***	0.037
Disorder/Violence Index (00)	–	–	0.010***	0.003
Peer Environment				
Support for Academic Effort	–	–	−0.005	0.020
Support for Intellectual Independence	–	–	−0.040	0.029
Support for Delinquency	–	–	−0.245***	0.027
Intercept	10.164***	0.144	16.358***	0.852
R^2	0.003**		0.121***	
N	3,922		3,133	

$*p < .05$ $**p < .01$ $***p < .001$

then, black students seem to be more sensitive to peer opinion because they come from poor backgrounds, attend segregated schools characterized by high levels of violence and disorder, and have parents who tend to be less involved in the cultivation of human and social capital.

Table 8.7 attempts to explain differences in the perception of social distance from minorities (blacks and Hispanics). As already noted, Latinos and especially African Americans perceive themselves to be socially much closer to minorities than whites, and the group-specific coefficients shown in the left-hand columns indicate that these differences are very significant statistically. Asians, in contrast, perceive even more social distance between themselves and minority groups than do whites.

TABLE 8.7
Effect of selected factors on perceived social distance from minorities

Independent Variables	Group Effects		Full Model	
	B	SE	B	SE
Race/Ethnicity				
White	–	–	–	–
Asian	0.764***	0.212	0.567*	0.295
Latino	−2.287***	0.216	−1.361***	0.280
Black	−3.360***	0.208	−2.019***	0.284
Demographic Characteristics				
Respondent Traits				
Male	–	–	0.836***	0.176
Religiosity	–	–	−0.102***	0.028
Number of Siblings	–	–	−0.034	0.099
Family Structure				
Two Parents All Ages	–	–	–	–
Two Parents Some Ages	–	–	0.116	0.240
Single Parent All Ages	–	–	0.175	0.352
Immigrant Origins				
Both Parents Natives	–	–	–	–
Foreign Born Parent	–	–	−0.172	0.233
Foreign Born Respondent	–	–	−0.215	0.285
Socioeconomic Background				
Household Income				
<$14,999	–	–	–	–
$15,000–$24,999	–	–	0.515	0.473
$25,000–$49,999	–	–	0.309	0.393
$50,000–$74,999	–	–	−0.640	0.407
$75,000+	–	–	0.028	0.393
Parental Education				
Neither Parent College Grad	–	–	–	–
One Parent College Grad	–	–	−0.341	0.223
Two Parents College Grad	–	–	0.541	0.299
One Parent Advanced Degree	–	–	0.036	0.241
Both Parents Advanced Degree	–	–	−0.487	0.296
Home Value				
Value in $100,000	–	–	0.324	0.402
Poverty Status				
Ever on Welfare	–	–	0.157	0.284
Parental Child-Rearing Strategies				
Cultivation of Human Capital	–	–	−0.008	0.012
Cultivation of Social Capital	–	–	−0.073*	0.031
Cultivation of Cultural Capital	–	–	0.000	0.013

TABLE 8.7 (cont.)

Independent Variables	Group Effects		Full Model	
	B	SE	B	SE
Parental Child-Rearing Strategies				
Cultivation of Intellectual Independence	–	–	0.006	0.011
Strictness of Discipline	–	–	−0.011	0.011
Use of Shame and Guilt	–	–	0.050**	0.018
Kind of School				
Private	–	–	−0.116	0.222
School Segregation				
<20% Minority	–	–	–	–
20–39% Minority	–	–	−0.759**	0.255
40–59% Minority	–	–	−1.859*	0.347
60–79% Minority	–	–	−1.891***	0.376
>80% Minority	–	–	−2.470***	0.330
School Quality				
Infrastructure	–	–	−0.036	0.028
Academic Support	–	–	−0.061	0.039
Disorder/Violence Index (00)	–	–	0.009**	0.003
Peer Environment				
Support for Academic Effort	–	–	−0.020	0.021
Support for Intellectual Independence	–	–	−0.073*	0.030
Support for Delinquency	–	–	−0.074**	0.029
Intercept	14.267***	0.149	17.412***	0.936
R^2	0.114***		0.170***	
N	3,876		3,107	

$*p < .05$ $**p < .01$ $***p < .001$

Although these intergroup differences in the perception of social distance are reduced by controlling for background characteristics, once again they are by no means eliminated. The closeness to minorities felt by Latinos and blacks and the distance perceived by Asians cannot be explained away by differences in demographic background, socioeconomic circumstances, neighborhood conditions, school circumstances, or peer influence. Indeed, perceived distance from minorities is largely unrelated to family structure, immigrant origins, income, parental education, family wealth, or poverty status. Males generally perceive more social distance from minorities than females, and perceived social distance from minorities is strongly reduced by rising religiosity. The most important determinant of social distance from minorities, however, is segregation: the more racially segregated the school the respondent attended while growing up, the less the perceived social distance from minority group members.

Child-rearing practices and peer environments also play a significant but much weaker role in determining perceptions of social distance from minorities. The involvement of parents in the cultivation of social capital generally reduces perceptions of social distance, while parental reliance on shame and guilt in child rearing increases them. Interestingly, peer support for intellectual independence and delinquency both seem to *reduce* perceived distance from minorities, although the former effect is not particularly strong. In general, perceptions of social distance from minorities are governed primarily by the degree of racial/ethnic segregation experienced while growing up.

Much the same can be said about the perception of social distance from whites, as shown in table 8.8. Moving from whites through Asians and Latinos to blacks, perceptions of social distance from whites increase significantly. Controlling for background variables reduces the perception of distance from whites for Asians and Latinos, but blacks continue to stand out in perceiving a substantial social distance from whites, even after controls are introduced.

As before, perceptions of social distance from whites are very strongly conditioned by segregation: those coming of age in segregated school environments generally perceive much greater social distance between themselves and whites, and the perception of social distance increases monotonically with each extra increment of segregation up to 60% minority. The perception of social distance is mitigated somewhat by parental involvement in the cultivation of human and social capital and by attending a school with high-quality infrastructure. Surprisingly, peer support for academic effort and delinquency both decrease perceived social distance from whites.

In sum, therefore, perceptions of social distance—either to minority or to majority members—are conditioned primarily on the degree of segregation experienced in the past, and to a lesser degree on the kind of school and peer environments experienced while growing up. Susceptibility to peer influence, in contrast, is governed largely by parental child-rearing practices, religiosity, and the quality of the school and peer environment.

Psychological Preparation

We begin our assessment of psychological preparation by considering self-esteem. As the left-hand columns table 8.9. show, Asians display significantly less self-esteem than whites, while blacks express significantly more

TABLE 8.8
Effect of selected factors on perceived social distance from whites

Independent Variables	Group Effects		Full Model	
	B	SE	B	SE
Race/Ethnicity				
White	–	–	–	–
Asian	0.248***	0.247	1.447***	0.335
Latino	2.246***	0.251	0.966**	0.318
Black	6.447***	0.242	4.516***	0.322
Demographic Characteristics				
Respondent Traits				
Male	–	–	−0.225	0.200
Religiosity	–	–	−0.074*	0.032
Number of Siblings	–	–	0.132	0.113
Family Structure				
Two Parents All Ages	–	–	–	–
Two Parents Some Ages	–	–	0.040	0.273
Single Parent All Ages	–	–	−0.232	0.399
Immigrant Origins				
Both Parents Natives	–	–	–	–
Foreign Born Parent	–	–	0.157	0.264
Foreign Born Respondent	–	–	0.144	0.324
Socioeconomic Background				
Household Income				
<$14,999	–	–	–	–
$15,000–$24,999	–	–	1.013	0.538
$25,000–$49,999	–	–	−0.183	0.446
$50,000–$74,999	–	–	−0.194	0.462
$75,000+	–	–	−0.375	0.447
Parental Education				
Neither Parent College Grad	–	–	–	–
One Parent College Grad	–	–	−0.145	0.254
Two Parents College Grad	–	–	0.163	0.339
One Parent Advanced Degree	–	–	0.468	0.274
Both Parents Advanced Degree	–	–	0.456	0.334
Home Value				
Value in $100,000	–	–	−0.334	0.456
Poverty Status				
Ever on Welfare	–	–	−0.583	0.323

(continued)

TABLE 8.8 (cont.)

Independent Variables	Group Effects		Full Model	
	B	SE	B	SE
Parental Child-Rearing Strategies				
Cultivation of Human Capital	–	–	−0.044***	0.013
Cultivation of Social Capital	–	–	−0.131***	0.035
Cultivation of Cultural Capital	–	–	0.010	0.015
Cultivation of Intellectual Independence	–	–	0.019	0.013
Strictness of Discipline	–	–	0.013	0.013
Use of Shame and Guilt	–	–	−0.024	0.020
Kind of School				
Private	–	–	0.777**	0.252
School Segregation				
<20% Minority	–	–	–	–
20–39% Minority	–	–	0.694*	0.290
40–59% Minority	–	–	1.363***	0.395
60–79% Minority	–	–	2.296***	0.427
>80% Minority	–	–	2.217***	0.375
School Quality				
Infrastructure	–	–	−0.083**	0.032
Academic Support	–	–	−0.133**	0.044
Disorder/Violence Index (00)	–	–	0.020***	0.003
Peer Environment				
Support for Academic Effort	–	–	−0.084***	0.024
Support for Intellectual Independence	–	–	−0.062	0.034
Support for Delinquency (000)	–	–	−0.152***	0.033
Intercept	8.624***	0.173	15.003***	0.615
R^2	0.161***		0.244***	
N	3,884		3,113	

*$p < .05$ **$p < .01$ ***$p < .001$

(Latinos have about the same level as whites). Controlling for background variables eliminates the significant group effect for Asians but not blacks. Indeed, after controls are introduced blacks express slightly more self-esteem than before. Self-esteem does not seem to be a serious issue for African Americans and does not represent a good candidate for explaining minority underachievement.

Self-esteem is not strongly related to demographic or socioeconomic background, except that males generally express more self-esteem than fe-

TABLE 8.9
Effect of selected factors on degree of self-esteem

Independent Variables	Group Effects		Full Model	
	B	SE	B	SE
Race/Ethnicity				
White	–	–	–	–
Asian	−1.695***	0.251	−0.584	0.337
Latino	0.269	0.254	0.319	0.320
Black	1.757***	0.245	2.058***	0.325
Demographic Characteristics				
Respondent Traits				
Male	–	–	0.878***	0.202
Religiosity	–	–	0.048	0.032
Number of Siblings	–	–	0.167	0.114
Family Structure				
Two Parents All Ages	–	–	–	–
Two Parents Some Ages	–	–	0.650*	0.274
Single Parent All Ages	–	–	0.725	0.402
Immigrant Origins				
Both Parents Natives	–	–	–	–
Foreign Born Parent	–	–	0.089	0.266
Foreign Born Respondent	–	–	−0.070	0.325
Socioeconomic Background				
Household Income				
<$14,999	–	–	–	–
$15,000–$24,999	–	–	1.156*	0.539
$25,000–$49,999	–	–	0.300	0.447
$50,000–$74,999	–	–	0.302	0.464
$75,000+	–	–	0.616	0.448
Parental Education				
Neither Parent College Grad	–	–	–	–
One Parent College Grad	–	–	0.204	0.255
Two Parents College Grad	–	–	−0.687*	0.341
One Parent Advanced Degree	–	–	−0.624*	0.276
Both Parents Advanced Degree	–	–	−0.571	0.339
Home Value				
Value in $100,000	–	–	0.668	0.461
Poverty Status				
Ever on Welfare	–	–	0.032	0.324

(continued)

TABLE 8.9 (cont.)

Independent Variables	Group Effects		Full Model	
	B	SE	B	SE
Parental Child-Rearing Strategies				
Cultivation of Human Capital	–	–	0.009	0.013
Cultivation of Social Capital	–	–	0.122***	0.035
Cultivation of Cultural Capital	–	–	−0.017	0.015
Cultivation of Intellectual Independence	–	–	0.050***	0.013
Strictness of Discipline	–	–	−0.024	0.013
Use of Shame and Guilt	–	–	−0.139	0.020
Kind of School				
Private	–	–	−0.855***	0.253
School Segregation				
<20% Minority	–	–	–	–
20–39% Minority	–	–	0.490	0.292
40–59% Minority	–	–	0.194	0.397
60–79% Minority	–	–	0.709	0.429
>80% Minority	–	–	0.866*	0.376
School Quality				
Infrastructure	–	–	0.086*	0.032
Academic Support	–	–	0.195***	0.045
Disorder/Violence Index (00)	–	–	−0.005	0.003
Peer Environment				
Support for Academic Effort	–	–	0.029	0.025
Support for Intellectual Independence	–	–	−0.038	0.035
Support for Delinquency (000)	–	–	0.068*	0.033
Intercept	32.003***	0.176	25.556***	1.034
R^2	0.047***		0.148***	
N	3,918		3,132	

$*p < .05$ $**p < .01$ $***p < .001$

males. Rather, self-esteem is determined primarily by child-rearing practices and school conditions. Self-esteem is more strongly enhanced by parental involvement in the cultivation of social capital and intellectual independence and is generally reduced by the parental use of discipline, shame, and guilt. With respect to schools, self-esteem is *enhanced* by greater segregation, and by going to a school with better infrastructure and academic support. Even controlling for these factors, however, blacks express far more self-esteem than other groups, indicating the degree to which they have developed internalized self-images that are resistant to racist cues that continue to pervade American society.

Interestingly, self-esteem and self-efficacy seem to be lower for those attending private than public schools (see table 8.10). This pattern could reflect a selection effect, whereby problem students with adjustment problems are taken out of public school and deliberately placed into private institutions. Or it might be that private schools have so many bright and talented students that students feel inadequate, even though they may feel prepared academically. The fact that there is a small negative effect of parental education supports this interpretation, as those with highly educated parents who attend very competitive schools may feel that they will never be as smart as their parents, and never achieve the level of academic excellence that they expect.

African Americans also stand out for having more self-efficacy once background variables are controlled, and once again Asians are notable for feeling significantly *less* self-efficacy than other groups. As before, this dimension of psychological preparation is not connected in any clear or consistent way to demographic or socioeconomic background. Rather, self-efficacy stems primarily from parental child-rearing strategies and school quality. Respondents who grew up in a religious household, who had parents who were involved in the creation of human and social capital, and who worked to promote intellectual independence generally felt greater self-efficacy, whereas those raised by parents who made frequent use of shame and guilt generally experienced lower levels of efficacy. Self-efficacy was generally higher in schools with better infrastructures and more academic support services, but, other things being equal, was lower in private schools.

Finally we consider the issue of self-confidence. As noted earlier, Asians, Latinos, and blacks all express a much higher degree of academic self-confidence than whites. As the left-hand columns of table 8.11 show, these differences are highly significant, and as the right-hand columns reveal, this pattern is not changed all that much by the introduction of controls. Before and after controls are introduced, blacks express by far the highest degree of self-confidence, followed by Asians, and Latinos. Academic self-confidence is lower for men than women and is enhanced by greater religiosity and immigrant origins. It is greater among those who have parents with advanced degrees and is increased by rising wealth. Self-confidence is marginally increased by parental involvement in the creation of human capital ($p = .07$) and is decreased by parental reliance on shame and guilt. As with self-esteem, self-confidence increases with the degree of school segregation, suggesting that racially isolated schools might serve as buffers from a hostile outside world, thereby helping to maintain psychological well-being. Self-confidence also increases as the quality of school

TABLE 8.10
Effect of selected factors on degree of self-efficacy

Independent Variables	Group Effects		Full Model	
	B	SE	B	SE
Race/Ethnicity				
White	–	–	–	–
Asian	−0.875***	0.135	−0.379*	0.180
Latino	−0.082	0.136	0.170	0.170
Black	0.171	0.131	0.478**	0.173
Demographic Characteristics				
Respondent Traits				
Male	–	–	0.122	0.108
Religiosity	–	–	0.046**	0.017
Number of Siblings	–	–	−0.013	0.061
Family Structure				
Two Parents All Ages	–	–	–	–
Two Parents Some Ages	–	–	0.064	0.146
Single Parent All Ages	–	–	−0.034	0.214
Immigrant Origins				
Both Parents Natives	–	–	–	–
Foreign Born Parent	–	–	0.157	0.142
Foreign Born Respondent	–	–	0.155	0.173
Socioeconomic Background				
Household Income				
<$14,999	–	–	–	–
$15,000–$24,999	–	–	0.377	0.287
$25,000–$49,999	–	–	−0.047	0.238
$50,000–$74,999	–	–	−0.071	0.247
$75,000+	–	–	0.196	0.239
Parental Education				
Neither Parent College Grad	–	–	–	–
One Parent College Grad	–	–	−0.077	0.136
Two Parents College Grad	–	–	−0.386*	0.182
One Parent Advanced Degree	–	–	−0.277*	0.147
Both Parents Advanced Degree	–	–	−0.289	0.181
Home Value				
Value in $100,000	–	–	0.144	0.245
Poverty Status				
Ever on Welfare	–	–	0.068	0.173
Parental Child-Rearing Strategies				
Cultivation of Human Capital	–	–	0.011	0.007
Cultivation of Social Capital	–	–	0.050**	0.019
Cultivation of Cultural Capital	–	–	−0.012	0.008

TABLE 8.10 (cont.)

Independent Variables	Group Effects		Full Model	
	B	SE	B	SE
Parental Child-Rearing Strategies				
Cultivation of Intellectual Independence	–	–	0.024***	0.007
Strictness of Discipline	–	–	−0.001	0.007
Use of Shame and Guilt	–	–	−0.074***	0.011
Kind of School				
Private	–	–	−0.544***	0.135
School Segregation				
<20% Minority	–	–	–	–
20–39% Minority	–	–	0.130	0.155
40–59% Minority	–	–	−0.571**	0.219
60–79% Minority	–	–	0.096	0.229
>80% Minority	–	–	0.046	0.201
School Quality				
Infrastructure	–	–	0.033*	0.017
Academic Support	–	–	0.121***	0.024
Disorder/Violence Index	–	–	−0.002	0.002
Peer Environment				
Support for Academic Effort	–	–	0.017	0.013
Support for Intellectual Independence	–	–	−0.002	0.019
Support for Delinquency (000)	–	–	0.024	0.018
Intercept	18.905***	0.094	15.657***	0.551
R^2	0.018***		0.114***	
N	3,918		3,132	

*$p < .05$ **$p < .01$ ***$p < .001$

academic support rises and as peer support for academic effort increases. But as already stated, none of these significant effects does much to explain intergroup differentials.

Differences in Preparation

In this chapter we have shown how the many differences in background and upbringing documented in earlier chapters translate into differences in college preparation along a variety of salient dimensions, not only academic, but economic, social, and psychological. We have shown that dif-

TABLE 8.11
Effect of selected factors on degree of self-confidence

Independent Variables	Group Effects		Full Model	
	B	SE	B	SE
Race/Ethnicity				
White	–	–	–	–
Asian	1.407***	0.207	1.114***	0.280
Latino	0.800***	0.209	0.520*	0.266
Black	1.724***	0.202	1.482***	0.270
Demographic Characteristics				
Respondent Traits				
Male	–	–	−0.679***	0.168
Religiosity	–	–	0.084**	0.026
Number of Siblings	–	–	−0.040	0.094
Family Structure				
Two Parents All Ages	–	–	–	–
Two Parents Some Ages	–	–	−0.159	0.229
Single Parent All Ages	–	–	−0.012	0.334
Immigrant Origins				
Both Parents Natives	–	–	–	–
Foreign Born Parent	–	–	0.711***	0.221
Foreign Born Respondent	–	–	0.940***	0.270
Socioeconomic Background				
Household Income				
<$14,999	–	–	–	–
$15,000–$24,999	–	–	0.428	0.448
$25,000–$49,999	–	–	−0.270	0.372
$50,000–$74,999	–	–	−0.534	0.385
$75,000+	–	–	0.166	0.372
Parental Education				
Neither Parent College Grad	–	–	–	–
One Parent College Grad	–	–	−0.256	0.212
Two Parents College Grad	–	–	0.083	0.284
One Parent Advanced Degree	–	–	0.441*	0.229
Both Parents Advanced Degree	–	–	0.931***	0.281
Home Value				
Value in $100,000	–	–	0.933**	0.383
Poverty Status				
Ever on Welfare	–	–	−0.417	0.269
Parental Child-Rearing Strategies				
Cultivation of Human Capital	–	–	0.020	0.011
Cultivation of Social Capital	–	–	0.017	0.029
Cultivation of Cultural Capital	–	–	0.002	0.013

TABLE 8.11 (cont.)

Independent Variables	Group Effects		Full Model	
	B	SE	B	SE
Parental Child-Rearing Strategies				
Cultivation of Intellectual Independence	–	–	−0.007	0.011
Strictness of Discipline	–	–	0.005	0.011
Use of Shame and Guilt	–	–	−0.050**	0.017
Kind of School				
Private	–	–	−0.177	0.211
School Segregation				
<20% Minority	–	–	–	–
20–39% Minority	–	–	0.423	0.242
40–59% Minority	–	–	0.292	0.330
60–79% Minority	–	–	0.936**	0.357
>80% Minority	–	–	0.002	0.313
School Quality				
Infrastructure	–	–	−0.010	0.027
Academic Support	–	–	0.140***	0.037
Disorder/Violence Index	–	–	0.002	0.003
Peer Environment				
Support for Academic Effort	–	–	0.118***	0.020
Support for Intellectual Independence	–	–	−0.033	0.029
Support for Delinquency (000)	–	–	−0.001	0.027
Intercept	34.631***	0.145	29.128***	0.859
R^2	0.020***		0.111***	
N	3,922		3,133	

$^*p < .05$ $^{**}p < .01$ $^{***}p < .001$

ferences in background and upbringing explain some but not all of the intergroup differences in academic preparation; eliminate most or all of the differences in economic preparation; and explain most of the differences in susceptibility to peer influence but account for relatively little of the perceived social distance between groups. Black and Latino students do not appear to be disadvantaged by a lack of self-esteem, self-confidence, or self-efficacy. On the contrary, they generally score highest on these scales and retain this high standing even when controls are introduced. Now that we understand something about where differences in academic, financial, social, and psychological preparation for college come from, our task in the next chapter is to measure the effects of these differences on early academic performance.

CHAPTER 9

SINK OR SWIM: THE FIRST SEMESTER

EVEN AFTER controlling for background differences with respect to family, neighborhood, school, and peer environments, we find that significant differences between groups persist along a variety of dimensions of preparation for higher education. In this chapter we measure the degree to which variation in background and preparation across groups translates into differentials in academic performance during the first semester of college study. Our purpose in doing so is to assess how much of the intergroup variation in early performance may be attributed to traits and characteristics that students brought with them the day they set foot on campus. At this stage of our analysis we deliberately do not take into account any differences between groups that emerge after their arrival on campus. These will be the subject of study in subsequent volumes. Here we seek only to establish a baseline against which campus-based sources of differential performance may be considered.

Psychological Vulnerabilities

In addition to differences in the degree of academic, financial, social, and psychological preparation among groups, we sought to measure the specific psychological vulnerabilities mentioned by social scientists as producing underachievement. For example, we developed two different measures of vulnerability to Claude Steele's (1998, 1999) notion of strereotype threat. First, we selected black and Latino students who simultaneously had two characteristics: they said they were extremely self-conscious about their teachers' perceptions of them, and they didn't think they were very good students (i.e., they said it was "not true" or "somewhat true" that they were good students). We reasoned that black and Latino students who doubted their own abilities and worried what their (mostly white) teachers thought of them would be particularly vulnerable to stereotype threat.

Second, we also selected blacks and Latinos who shared two other characteristics: they reported their identity to be "American" rather than some group-specific racial or ethnic identity, and they assigned their own group an unintelligence rating of 5 or greater on a 10-point scale. In this case, we reasoned that minority students who strongly identified with the mainstream (by labeling themselves "American") but who harbored doubts about their group's intelligence would be especially afraid of living up to the myth of intellectual inferiority.

We also attempted to measure vulnerability to "racelessness," as described by Signithia Fordham and John Ogbu (1986), who argued that minority students may perceive academic success as "acting white," and that doing well in school will lead to a state of "racelessness" where they betray their black identity while not really being accepted as white. To isolate those vulnerable to this psychological threat, we also developed two measures. First, we selected those black and Latino students who said they were very self-conscious about how others in their group viewed them and simultaneously said that their friends perceived studying hard outside of class as "uncool." We figured that students who believed their peers denigrated academic work and were notably sensitive to peer opinion would be motivated to hide their true academic abilities through underachievement.

Second, we selected black and Latino respondents who reported an exclusive ingroup identity (saying they were black or Latino rather than "American" or "both") and who simultaneously gave blacks an unintelligence rating of 5 or more on the stereotype scale. These people, we felt, would also be quite likely to think that high levels of academic performance would be perceived as "acting white."

Finally, we sought to address one additional psychological vulnerability not mentioned by Fordham, Steele, or Ogbu. As noted earlier, a significant fraction of black respondents simultaneously expressed high levels of confidence about academic success despite having few AP credits, achieving low high school GPAs, and having gone to poorly rated high schools. This discrepancy suggested to us that perhaps they might be a little *too* confident—possessing an unrealistic appraisal of the difficulties they would face in college. Students who are *overconfident* might expect to do well but then find the courses more difficult than they imagined and suffer a psychological letdown that would impede performance. In an attempt to assess this potential vulnerability, we defined overconfident subjects as those who expressed 100% surety of graduating from college but had not taken *any* Advanced Placement courses in high school.

Into the Current

A full-blown analysis of academic performance across a variety of outcomes will be the subject of future studies that follow respondents into the spring of their freshmen year and beyond. Here we focus on three simple indicators of academic achievement measured during the first semester of the freshman year: grade point average, whether or not a class was dropped, and whether or not a class was failed. We undertake the analysis in two phases. First we regress each academic outcome on a set of dichotomous variables indicating group membership; then we add controls for the three dimensions of preparation and three psychological vulnerabilities. This procedure enables us to examine intergroup differentials before and after the addition of the controls.

Grade Point Average

For example, table 9.1 considers the GPA that respondents earned during their first semester of college (recall that earlier analyses showed that respondents are able to offer reliable and accurate self-reports of their fall-term grades). As the left-hand columns of table 9.1 reveal, significant differences in academic performance were already evident between groups at this early phase of college education. On average, whites earned a grade point average of 3.31 in their first term of college (see the intercept in the left-hand column of the table). The Asian GPA was nearly identical at just 0.02 point below that of whites (3.29); but Latino and black GPAs were considerably lower—0.26 and 0.36 points, respectively—yielding associated GPAs of 3.05 and 2.95. Thus, whereas the average white and Asian students earned a solid "B" in their first term of college-level work, the typical Latino earned a B− and the average African American a C+.

Controlling for differences in preparation and vulnerabilities reduces but does not eliminate this intergroup variation in GPA (see the right-hand columns). Although all groups are brought into the B range once background differences are held constant, the GPA of blacks is still 0.225 point below that of whites, while that of Latinos is 0.175 point lower. The variables included in the model explain roughly 22% of the total variation in grade point average during the fall term, up from just 8% in the group-only model (see the R^2 values of .079 and .223).

Grades earned during the first term of college were most strongly predicted by indicators of academic preparation, which is what one would expect at selective schools such as those in our survey. GPA was positively associated with grades earned in high school, degree of self-perceived academic preparation, and the number of AP courses taken. It was also positively related to the family's financial capacity to absorb the costs of college, and to two aspects of social preparation: sensitivity to peer influence and degree of self-confidence. The effect of peer susceptibility on grade point is strong and positive, which is perhaps not surprising as the peers of these freshmen are, by definition, high achievers.

Although self-confidence also played a modest role in promoting higher grades, we could detect no significant effect of overconfidence. It seems as

TABLE 9.1
Effect of indicators of preparation on first-semester grade point average

Independent Variables	Group Effects		Full Model	
	B	SE	B	SE
Race/Ethnicity				
White	–	–	–	–
Asian	−0.023	0.025	−0.015	0.024
Latino	−0.258***	0.025	−0.175***	0.026
Black	−0.360***	0.024	−0.225***	0.029
Level of Preparation				
Academic				
AP Courses Taken	–	–	0.013**	0.005
High School GPA	–	–	0.441***	0.029
Self-Rated Preparation	–	–	0.045***	0.003
Financial				
Share of Cost Paid by Family	–	–	0.048*	0.024
Social				
Susceptibility to Peer Influence	–	–	0.011***	0.002
Social Distance from Minorities	–	–	0.004	0.002
Social Distance from Whites	–	–	0.002	0.002
Psychological				
Self-Esteem	–	–	0.003	0.002
Self-Efficacy	–	–	−0.002	0.004
Self-Confidence	–	–	0.004*	0.002
Vulnerabilities				
Overconfidence	–	–	0.042	0.310
Stereotype Threat Index 1	–	–	−0.122**	0.046
Stereotype Threat Index 2	–	–	0.004	0.111
Raceless Index 1	–	–	0.099	0.068
Raceless Index 2	–	–	0.041	0.110
Intercept	3.307***	0.017	0.910***	0.133
R^2	0.079***		0.223***	
N	3,641		3,441	

$^*p < .05$ $^{**}p < .01$ $^{***}p < .001$

though one can never have too much confidence. Likewise we found no significant effect of racelessness, no matter which index we considered. We did, however, find a rather strong and negative effect of stereotype vulnerability, at least as measured by the first index. Those black and Latino students who doubted their own abilities and were simultaneously sensitive to the views of their teachers earned a GPA that was 0.122 point lower than that earned by other minority students.

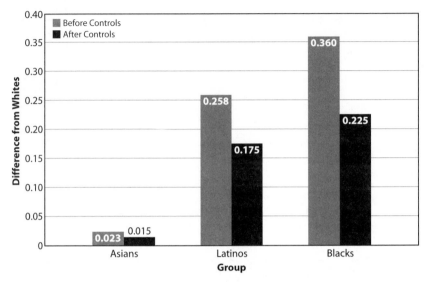

Figure 9.1. Deficit in grade point earned by minorities compared with whites

All in all, the foregoing results suggest that early grade performance is determined largely by academic preparation, socioeconomic status, susceptibility to peer influence, and, among Latinos and blacks, stereotype threat—the fear of minorities that they will confirm stereotypes about their intellectual inferiority. Figure 9.1 shows the residual effect of group membership before and after differences in these factors are controlled. As can be seen, the small gap in GPA between whites and Asians pretty much disappears in the wake of controls for differences in preparation and vulnerability, the Latino-white differential drops from 0.258 to 0.175, and the black differential falls from 0.360 to 0.225.

In other words, were all group members to have exactly the same background characteristics coming into college, blacks would earn a GPA of 3.09 in their first semester and Latinos one of 3.14, compared with an average of 3.31 for whites. While still significant in statistical terms, these small differences probably have few practical implications in determining the likelihood of future academic progress.

Dropping a Course

Whereas small differences in grade point average may have few practical implications for the prospects of finishing college, dropping a course has more serious consequences, particularly for students on financial aid. For them, dropping a course may render them ineligible to receive the full aid they might otherwise receive, in addition to whatever effect taking one fewer course might have in slowing down progress toward graduation. Table 9.2 therefore undertakes a logistic regression analysis to predict the odds of dropping a course during the fall term. As before, the left-hand columns present the analysis of group effects with no controls added, whereas the estimates displayed on the right control for differences with respect to preparation and vulnerability.

TABLE 9.2

Effect of indicators of preparation on likelihood of dropping a course during first semester of freshman year

Independent Variables	Group Effects		Full Model	
	B	SE	B	SE
Race/Ethnicity				
White	–	–	–	–
Asian	−0.037	0.119	−0.064	0.131
Latino	−0.363***	0.115	0.176	0.132
Black	−0.667***	0.108	0.253	0.146
Level of Preparation				
Academic				
AP Courses Taken	–	–	−0.049	0.027
High School GPA	–	–	−0.606***	0.136
Self-Rated Preparation	–	–	−0.065***	0.014
Financial				
Share of Cost Paid by Family	–	–	−0.194	0.121
Social				
Susceptibility to Peer Influence	–	–	0.005	0.010
Social Distance from Minorities	–	–	−0.011	0.010
Social Distance from Whites	–	–	0.011	0.008
Psychological				
Self-Esteem	–	–	−0.018*	0.009
Self-Efficacy	–	–	0.016	0.018
Self-Confidence	–	–	0.010	0.010
Vulnerabilities				
Overconfidence	–	–	0.024	0.310
Stereotype Threat 1	–	–	0.405*	0.196
Stereotype Threat 2	–	–	−1.905	1.038
Raceless 1	–	–	−0.046	0.321
Raceless 2	–	–	−0.337	0.571
Intercept	21.462***	0.084	1.376***	0.647
χ^2	58.427***		123.828***	
N	3,728		3,511	

*$p < .05$ **$p < .01$ ***$p < .001$

As can be seen, in the absence of controls for preparation and vulnerability, the probability of dropping a course was lowest for whites and Asians, higher for Latinos, and highest for African Americans. The logistic regression coefficient of $-.037$ for Asians indicates that their likelihood of dropping a course was slightly lower than for whites. In contrast, the coefficients of .363 for Latinos and .667 for blacks mean that the odds of dropping were considerably greater for members of these groups. Once controls are introduced, however, the Latino and black coefficients shrink and lose statistical significance. The effect of Latino group membership in elevating the risk of dropping a course is cut in half, falling from .363 to .176, and the effect of African American status is reduced by more than 60%, dropping from .667 to .253.

Although the coefficients depicted in the table do not have any easy intuitive interpretation, they can be used to generate *predicted probabilities* of dropping a course during the first term. Probabilities predicted from models estimated before and after the addition of controls are shown in figure 9.2. The baseline probability of course-dropping was .188 for whites, compared with .183 for Asians, .250 for Latinos, and .311 for blacks. After controls for preparation and vulnerability are added, the probability of dropping a course goes to .160 for Asians (a marginal change of just 13%), whereas it drops to .195 for Latinos (a 22% change) and .207 for blacks (a 33% decline).

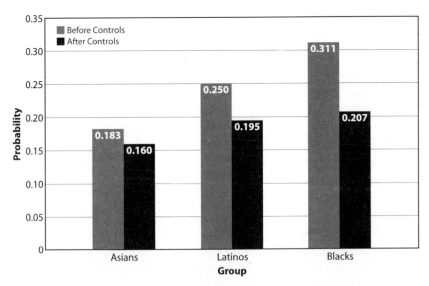

Figure 9.2. Predicted probability of dropping a class during
fall of freshman year

Were black and Latino students to enter college with the same level of academic, social, and psychological preparation as the average white student, and not experience any psychological pressure attributable to stereotype vulnerability, their likelihood of dropping a course in the first term would be very similar—in the range of 19% to 20%. To a great extent, then, early differences in grades earned is explained by different susceptibilities to stereotype threat and by the different levels of preparation for college that students in different groups bring with them when they arrive on campus.

Failing a Course

Of all the academic outcomes we consider, the last is probably the most important. Failing a course during the first term of college work cannot help but be a harbinger of academic problems to come. Unfortunately, as table 9.3. shows, there are significant differences between groups in the probability of failing a course. Although the odds are never very high for any group, the chances of failing a course in the fall term are substantially higher for blacks and Latinos than for whites and Asians. The coefficients in the group-only model are 1.210 for Latinos and 1.369 for blacks, both of which are large and highly significant; that for Asians is -0.249, slightly *below* that of whites.

The origins of these differential failure rates are suggested by the estimates of the model shown on the right side of the table. Adding controls for preparation and vulnerability reduces the size of the black coefficient to insignificance (although it is still rather close to significance at $p = .08$); and the Latino coefficient also drops substantially. The apparent effect of Latino status goes from 1.210 to .745 (a drop of 40%) while the black effect goes from 1.369 to .669 (a decline of 50%). The strongest predictors of course failure across all groups are high school GPA, self-rated academic preparation, self-esteem, and self-confidence. Since blacks score *higher* than whites on indicators of self-esteem and self-confidence, these factors cannot be the source of their poorer performance. Rather, the minority-white gap stems more from the lower academic preparation of black and Latino freshmen, as measured by their lower high school GPAs and their own lower self-assessments of preparation.

Whereas some whites and Asians share the disadvantage of poor academic preparation, a unique burden faced by black and Latino students is that of stereotype vulnerability. The two indicators we developed to assess this vulnerability are both large and statistically significant. The first indicator identified minority students who expressed doubts about their own intellectual abilities and who were also sensitive to the opinion of their teachers. Such students were much more likely to fail a course than

TABLE 9.3
Effect of indicators of preparation on likelihood of failing a course during first semester of freshman year

Independent Variables	Group Effects		Full Model	
	B	SE	B	SE
Race/Ethnicity				
White	–	–	–	–
Asian	−0.249	0.423	−0.580	0.460
Latino	1.210***	0.324	0.745*	0.350
Black	1.369***	0.313	0.669	0.380
Level of Preparation				
Academic				
AP Courses Taken	–	–	−0.013	0.070
High School GPA	–	–	−1.041***	0.278
Self-Rated Preparation	–	–	−0.139***	0.033
Financial				
Share of Cost Paid by Family	–	–	−0.129	0.286
Social				
Susceptibility to Peer Influence	–	–	−0.036	0.024
Social Distance from Minorities	–	–	−0.028	0.022
Social Distance from Whites	–	–	0.027	0.018
Psychological				
Self-Esteem	–	–	−0.043*	0.021
Self-Efficacy	–	–	0.021	0.041
Self-Confidence	–	–	−0.052**	0.019
Vulnerabilities				
Overconfidence	–	–	0.024	0.333
Stereotype Threat 1	–	–	0.748*	0.329
Stereotype Threat 2	–	–	1.345*	0.722
Raceless 1	–	–	0.468	0.589
Raceless 2	–	–	0.012	1.081
Intercept	−4.262***	0.279	3.872**	1.335
χ^2	45.861***		113.529***	
N	3,728		3,511	

*$p < .05$ **$p < .01$ ***$p < .001$

others (see the coefficient of .748). The second index identified minority students who subscribed to a mainstream identity ("American") but harbored some doubts about their group's intellectual capacities. These students were also more likely to fail a course (see the coefficient of 1.345).

Because it is difficult to derive much meaning from coefficients themselves, we used the models to generate predicted probabilities of failing a

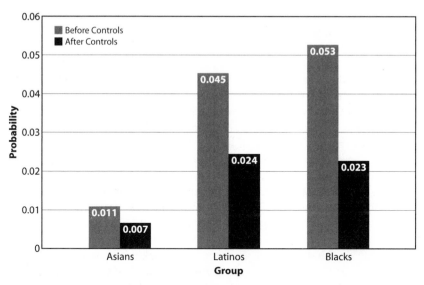

Figure 9.3. Predicted probability of failing a course during fall of freshman year

course under different conditions. These are summarized in figure 9.3. In the absence of controls for background differences, Asians display a failure probability of .011, compared with .045 among Latinos and .053 among blacks. The respective likelihood was .014 for whites. Controlling for differences in preparation and stereotype vulnerability, however, dramatically reduces odds of course failure for Latinos and blacks. The predicted probability that a Latino freshman would fail is only .024 and that for black freshmen is .023. Were blacks and Latinos to enter college with the same academic preparation as whites and be free from the burdens of stereotype vulnerability, their likelihood of failing a course during their first term of college would be only be around 2%, compared with the 4–5% we observe.

Sources of Minority Underachievement

Our analysis of early performance in higher education contains both discouraging and encouraging findings for those concerned with promoting the educational progress of disadvantaged minorities. The discouraging news is that during the very first semester of college there are clear and significant differences in academic performance that emerge between groups. Whether measured in terms of grade point average, courses dropped, or courses failed, whites and Asians perform significantly better than Latinos and blacks. In general, the grades earned by Latinos in their first college courses averaged about a quarter of a grade point lower than those of whites, whereas the grades earned by black students were more than a third of a point lower. Likewise about a quarter of all Latinos and a third of all blacks ended up dropping a fall-term class, compared with only a fifth of white and Asian students. The encouraging news, however, is that despite these overall differences, the vast majority of all group members did very well during their first term of college-level work. Upwards of 97% passed all the courses they took, 70% did not drop a class, and most earned grades of B or above.

Our assessment of the sources of intergroup differentials in academic performance likewise yielded reasons for hope and concern. On the bright side, variation in the degree of academic preparation was very strongly correlated with differences in grades earned and with variation in the odds of dropping or failing courses. The quality of schools attended and education received naturally varied systematically between groups, yielding differences in the degree of preparation for work in the nation's best academic institutions. In theory, such differences can be overcome simply by providing better support services, such as counseling, tutoring, and training. In future work with the NLSF we will, in fact, be able to measure exactly how well such interventions may compensate for weaker preparation to produce equal or better outcomes for minority students.

Also on the bright side, our findings show that self-esteem and self-confidence play a significant role in early academic performance. In general, students who hold themselves in higher regard and who express greater confidence in completing academic goals do indeed go on to earn higher grades, drop fewer classes, and fail courses less frequently. This is good news for disadvantaged minorities such as blacks and Latinos because their levels of self-confidence and self-esteem are generally quite high, often even higher than those expressed by whites and Asians. Although we originally harbored some concern that minority students may be *overconfident*, we found no empirical evidence to justify this worry. Their high level of confidence may simply reflect the fact that many students overcame disordered schools, unstable families, and violent neighborhoods to make it to college, making life on campus seem like a breeze, even if it is a bit of an adjustment. As far as we can tell, therefore, minority students entering elite colleges and universities in the fall of 1999 seemed to possess precisely the kind of positive mental attitude conducive to academic success.

Likewise encouraging is the fact that we found no evidence whatsoever of "the burden of acting white" among either black or Latino students. As high school students, the vast majority had peers that strongly supported hard work, diligence, and getting good grades, and if anything the peer environment on campus was even more supportive of academic success. Neither of the two definitions we developed to identify students susceptible to the condition of racelessness was significant in predicting academic performance. In a way this negative finding should not be surprising, as the hypothesis of racelessness was derived from observations of socioeconomic disadvantaged students attending segregated schools of very poor quality. The peer environment in which our respondents perform could not be more different.

On the dark side, however, we found clear and consistent statistical evidence that stereotype vulnerability worked to undermine the academic performance of black and Latino students above and beyond whatever deficits they experienced with respect to academic, financial, social, or psychological preparation for college. Although Steele et al. (in press) have shown it is not impossible, it is nonetheless difficult to design programs to overcome "the threat in the air" that is the hallmark of stereotype vulnerability, for this involves a manipulation of students' deepest feelings, which are often unconscious or unacknowledged.

Admittedly, our markers of stereotype vulnerability are rather crude. Basically we hypothesized that blacks or Latinos who expressed reservations about their academic abilities and were unusually self-conscious of teachers would be at elevated risk of stereotype threat, along with students who expressed doubts about their group's ability while adhering to a mainstream "American" identity. Among Latinos surveyed by the NLSF, 6.3% fell into the former risk category, whereas 1% were in the latter and a very small fraction (0.1%) fell into both. Among blacks, 7.6% fell into the former, 1.2% into the latter, and 0.1% into both. Thus around 9% of blacks and 7% of Latinos evinced some vulnerability to stereotype threat.

Happily, these figures imply that 91% of blacks and 93% of Latinos are not at serious risk of succumbing to stereotype vulnerability, at least as we have crudely defined it. For those students possessing the relevant psychological dispositions, however, the effects on performance can be profound. Consider, for example, the catastrophic outcome of failing a course during the first term of college study. Aside from undermining confidence and self-esteem, it immediately puts students into serious academic difficulty vis-à-vis the institution, perhaps even academic probation. Our analysis suggests that stereotype vulnerability has a pronounced influence on the risk of course failure.

Figure 9.4 illustrates this fact by presenting a bar chart indicating the probability of failing a course for Latinos and blacks who do and do not meet our criteria for stereotype vulnerability. For the vast majority who satisfy neither of our two criteria, the likelihood of failing a course during the first term was small, on the order of 3% to 4%. While higher than the 1% to 2% characteristic of whites and Asians, in absolute terms the rate is still rather small. For those 6–7% of minority students who met the first

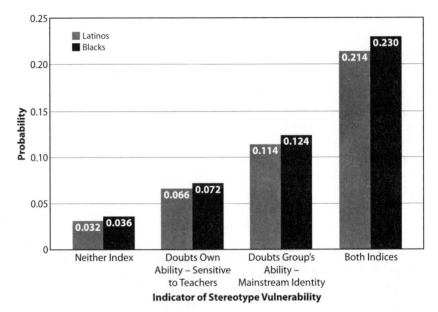

Figure 9.4. Predicted probability of failing a class by
indicator of stereotype vulnerability

definition for stereotype vulnerability, however (i.e., they doubted their own ability and were sensitive to the views of teachers), the probability of course failure rose to around 7%. Likewise for those students meeting the second set of criteria (not identifying as a minority and doubting the ability of the group), the likelihood of course failure was even higher, around 11% or 12%. Finally, for those very unlucky few (under 1%) who simultaneously met both sets of criteria, the probability of course failure became very high indeed, rising to 21% for Latinos and 23% for blacks.

To this point in our study, we have considered only the qualities and characteristics that the students brought with them when they arrived on campus. We have not measured anything about experiences on campus and how these might influence academic performance. We have only provided a baseline against which to compare future studies. Taking fall GPA as an example, our models account for only a quarter of the variation in academic performance. This leaves a considerable amount of variation yet to be explained, and while controlling for preexisting differences in preparation and vulnerabilities substantially reduces the differentials in group performance, it usually does not eliminate them. As we move on to analyze data gathered from students in their freshman and sophomore years, therefore, we have our work cut out for us.

CHAPTER 10

LESSONS LEARNED

I T IS HARDLY surprising that we have failed to explain away all the intergroup differences in academic performance. After all, we focused only on traits and characteristics that respondents brought with them when they arrived on campus. Although our documentation of differences between whites, Asians, Latinos, and blacks with respect to family, neighborhood, school, and peer circumstances was rather exhaustive, and even though we developed detailed data about their attitudes, expectations, and values, we only considered performance during the very first term of college, which is bound to be a bit of an experiment. We also made no effort to consider how students actually *behaved* once they arrived on campus, which naturally can be expected to have a bearing on how well they perform.

Our purpose was simply to construct a detailed portrait of freshmen entering selective colleges and universities throughout the United States, and to use this knowledge to shed light on group differences in academic achievement. We trust this information will prove useful to professors and administrators as they teach, advise, and counsel students working hard to adapt to the realities of life in a competitive academic environment. We hope that the information we have adduced about the contrasting backgrounds of whites and Asians, on the one hand, and Latinos and blacks, on the other, puts their differential rates of academic success into a broader and more understandable context. We offer the NLSF to other researchers as a new source of data to help them untangle the complicated teleology of success or failure in higher education. In the ensuing sections, we close by summarizing the important lessons learned from our foray into social, economic, and academic origins of people who will inevitably become the leaders of science, industry, business, and public affairs in the next generation.

The Study and the Data

Whatever the long-term contributions of our study to public understanding of issues surrounding academic achievement, we will have provided to the field a rich and reliable source of new data on the subject in the National Longitudinal Survey of Freshmen. In the fall of 1999, we interviewed 3,924 freshmen as they entered twenty-eight selective colleges and universities throughout the United States. The sample included public and private institutions, research universities as well as liberal arts colleges, women's schools, and one historically black institution. The baseline sample included 998 whites, 959 Asians, 916 Latinos, and 1,051 African Americans. Of those academic institutions approached for permission to interview on campus, 80% agreed to cooperate, and of those students we asked to join the study 86% agreed to be interviewed. The response rate varied from a low of 83% among whites to a high of 89% among African Americans.

The fall 1999 survey was designed to be the initial panel in a longitudinal survey that would reinterview students successively during the springs of 2000, 2001, 2002, and 2003 to follow them as they progressed through higher education. This book is based almost entirely on data from the baseline survey, which gathered detailed background information on students at three important junctures in their lives—at ages 6, 13, and 18. At each age, we compiled detailed information about the composition of the respondent's family, neighborhood, and school, and ascertained the frequence of different parental behaviors relevant to education, training, and discipline. We asked particularly detailed questions about the respondent's senior year in high school, including batteries of items on school quality, the nature of the peer environment, and personal values and attitudes. If we visualize the cohort of college freshmen as a river moving through life, the data analyzed in this book focus on the source of that river.

Homogeneity and Diversity

Entry into exclusive colleges and universities is obviously governed by rather rarefied selection processes. While we are not privy to actual admissions processes, we do know that they operate to produce a freshman class composed of two very distinct subpopulations. On the one hand are whites and Asians and on the other are Latinos and blacks. Aside from the fact that Asians are heavily of immigrant origin while whites are not, the two groups are similar to one another socially and economically. Likewise, although immigrants are more predominant among Latinos than among blacks, these two groups of students are also very similar to one another. Moreover, even though persons of immigrant origin may be less prevalent among African American college students, immigrant origins are nonetheless substantially overrepresented among blacks admitted to selective schools. In many ways, therefore, black-Latino differences are more apparent than real.

The overwhelming majority of white and Asian students come from families with two well-educated parents, both of whom occupy upper managerial or professional positions. Nearly all fathers and more than two-thirds of mothers are college graduates, and absolute majorities of white and Asian fathers hold advanced degrees. Half of all white students and more than 40% of Asian students come from households earning over $100,000 per year. These students generally attended suburban public schools or some kind of private institution. White students had little or no contact with minorities while growing up, and although Asians had substantial contact with other Asians, their exposure to blacks and Latinos was equally as limited.

In contrast, black and Latino students came from a diverse array of social origins. Although many replicate the rather privileged socioeconomic background of whites and Asians, many others do not. Only two-thirds of Latinos and just 60% of blacks had a father with a college degree, and a third or fewer had a father with an advanced degree. Almost half of the mothers of black and Latino students were not themselves college graduates, and a substantial plurality of their parents—more than 40%—did not hold managerial or professional jobs. Relatively few students came from households with incomes over $100,000 (just a third of Latinos and a quarter of blacks). Indeed, 12% of Latinos and 17% of blacks came from a welfare background (compared with just 4% of whites).

A significant share of both Latino and black students (40% of the former and nearly half of the latter) grew up in a household in which the father was absent (in contrast, well over 80% of whites and Asians grew up in households with both parents present). Most Latinos and African Americans attended public schools, although the former displayed a stronger proclivity toward parochial education than other groups. A significant share of Latinos and blacks (nearly 40% of the latter and 20% of the former) grew up in segregated neighborhood circumstances that did not expose them to other races or ethnicities. The remainder grew up in mixed or integrated neighborhoods that provided considerable exposure to members of other racial and ethnic groups, minority and majority. Whereas the share of foreign origins among African Americans is around 5% in the population at large, roughly a quarter of those entering selective schools were immigrants or children of immigrants.

In sum, whereas white and Asian students are characterized by great social, economic, and demographic homogeneity, Latinos and blacks are typified by tremendous heterogeneity. Picking a white student at random, one can guess with some confidence that he or she grew up in stable family circumstances, in an upper-middle-class environment, attending good schools that provided little direct contact with blacks or Latinos. If one were to make this attribution to all white students, one would be right in the vast majority of cases, and to the extent that one conditioned behavior on such assumptions, one would be unlikely to cause offense. To the extent that a poor white student gets treated as rich and privileged, whatever alienation results will likely be experienced as an individual rather than a group phenomenon.

Picking a black student at random, however, one would be hard-pressed to make an accurate guess about his or her background. He or she could be the heir to a sizable fortune, the child of affluent, married professionals, the son or daughter of high-school-educated, working-class parents, or the child of a single welfare mother who dropped out of school in the tenth grade. If one were to assume *anything* about a randomly selected black student, one would be wrong most of the time, and if one's behavior toward that student were conditioned on this assumption, it would be very likely to cause offense. To the extent that affluent blacks resent being treated like they are poor and poor blacks resent being treated as if they are rich, all will find plenty of company with whom to share their resentments. For them, class marginalization will be a distinctly *social* experience.

The obvious lesson for professors, administrators, and students is to resist making assumptions and attributions about the backgrounds of black or Latino students. Rather, one should suspend judgment until relevant personal facts can be gathered. Assumptions made about the class origins of Latino and black students are very likely to be wrong, creating considerable potential for miscommunication, misunderstanding, and resentment. The wisest course is to resist the natural human tendency to make attributions according to group markers, and to treat Latinos and African Americans as individuals rather than representatives of social categories. Come to think of it, this is not bad advice for navigating social life in general.

The heterogeneity of the black and Latino student bodies creates considerable potential for conflict around identity issues among the groups themselves, with salient cleavages along the lines of class, gender, and immigrant origins. For many black and Latino freshmen from segregated inner cities, it will be the first time they have ever encountered rich minority members who may not share the same linguistic or cultural styles. For others coming from affluent, integrated settings, college will be their first chance to move through black or Latino worlds (in theme dorms and student organizations). For some rich black and Latino students, campus life offers the first opportunity for sustained exposure to lower-class group members. Moreover, many African Americans will not have known black immigrants before. Under such circumstances group membership becomes problematic, and conflict over what constitutes a "real" or "authentic" African American or Latino identity is like to occur. Given the heterogeneity of the black and Latino student bodies, it is hardly surprising that "identity politics" have been so common on college campuses.

The Tyranny of Demography

Compared with white, Asian, and even Latino freshmen, those of African ancestry encounter a student population characterized by a very imbalanced sex ratio in which women decidedly outnumber men. Indeed, the class of black freshmen at the twenty-eight selective institutions we studied was two-thirds female and just one-third male, yielding a sex ratio of 2.05, compared with figures of 1.12 for whites, 1.25 for Latinos, and 1.18 for Asians. Given that a third to a half of college-age black men are in prison, on parole, or under court supervision (Tonry 1995), their relative absence within institutions of higher education, however tragic, should not be surprising.

The demographics of the black student population, however, have rather strong implications for patterns and processes of mating and dating and inevitably for issues of racial identity. Given their two-to-one numerical superiority to black males, in the absence of black male polygamy, cross-class pairing, or racial exogamy at least half of college-educated black women will remain single. If they have any hope of forming a romantic partnership with a member of the opposite sex, roughly half of all black women will have to date someone who is nonblack or someone who is much less educated (given that polygamy is illegal).

William Julius Wilson (1987) developed the "marriageable male hypothesis" to explain the dissolution of marriage within inner-city black communities and the rise of unwed childbearing among poor black women. Whereas the disappearance of factory jobs reduced the number of black men capable of supporting a family, the war on drugs removed others from the marriage pool through incarceration. As a result, poor black women were virtually forced into unwed childbearing if they wished to become mothers. Our snapshot of African Americans attending the most elite segment of American higher education paradoxically suggests that the marriage squeeze may be equally or more severe for upper-class black women, who face a clear dearth of black men of comparable educational status.

The tyranny of demography thus places a sizable share of well-educated black women in a difficult structural position. For about half of all African American women attending elite colleges, the possible outcomes will be fourfold: (1) date infrequently, never marry, and never have children; (2) date sporadically, never marry, and at some point become a single mother;

(3) cross class lines, date more often, marry someone of lesser education, and thus leave open the possibility of marital childbearing; or (4) cross racial lines, date more often, possibly marry someone of different race but similar education, and potentially bear multiracial children within the bounds of matrimony.

Assuming that women are motivated toward pair bonding and that the incidence of lesbianism is rather small, then the pressures for interracial dating by black women will be significant. To the extent that such dating is frowned upon by the black community or perceived as threatening by black men, it will add a distinct sexual edge to campus identity politics. To the extent that interracial dating is perceived as undesirable and neg-atively sanctioned by other groups, such as whites or Asians, then the dis-tinctive demography of African American students may heighten inter-group conflicts. Of course, to the extent that interracial dating and mating occur in response to demographic pressures, it might also help break down barriers and lead to greater communication and understanding be-tween groups. One way or another, however, demography will exert its force.

The Continuing Reality of Segregation

When it comes to the kind and quality of experiences gleaned while grow-ing up, college freshmen at elite schools can be divided into two basic groups. On the one hand are whites, Asians, and those blacks and Lati-nos who lived in integrated neighborhoods and/or attended integrated schools. On the other hand are blacks and Latinos who attended segre-gated schools or who grew up in segregated, racially isolated neighbor-hoods. The experiences of these two sets of people could not have been more different.

Whites, Asians, and people of color growing up in integrated neigh-borhoods experienced low levels of social disorder and were exposed to little in the way of violence. In contrast, blacks and Latinos growing up in segregated communities were exposed to high rates of both violence and social disorder. Using severity-weighted indices that we developed, we found that minorities growing up in a segregated neighborhood experi-enced 4 times the social disorder of the typical white respondent and 5.5 times more violence.

Within schools, meanwhile, minority students attending segregated in-stitutions experienced 17% more disorder and 55% more violence than either whites or those blacks and Latinos attending integrated schools. School quality also varied systematically by segregation. According to re-liable indices that we developed to measure different school attributes, the quality of infrastructure was 22% lower in segregated than integrated schools, whereas the quality of teaching was about 7% lower.

In sum, whereas white and Asian freshmen could count on safe neighborhoods as a virtual birthright, and whereas their schools were universally secure and offered high-quality academic support, the experience of blacks and Latinos was highly structured by segregation. Whether or not they experienced safe schools and neighborhoods and attended high-quality schools with good teachers and supportive staff depended on whether they grew up under integrated or segregated circumstances. Unfortunately, the residential segregation of African Americans and dark-skinned Latinos is a sad but persisting reality in American society (Massey and Denton 1993). About half of black freshmen at selective institutions and a quarter of all Latinos grew up under residential segregated circumstances, and a third of blacks and a quarter of Latinos attended segregated schools. Thus segregation constitutes a major cleavage among students in selective colleges and universities, as it does in U.S. society generally.

Peers and Parents

Despite the disadvantages imposed on a substantial fraction of African American and Latino students by prior residential and school segregation, members of these groups selected themselves into peer subcultures that were generally supportive of academic effort and intellectual independence. In general, there were few differences between groups in terms of peer support for academic achievement, and among minorities there was little variation in peer culture by level of segregation. Of course, NLSF respondents are highly self-selected by virtue of having been admitted into some of the most selective schools in the country. Those minority students with unsupportive peers simply did not survive the rigors of high school grading and college application to become a part of our study.

Whatever the reasons for the homogeneity of peer environments—selection or a real absence of difference between the groups in high school— explanations for minority underachievement that center on "racelessness" and "the burden of acting white" nonetheless would not appear to have much potential for explaining intergroup differences in academic performance in college, since such explanations require an audience of peers who denigrate educational achievement along with the attitudes and behaviors that support it, none of which are in evidence among black or Latino freshmen at selective institutions.

We did find, however, that freshmen of different races and ethnicities experienced very different patterns of child rearing while growing up. Although differences in child-raising strategy in part reflect intergroup variation with respect to social class and neighborhood circumstances, we also found durable differences between the four groups even after such factors were controlled. White students generally experienced a supportive, companionate style of child rearing. Their parents were very involved in their lives, talked to them frequently, knew their friends, and took an active role in developing their cognitive skills and cultural knowledge. They were unlikely to use strict discipline or make use of shame and guilt to secure complaint behavior, favoring rewards and reasoning instead.

Black parents, in contrast, were less directly involved in cultivating human or cultural capital, or in monitoring their children's social relationships. Among all groups, they were the most likely to rely on a regime of rewards and punishments and to set strict limits on behavior, partly in response to the fact that their neighborhood and school environments were more threatening and dangerous and partly because black parents feel that strict discipline is required to prepare students for life in a racist world. Like white parents, however, they were unlikely to rely on shame or guilt in child rearing.

Asian parents were the least companionate and the most strict of all groups. Except for blacks, they were the most likely to mete out punishments and were by far the most likely to rely on shame and guilt as a strategy of child raising. Asian parents were generally uninvolved in the cultivation of their children's human or cultural capital and were relatively unlikely to interact with their children's friends.

Finally, Latino parents were more authoritarian and less companionate. Compared with white parents Latino parents tended not to know or interact with respondents or their friends, and they emphasized obedience and authority rather than independence. Latinos, however, were relatively likely to pair their demand for obedience with an explanation for decisions; and despite a rather hierarchical relationship with their parents, Latino respondents were very likely to report that their parents interacted with them socially and relied only modestly on shame and guilt as tools of child raising.

Differences in Preparation

The diverse backgrounds of white, Asian, Latino, and black students are associated with different levels of preparation on a variety of dimensions. We conceptualized preparation for college as occurring with respect to academic, economic, social, and psychological criteria. Whites and Asians were the best prepared academically for college work, followed by Latinos and then blacks, and roughly the same ordering occurred with respect to the ability of families to absorb the costs of college.

All groups were relatively unprepared for the diversity of social interactions they would encounter in college. Whites and Asians were least prepared, having little prior experience with minorities and perceiving a high
degree of social distance between themselves and groups such as blacks
and Latinos. Despite the fact that a large share of African Americans had
interacted with whites in the past, they nonetheless perceived a high degree of social distance from them, combined with low perceived distance
with respect to minorities. Latinos perceived a relatively low degree of distance from whites and only slightly greater distance from minorities. Of
all the groups, they seemed most prepared for the diversity of the college
campus.

The best-prepared group psychologically appear to be African Americans, who generally reported the highest levels of self-confidence, self-
esteem, and self-efficacy. Least prepared were Asians, who expressed the
lowest levels of self-esteem and self-efficacy. Latinos were generally close
to blacks in terms of these attributes, whereas whites were more like
Asians, and it was whites who expressed the lowest confidence in academic success. We found that differences in background and upbringing explained some but not all of the intergroup differences in academic preparation; eliminated the differences in economic preparation; and accounted
for most of the differences in susceptibility to peer influence. However,
background differences accounted for little in the way of perceived social
distances, in spite of the fact that these perceptions were rather strongly
related to prior school and residential segregation.

Minority Underachievement Revisited

In the first term of college work, we could already detect differences between groups with respect to academic performance. Fortunately, grades
for all group generally ran in the B range, and failing courses was a relatively rare event. Nonetheless, the differentials in performance across
groups were significant, with whites and Asians generally being highest
and very close to one another, followed by Latinos, and finally by blacks.
As one would expect, these performance differentials were most strongly
and consistently predicted by level of academic preparation, which we
measured in terms of high school GPA, Advanced Placement credits, and
self-assessment. They were also influenced by socioeconomic background,
with students from more privileged background generally doing better, as
well as by various combinations of self-esteem and self-confidence.

The foregoing results are generally in line with the theory of capital deficiency outlined in the first chapter. Students in general perform poorly
in college when the circumstances of their upbringing have denied them

access to some form of capital—human, social, cultural, psychic, or financial—that is important in producing success in higher education. Minority students generally do not lack for self-esteem and self-confidence, so it is not psychic capital that is the problem, and socially blacks and Latinos are probably more prepared for campus diversity than either Asians or whites, at least on average. The capital they lack is generally financial and human, which reflects the fact that many blacks and Latinos come from backgrounds of residential segregation, school isolation, and socioeconomic disadvantage.

In addition to theories of capital deficiency, we also considered explanations rooted in the psychological dynamics of group stereotyping and identity. We found no support whatsoever for the view that blacks and Latinos performed poorly because they felt that working hard and earning good grades would be a betrayal of their group identity, something to be avoided because it would be seen as "acting white." The peer milieu that black and Latino students experienced in high school was highly supportive of academic achievement and less tolerant of delinquency than that of whites. Indices we developed to measure vulnerability to the burden of acting white had no significant effect on any indicator of academic performance. Whatever the merits of Fordham and Ogbu's (1986) theory in explaining the poor performance of blacks in segregated inner-city high schools, the psychological dynamics of "racelessness" are clearly not in play among minority students attending selective colleges and universities.

We did find substantial support, however, for Claude Steele's (1988, 1999) hypothesis of stereotype vulnerability—the disengagement from school work that stems from fears of living up to negative stereotypes of minority intellectual inferiority. We developed a very rough definition of those who, by virtue of their attitudes and feelings upon entry, we judged to be unusually vulnerable to stereotype threat—those who had doubts about their own abilities and were self-conscious about the views of teachers, or those doubted their own group's ability and identified more with the majority than the minority. About 9% of blacks and 7% of Latinos entered college with one of these predispositions. In their first term of college work, those who did earned significantly lower grades and failed courses at much high rates than other minority students. For the few blacks and Latinos who had both predispositions, the likelihood of failing a course in the first term was over 20%. To our knowledge, this constitutes the first demonstration of the effect of stereotype vulnerability on academic performance outside of an experimental situation using survey-based measurements on a large, representative population of minority students.

Despite this exhaustive study of the source of the river of students that annually flows into America's elite colleges and universities, we have barely scratched the surface in developing a full and satisfying explanation for differentials in group performance. So far we have only made use of qualities, characteristics, and differences that minority and majority group members possessed when they walked onto campus on the first day of the fall term. These preexisting circumstances explain some, but by no means all, of the observed differentials in academic achievement among whites, blacks, Asians, and Latinos. Our goal in future volumes based on successive follow-up surveys will be to understand how preexisting traits and characteristics do or do not yield differences in attitudes and behavior on campus, and how these campus-based actions, in turn, produce different academic outcomes. The journey down the river has only just begun.

APPENDIX A

SURVEY OF COLLEGE LIFE

AND EXPERIENCE:

FIRST-WAVE INSTRUMENT

Grade School Environment

To begin, please think back to when you were about 6 years old. You may have been in the first grade. I'd like to find out a little about the family, neighborhood, and school environment that you experienced when you were 6.

1. Let's start with your household. What is the first name and the relationship to you of everyone who was living with you at that time? Include everyone who lived in your household for at least one month during the time you were 6, even if they didn't spend the entire year with you and even if they weren't a relative. Please begin with your parents, guardians, or the people most responsible for raising you.

Relation to Respondent	Sex	Age	In School?	Working? Part or Full Time?	Present All Year?
Parent or Guardian					

2. To make it easier for you to answer some questions, I will be giving you cards with responses to look at during the interview. You may just choose the answers that come closest to how you feel. (HAND R CARD 1) Still thinking about when you were 6 years old, how often did your parents, older siblings, or other adults in your house read to you? Please look at the card and tell me if it was never, rarely, sometimes, often, or very often. You can just tell me the number of your answer.

Never | Rarely | Sometimes | Often | Very Often

Read to you?
Check if you'd done your homework?
Participate in a Parent-Teacher Association?
Help you with your homework?
Reward you for good grades?
Punish you for bad grades?
Punish you for disobedience?
Limit your TV watching?
Ask you to do household chores?
Take you to an art museum?
Take you to a science center or museum?
Take you to a library?
Take you to the zoo or aquarium?
Take you traveling within the U.S.?
Take you on foreign trips?

3. Did you attend all or most of first grade in:

   ( ) a public school
   ( ) a religious school
   ( ) a private nonreligious school
   ( ) other (specify)

4. During the summer when you were 6 (after your first-grade year), did you participate in:

Summer school	Yes / No
Recreational day camp	Yes / No
Educational day camp	Yes / No
Sleep-away camp	Yes / No
Organized day care	Yes / No
Family vacation	Yes / No
Academic enrichment program (specify)	Yes / No

5. When you were in first grade, what was the ethnic and racial composition of all first graders in your school? I'll be asking you about all ethnic and racial groups, one group at a time. Out of a total of 100% of all first graders:

   What percentage were African American? _____
   What percentage were Hispanic or Latino? _____
   What percentage were Asian? _____

What percentage were white? _____

What percentage were of other racial or ethnic

backgrounds I have not already mentioned? _____

6. Now think back to the ethnic and racial composition of the three-block radius where you lived when you were about 6 years old.

What is your estimate of the percentage of African Americans? _____

What percentage were Hispanic or Latino? _____

What percentage were Asian? _____

What percentage were white? _____

What percentage were of other racial or ethnic

backgrounds I have not already mentioned? _____

7. In your grade school, when you were between the ages of 6 and 10, did you see

Students fighting?	Yes / No
Students smoking?	Yes / No
Students cutting class?	Yes / No
Students cutting school?	Yes / No
Students verbally abusing teachers?	Yes / No
Did you see physical violence directed at teachers by students?	Yes / No
Vandalism of school or personal property?	Yes / No
Theft of school or personal property?	Yes / No
Students consuming alcohol?	Yes / No
Students taking illegal drugs?	Yes / No
Students with knives as weapons?	Yes / No
Students with guns?	Yes / No

8. In your neighborhood, before you were 10, do you remember seeing

Homeless people on the street?	Yes / No
Prostitutes on the street?	Yes / No
Gang members hanging out on the street?	Yes / No
Drug paraphernalia on the street?	Yes / No
People selling illegal drugs in public?	Yes / No
People using illegal drugs in public?	Yes / No
People drinking or drunk in public?	Yes / No
Physical violence in public?	Yes / No
Hearing the sound of gunshots?	Yes / No

Middle School Environment

Now I'd like you to think back to when you were 13 years old. I'd like to find out something about the family, school, and neighborhood conditions you experienced when you were 13 years old. These questions are about the people who lived in your household at least one month during the year you were 13.

9. Could you please tell me who was living with you at that time? Once again, include *everyone* who lived in your home or apartment at age 13, even if they weren't a relative and even if they didn't spend the entire year with you. Begin with your parent, guardian, or closest relative.

Relation to Respondent	Sex	Age	In School?	Working? Part or Full Time?	Present All Year?
Parent or Guardian					

10. At age 13, did you attend all or most of the year in:

    ( ) a public school
    ( ) a religious school
    ( ) a private nonreligious school
    ( ) other (specify)

11. (HAND R CARD 1) Still thinking about when you were 13 years old, how often did your parents or other adults in your household check

if you'd done your homework? You can just tell me the number of your answer.

Never | Rarely | Sometimes | Often | Very Often | Always

Help you with your homework?
Participate in a Parent-Teacher Association?
Talk with your friends?
Reward you for good grades?

Did your parents or other adults:
Punish you for bad grades?
Punish you for disobedience?
Limit your TV watching?
Limit your playing of video games?
Limit the time you spent with friends?
Set an hour to return home at night?
Ask you to do household chores?
Take you to an art museum?
Take you to a science center or museum?
Take you to a library?
Take you to plays or concerts?
Take you to sporting events?
Take you traveling within the U.S.?
Take you on trips to foreign countries?

12. About how often did you participate in the following activities when you were 13 years old:

Never | Rarely | Sometimes | Often | Very Often

Organized sports at school?
Organized sports outside of school?
Dance lessons?
Music lessons?
Art lessons?
Scouting activities?
4H Club?

13. During the summer after your 13th birthday, did you participate in:

Summer school?	Yes / No
Recreational day camp?	Yes / No
Educational day camp?	Yes / No
Sleep-away camp?	Yes / No
A family vacation?	Yes / No
A summer job?	Yes / No

14. The next question is about the ethnic and racial composition of your school when you were 13.

   Let's start with your estimate of the percentage of
   African Americans. _____

   What percentage were Hispanic or Latino? _____

   What percentage were Asian? _____

   What percentage were white? _____

   What percentage were of other racial or ethnic
   backgrounds I have not already mentioned? _____

15. Now think back to the ethnic and racial composition of the three-block radius of where you lived when you were 13.

   Let's start with your estimate of the percentage of
   African Americans. _____

   What percentage were Hispanic or Latino? _____

   What percentage were Asian? _____

   What percentage were white? _____

   What percentage were of other racial or ethnic
   backgrounds I have not already mentioned? _____

16. When you were 13, how often do you recall witnessing students fighting in school, that is, on school property during school hours? You can just tell me the number of your answer.

   Never | Rarely | Sometimes | Often | Very Often

   Students smoking?

   Students kissing or "making out"?

   Students being late for class?

   Students cutting class?

   Students cutting school?

   Verbal abuse of teachers by students?

   Physical violence directed at teachers by students?

   Vandalism of school or personal property?

   Theft of school or personal property?

   Students consuming alcohol?

   Students taking illegal drugs?

   Students carrying knives?

   Students carrying guns?

   Robbery of students by other students?

17. In your neighborhood, when you were 13, how often do you recall seeing homeless people on the street?

Never | Rarely | Sometimes | Often | Very Often

Prostitutes on the street?

Gang members hanging out on the street?

Drug paraphernalia on the street?

People selling illegal drugs in public?

People using illegal drugs in public?

People drinking or drunk in public?

Physical violence in public?

The sound of gunshots?

High School Experiences: Home

Now, I'd like to ask you about last year. I'd like to find out something about the family, school, and neighborhood conditions you experienced last year. These questions are about the people who lived in your household at least one month last year.

18.   Could you please tell me who was living with you at that time? Once again, include *everyone* who lived in your home or apartment during your senior year of high school, even if they weren't a relative and even if they didn't spend the entire year with you. Begin with your parent, guardian, or closest relative.

| | | | | Working? | |
Relation to Respondent	Sex	Age	In School?	Part or Full Time?	Present All Year?
Parent or Guardian					

19. Did you attend all or most of your senior year in:

   ( ) a public school
   ( ) a religious school
   ( ) a private nonreligious school
   ( ) other (specify)

20. (HAND R CARD 1) Last year, how often did your parents or other adults in your household check if you had done your homework? Just tell me the number of your answer.

Never | Rarely | Sometimes | Often | Very Often | Always

Meet personally with your teachers?
Help you with your homework?
Talk with your friends?
Reward you for good grades?
Punish you for bad grades?
Punish you for disobedience?
Limit your TV watching?
Limit your playing of video games?
Limit the time you spent with friends?
Set an hour to return home at night?
Ask you to do household chores?
Take you to museums?
Take you to plays or concerts?
Take you to sporting events?
Take you traveling in the U.S.?
Take you on foreign trips?

21. Last year, about how often did you participate in sports at school?

Never | Rarely | Sometimes | Often | Very Often

Organized sports outside of school?
Drama or theater activities?
School band or orchestra?
School debate?
School cheerleading?
Pep club or related activities?
Student government?
Dance lessons?
Private music lessons?
Private art lessons?
Scouting activities?
4H Club?
Volunteer work in community?

22. (HAND R CARD 2) How often did you make use of a daily newspaper last year?

Never | Rarely | Sometimes | Often | Very Often | Didn't Have Access

A Sunday newspaper?
A weekly news magazine?
An encyclopedia?
A dictionary?
An atlas?
A typewriter or word processor?
A computer?
The Internet?
A pocket calculator?
A piano?
Another musical instrument?

23. How often did your mother, father, or other adult most responsible for you read/make use of a daily newspaper last year?

Never | Rarely | Sometimes | Often | Very Often | Didn't Have Access

A Sunday newspaper?
A weekly news magazine?
An encyclopedia?
A dictionary?
An atlas?
A typewriter or wordprocessor?
A computer?
The Internet?
A pocket calculator?
A piano?
Another musical instrument?

24. Last year, approximately how late were you allowed to stay out on a weeknight?

Approximate time: _____

25. Last year, approximately how late were you allowed to stay out on a weekend night?

Approximate time: _____

26. Did you have a room of your own last year?   Yes / No

27. Did you have a specific place where you could study without being disturbed?   Yes / No

28. Last year, about how many books were in your household?

    ( ) None
    ( ) 1–25
    ( ) 26–50
    ( ) 51–75
    ( ) 76–100
    ( ) >100

29. How many televisions were in your household?

                                                        Number: _____

30. How many VCRs?   Number: _____

31. I'm going to ask you about a typical seven-day week last year. There are 168 hours in a seven-day week. Thinking only of the time you were awake, please estimate the number of hours you watched TV or videos during a typical seven-day week last year.

    Played video games.   _____
    Studied or did homework outside of school.   _____
    Read for information or pleasure.   _____
    During a typical seven-day week, please estimate the
        number of hours you listened to recorded music last year. _____
    Did chores or housework.   _____
    Looked after brothers or sisters at home.   _____
    Were employed outside the house.   _____
    Socialized with friends (outside of school).   _____

32. During a typical seven-day week, please estimate the number of hours your mother or the woman most responsible for you (READ ITEM BELOW) last year:

    Watched TV or videos.   _____
    Read for information or pleasure.   _____
    Listened to recorded music.   _____
    Did chores or housework.   _____
    Was employed outside the home.   _____

33. During a typical seven-day week, please estimate the number of hours your father or the man most responsible for you (READ ITEM BELOW) last year:

Watched TV or videos.   _____

Read for information or pleasure.   _____

Listened to recorded music.   _____

Did chores or housework.   _____

Was employed outside the home.   _____

34. (HAND R CARD 3) Please tell me how much you agree or disagree with the following statements about how your mother or the woman most responsible for you treated you last year. You can just tell me the number of your answer.

	Strongly Agree	Somewhat Agree	Somewhat Disagree	Strongly Disagree
I could count on her to help me out with problems.				
She thought you shouldn't argue with adults.				
She pushed me to do my best.				
She thought you should give in on arguments rather than make people angry.				
She pushed me to think independently.				
When I got a poor grade in school, she made life miserable.				
She helped me with schoolwork whenever I didn't understand.				
She thought she was always right and that I shouldn't question her.				
When she wanted me to do something, she always explained why.				
Whenever I argued with her, she said "You'll understand when you grow up."				
Whenever I got a poor grade in school, she encouraged me to try harder.				
She knew who my friends were.				
She acted cold and unfriendly if I did something she didn't like.				
She spent a lot of time just talking with me.				
If I got a poor grade in school, she made me feel guilty.				
She and I did fun things together.				
She wouldn't let me do things with her whenever I did something she didn't like.				

35. (HAND R CARD 3) Please tell me how much you agree or disagree with the following statements about how your father or the man most responsible for you treated you last year. You can just tell me the number of your answer.

	Strongly Agree	Somewhat Agree	Somewhat Disagree	Strongly Disagree
I could count on him to help me out with problems.				
He thought you shouldn't argue with adults.				

He pushed me to do my best.

He thought you should give in on arguments rather than make people angry.

He pushed me to think independently.

When I got a poor grade in school, he made life miserable.

He helped me with schoolwork whenever I didn't understand.

He thought he was always right and that I shouldn't question him.

When he wanted me to do something, he always explained why.

Whenever I argued with him, he said "You'll understand when you grow up."

Whenever I got a poor grade in school, he encouraged me to try harder.

He knew who my friends were.

He acted cold and unfriendly if I did something he didn't like.

He spent a lot of time just talking with me.

If I got a poor grade in school, he made me feel guilty.

He and I did fun things together.

He wouldn't let me do things with him whenever I did something he didn't like.

(TAKE BACK CARD 3)

High School Environment: School

36. What was the name and address of the last high school you attended? (Get as specific an address as possible, but at least name, city, and state.)

37. The next question is about the ethnic and racial composition of the student body of your last high school.

    Let's start with your estimate of the percentage of
        African Americans: _____
    Estimated percentage of Latinos or Hispanics: _____
    Estimated percentage of Asians: _____
    Estimated percentage of whites: _____
    What percentage of other racial or ethnic
        backgrounds I have not already mentioned? _____

38. To give us an idea of what your high school was like, please tell me, did it, during your senior year, have

    A swimming pool?   Yes / No
    Tennis courts?   Yes / No
    A track?   Yes / No

An indoor gym?	Yes / No
A weight room	Yes / No
A library?	Yes / No
A TV or radio station?	Yes / No
A foreign language lab?	Yes / No
Computers for student use?	Yes / No
A theater for dramatic productions	Yes / No
Nonteaching guidance counselors?	Yes / No
A school psychologist?	Yes / No
An orchestra or band rehearsal room?	Yes / No
Organized visits from college recruiters?	Yes / No
Uniformed security officers?	Yes / No
Metal detectors at school entrances?	Yes / No

39. (HAND R CARD I) As a high school student, how often do you recall witnessing students fighting in your school, that is, on school property during school hours? Just tell me the number of your answer.

Never | Rarely | Sometimes | Often | Very Often

Students smoking?
Students being late for class?
Students cutting class?
Students cutting school?
Students verbally abusing teachers?
Physical violence directed at teachers by students in your school during school hours?
Vandalism of school or personal property?
Graffiti on school property?
Theft of school or personal property?
Gang activity?
Students consuming alcohol?
Students taking illegal drugs?
Students carrying knives as weapons?
Students carrying guns?
Robbery of students by other students?

40. By the beginning of the senior year in high school, what percentage of male students in your school do you think had engaged in sexual intercourse at least once? _____

41. By the beginning of the senior year in high school, what percentage of female students in your school do you think had engaged in sexual intercourse at least once? _____

42. (HAND R CARD 4) In the past four years/ In high school, how much course work did you take in each of the following subjects:

None | ½ Year | 1 Year | 1½ Years | 2+ Years

Mathematics
Algebra
Geometry
Trigonometry
Calculus
General mathematics

Natural Sciences
Biology
Chemistry
Physics
Computer science
Earth science or geology
Other or general sciences

Social Studies
U.S. history
World history
Economics
Business
Government, politics, or civics
Sociology
Psychology

Arts and Humanities
English language or literature
Foreign language or literature
Religious studies or philosphy
Music
Drama
Art

Life Skills
Typing
Computing
Wood or metal shop
Auto shop
Home economics
Health
Sex education

43. In which subjects, if any, did you take an Advanced Placement class? If you took more than one, please name one at a time.

First Mention Advanced Placement Class

44.   Did you pass the Advanced Placement test for this course?

( ) Yes
( ) No
( ) Didn't take AP test

45.   For each of the following subjects, did you get mostly A's, mostly B's, mostly C's, mostly D's, or mostly grades below D in:

	Mostly A's	Mostly B's	Mostly C's	Mostly D's	Mostly Below D	Not Applicable
English						
History						
Mathematics						
Natural sciences						
Social studies						
Foreign languages						

46.   Measuring the degree of difficulty on a scale of 0 to 10, where 0 is not difficult at all and 10 is extremely difficult, how hard were each of the following subjects for you? Feel free to use any number between 0 and 10.

0 Not Difficult at All . . . . 10 Extremely Difficult

English
History
Mathematics
Natural sciences
Social studies
Foreign languages

High School Environment: Peers

47.   (HAND R CARD) In your high school, do you think your friends and acquaintances viewed the following behaviors as very uncool, neither cool nor uncool, somewhat cool, or very cool, where "cool" refers to behavior that is respected or admired by students?

	Very Uncool	Somewhat Uncool	Neither Cool nor Uncool	Somewhat Cool	Very Cool
Studying hard outside of class?					
Asking challenging questions in class?					
Volunteering information in class?					
Answering teachers' questions in class?					
Solving problems using new and original ideas?					
Helping other students with their homework?					
Getting good grades in difficult subjects?					
Planning to go to college?					

48. (HAND R CARD 6) Among the friends you hung out with last year, was it not at all important, a little important, somewhat important, or very important to attend classes regularly?

	Not at All Important	A Little Important	Somewhat Important	Very Important
Study hard?				
Play sports?				
Get good grades?				
Be popular or well-liked?				
Finish high school?				
Go to college?				
Have a steady boyfriend or girlfriend?				
Be willing to party and get wild?				
Participate in religious activities?				
Do community or volunteer work?				
Hold a steady job?				

49. (HAND R CARD 3) To what extent do you agree or disagree with the following statements about your experiences last year:

	Strongly Agree	Somewhat Agree	Somewhat Disagree	Strongly Disagree	Neither
You acted and thought like most people your age.					
You hung out where most people your age went.					
You felt comfortable around other people your age.					
You valued the same things as other students.					

50. To what extent would you have agreed or disagreed with the following statement:

	Strongly Agree	Somewhat Agree	Somewhat Disagree	Strongly Disagree
Doing well in school helps you later in life.				
You feel your future is limited.				
What you are taught in school is pretty useless once you graduate.				
There are better things to do than spend your time on school work.				
Trying hard in school is a waste of time.				

51. By the time you turned 18, how many of your closest friends had/ have dropped out without graduating? Was it:

None | Some | Most | All

How many used illegal drugs at least once?				
Got drunk on alcohol at least once?				
Had sexual intercourse at least once?				

52. By the time you turned 18 had/have you engaged in sexual intercourse at least once?

( ) Yes
( ) No

53. Now I would like you to think of your ten closest friends last year. How many were:

African American?	_____
Hispanic or Latino?	_____
Asian?	_____
White?	_____
Some other race or ethnicity?	_____

54. (HAND R CARD 7) Please think of your very best friend last year. Are the following statements not at all true, somewhat true, or very true about this person?

	Not at All True	Somewhat True	Very True
Got good grades			
Was interested in school			
Studied hard			
Attended classes regularly			
Planned to go to college			
Was popular with others			

Played sports
Read a lot
Watched TV a lot
Had sexual intercourse
Took illegal drugs
Got drunk on alcohol

55. Were the following characteristics not at all true, somewhat true, or very true of you last year?

	Not at All True	Somewhat True	Very True

Socially popular
Good athlete
Good student
Class leader
Troublemaker
Class clown
Politically active

56. (HAND R CARD 8) Thinking of the high school you attended in your senior year, please rate the quality of the following characteristics as poor, fair, good, or excellent. Let me know if the school didn't have the item when I read it. How would you rate the school's buildings?

	Poor	Fair	Good	Excellent	Didn't Have

Classrooms?
Audio-visual equipment?
Library?
Computers for students' use?
Teacher interest?
Teacher preparedness?
Strictness of discipline?
Fairness of discipline?
School spirit?
Overall quality of school?
School's reputation in community?

57. (HAND R CARD 1) How often did you find yourself not telling your friends when you got good grades last year?

	Never	Rarely	Sometimes	Often	Very Often

Acting less intelligent than you really were?
Worrying about what others thought of you?

Doing things so that others would like you?

Worrying about being called a "nerd" or "brainiac"?

58. To what extent did your high school teachers encourage independent and critical thinking?

   ( ) Never
   ( ) Rarely
   ( ) Sometimes
   ( ) Often
   ( ) Very Often
   ( ) Always

59. On a scale of 0 to 10, how self-conscious were you about how
African American students perceived you, with 0 meaning you were
not self-conscious at all and 10 meaning that you were extremely
sensitive to what they thought? Feel free to use any number between
0 and 10.

   0 Not conscious at all . . . . 10 Extremely sensitive

60. How self-conscious were you about the way that Hispanic or Latino
students perceived you, with 0 meaning that you were not self-conscious at all and 10 meaning that you were extremely sensitive to
what they thought?

   0 Not conscious at all . . . . 10 Extremely sensitive

61. How self-conscious were you about the way that Asian students perceived you?

   0 Not conscious at all . . . . 10 Extremely sensitive

62. How about the way that white students perceived you?

   0 Not conscious at all . . . . 10 Extremely sensitive

63. Finally, how self-conscious were you about the way that your teachers perceived you?

   0 Not conscious at all . . . . 10 Extremely sensitive

High School Environment: Neighborhood and Work

64. What was the complete address of the place where you lived in May of this year? Let's start with the number and street name.

    _____

65. Now think back to the ethnic and racial composition of the three-block radius of where you lived last year.

    Let's start with your estimate of the percentage of
    African Americans.   _____
    What percentage were Hispanic or Latino?   _____
    What percentage were Asian?   _____
    What percentage were white?   _____
    What percentage were of other racial or ethnic
    backgrounds I have not already mentioned?   _____

66. (HAND R CARD 1) In your neighborhood, how often do you recall seeing homeless people on the street last year?

                            Never | Rarely | Sometimes | Often | Very Often

    Prostitutes on the street?
    Drug paraphernalia on the street?
    People selling illegal drugs in public?
    People using illegal drugs in public?
    People drinking or drunk in public?
    Graffiti on neighborhood businesses?
    Graffiti on neighborhood homes?
    Gang members hanging out on the street?
    Physical violence in public?
    The sound of gunshots?
    Someone stabbed by a knife?
    Someone shot by a gun?
    Someone getting mugged?

67. Did you ever get paid for doing work outside your own home last year? Include holidays and breaks, but not summertime.

                                                            Yes / No

    If yes, what was it that you usually did or were?

( ) Baby-sitting
( ) Construction worker
( ) Factory worker
( ) Fast-food worker
( ) Hospital or health worker
( ) Housecleaning
( ) Lawn or garden worker
( ) Manual laborer
( ) Mechanic
( ) Odd jobs
( ) Office or clerical worker
( ) Store clerk or salesperson
( ) Waiter or waitress
( ) Coach/other sports-related activity
( ) Tutor/teaching asst./teacher
( ) Worked in a bank
( ) Other food service related: busboy, dishwasher, hostess
( ) Camp or after-school counselor, child-care aide
( ) Music/dance-related: playing, music/dancing, teaching
( ) Music/dance
( ) Research/lab/survey worker
( ) Food manufacturing-baker, etc.
( ) Computer-related technician, consultant, etc.
( ) Other: specify   _____

68. During a typical week last fall, how many hours did you work for
     pay outside of your home?   _____

69. During the summer after your graduation, about how many weeks
     did you spend in each of the following activities:

     Working at a summer job?   _____
     Precollege program?   _____
     Summer school?   _____
     Day camp?   _____
     Sleep-away camp?   _____
     Vacation or travel?   _____
     Volunteer work in community?   _____
     Other (specify)?   _____

70. On the last job for which you were paid before coming to college,
     how much did you earn per hour?   _____

Thinking about College

71. On a scale of 0 to 10, how important were the following considerations in choosing where to attend college, where 0 indicates it was extremely unimportant and 10 indicates it was extremely important. Please feel free to use any number between 0 and 10.

0 Extremely unimportant . . . . 10 Extremely important

Cost?
Availability of financial aid?
Availability of athletic scholarship?
Sports opportunities?
Availability of academic support programs?
Recruitment efforts made by school?
Availability of specific courses?
Overall academic reputation?
Overall athletic reputation?
Overall social prestige?
School social life?
Availability of specialized or "theme" dorms?
Distance to home?
Religious environment?
Security and safety on campus?
Job placement record?
Graduate school placement record?
Professional school placement record?
Admissions standards?
Enough members of my own group to feel comfortable?
Enough members of my group in surrounding community?
Size of school and number of students?
Parents' connection to school?
Parents' opinion of school?
Friendship with students or alumni?

72. Please estimate the probability that you will complete each of the following educational milestones. That is, on a scale from 0 to 10, where 0 means it is extremely unlikely and 10 means it is extremely likely, what is the likelihood that you will finish one year of college? Feel free to use any number between 0 and 10.

Finish two years of college?   _____

Graduate from college?   _____

Go on for more education after college?   _____

Complete a graduate or professional degree?   _____

73. Have you already chosen a major? If yes, what?   _____

Group Stereotypes

Now I have some questions about different racial and ethnic groups in our society. I want you to rate each group on a seven-point scale on which the characteristics of people in a group can be rated.

74. In the first statement, a score of 1 means that you think almost all of the people in that group are "rich." A score of 7 means that you think that almost everyone in the group is "poor." A score of 4 means you think that the group is not toward one end or the other, and, of course, you may choose any number in between that comes closest to where you think people in the group stand.

Where would you rate whites on this scale, where 1 means tends to be rich and 7 means they tend to be poor?

1 Poor . . . . .7 Rich

Asians?

African Americans?

Hispanics or Latinos?

75. Next, for each group I want to know whether you think they tend to be lazy or hard-working. A score of 1 means that you think almost all of the people in that group are "lazy." A score of 7 means that you think almost everyone in the group is "hard-working." A score of 4 means you think that the group is not toward one end or the other, and, of course, you may choose any number in-between that comes closest to where you think people in the group stand.

Where would you rate whites on this scale, where 1 means tends to be lazy and 7 means they tend to be hard-working?:

1 Lazy . . . . .7 Hard-working

Asians?

African Americans?

Hispanics or Latinos?

76. Next, for each group I want to know whether you think they tend to be peaceful or tend to be prone to violence. A score of 1 means that you think almost all of the people in that group are "peaceful." A score of 7 means that you think almost everyone in the group is "prone to violence." A score of 4 means that the group is not toward one end or the other, and, of course, you may choose any number in-between that comes closest to where you think people in the group stand.

    Where would you rate whites on this scale, where 1 means to be peaceful and 7 means to be prone to violence?

    1 Peaceful . . . . .7 Prone to violence

    Asians?
    African Americans?
    Hispanics or Latinos?

77. Next, for each group I want to know whether you think they tend to be unintelligent or tend to be intelligent. A score of 1 means that you think almost all of the people in that group are "unintelligent." A score of 7 means that you think almost everyone in the group is "intelligent." A score of 4 means you think that the group is not toward one end or the other, and, of course, you may choose any number in-between that comes closest to where you think people in the group stand.

    Where would you rate whites on this scale, where 1 means tends to be unintelligent and 7 means tends to be intelligent?

    1 Unintelligent . . . . .7 Intelligent

    Asians?
    African Americans?
    Hispanics or Latinos?

78. Next, for each group I want to know whether you think they tend to prefer to be self-supporting or tend to prefer to live off welfare. A score of 1 means that you think almost all of the people in that group "prefer to be self-supporting." A score of 7 means that you think almost everyone in the group "prefers to live off welfare." A score of 4 means you think that the group is not toward one end or the other, and, of course, you may choose any number in-between that comes closest to where you think people in the group stand.

Where would you rate whites on this scale, where 1 means tends to prefer to be self-supporting and 7 means tends to prefer to live off welfare?

1 Self-supporting . . . . 7 Live off welfare

Asians?

African Americans?

Hispanics or Latinos?

79. Next, for each group I want to know if you think they tend to be hard to get along with or tend to be easy to get along with. A score of 1 means that you think almost all of the people in that group are "hard to get along with." A score of 7 means that you think that everyone in the group is "easy to get along with." A score of 4 means you think that the group is not toward one end or the other, and, of course, you may choose any number in-between that comes closest to where you think people in the group stand.

Where would you rate whites on this scale, where 1 means to be hard to get along with and 7 means tends to be easy to get along with?

1 Hard to get along with . . . . 7 Easy to get along with

Asians?

African Americans?

Hispanics or Latinos?

80. Next, for each group I want to know whether you think they tend to be honest or dishonest. A score of 1 means that you think almost everyone in the group is "dishonest." A score of 7 means that you think almost everyone in the group is "honest." A score of 4 means you think that the group is not toward one end or the other, and, of course, you may choose any number in-between that comes closest to where you think people in the group stand.

Where would you rate whites on this on this scale, where 1 means to be dishonest and 7 means tends to be honest?

1 Dishonest . . . . 7 Honest

Asians?

African Americans?

Hispanics or Latinos?

81. Now, for each group I want to know whether you think they tend to give up easily or if you think they tend to stick with a task until the end. A score of 1 means that you think almost all of the people in that group tend to "give up easily." A score of 7 means that you think that all of the people in that group tend to "stick with a task until the end." A score of 4 means you think that the group is not toward one end or the other, and, of course, you may choose any number in-between that comes closest to where you think people in the group stand.

Where would you rate whites on this scale, where 1 means tends to give up easily and 7 means tends to stick with a task until the end?

1 Give up easily . . . . .7 Stick with it

Asians?
African Americans?
Hispanics or Latinos?

82. Finally, for each group I want to know whether you think they tend to treat members of other groups equally or tend to discriminate against members of other groups. A score of 1 means that you think almost all of the people in that group "treat members of other groups equally." A score of 7 means that you think that everyone in that group "discriminates against members of other groups." A score of 4 means you think that the group is not toward one end or the other, and, of course, you may choose any number in-between that comes closest to where you think people in the group stand.

Where would you rate whites on this scale, where 1 means tends to treat members of other groups equally and 7 means tends to discriminate against members of other groups?

1 Treat equally . . . . .7 Discriminate against others

Asians?
African Americans?
Hispanics or Latinos?

Perceptions of Social Distance

The next questions ask about various facets of interaction with different groups to get a sense of how close to or distant you feel from them. I would like you to imagine a neighborhood that had the ethnic and racial mix you personally would feel most comfortable in.

(HAND R THE NEIGHBORHOOD CARD) Here is a blank card designed to represent a neighborhood. Using the letters "A" for Asian, "B" for African American or Black, "H" for Hispanic or Latino, and "W" for white, please put a letter in each of these houses to represent the neighborhood you'd most like to live in. Please give me the card after you've recorded a letter in every house.

INTERVIEWER: AFTER R GIVES YOU THE CARD, BE SURE THAT THERE IS A LETTER IN EVERY HOUSE. IF NOT, ASK R TO FILL IN THE BLANK HOUSE(S).

(READ TO R:) It will take a minute or so for me to enter the codes in the computer.

83. FROM THE NEIGHBORHOOD CARD, ENTER THE LETTER OF EACH HOUSE NEXT TO THE NUMBER OF THE HOUSE.

House #1

⟨A⟩ Asian
⟨B⟩ Black
⟨H⟩ Hispanic
⟨W⟩ White
⟨S⟩ Something else
⟨R⟩ Refused/don't know

House #2–House #14

84. What is the lowest percentage of (R's Race) you would be willing to have in your neighborhood?

Now consider schools. If you had children, what racial or ethnic mix would you personally most like your child's classroom to have?

(HAND R SCHOOL CARD) Here is a blank card similar to the neighborhood card you just completed. Using the letters A for Asian, B for African American or Black, H for Hispanic, and W for white, please put a letter in each of these desks to represent the classroom you'd most like your children to be in. Please give me the card after you've recorded a letter on every desk.

85. INTERVIEWER: AFTER R GIVES YOU THE CARD, BE SURE THAT THERE IS A LETTER ON EVERY DESK. IF NOT, ASK R TO FILL IN THE BLANK DESK(S).

(READ TO R): It will take a minute or so for me to enter the codes in the computer.
FROM THE SCHOOL CARD, ENTER THE LETTER OF EACH DESK NEXT TO THE NUMBER OF THE DESK.

Desk #1

⟨A⟩ Asian
⟨B⟩ Black
⟨H⟩ Hispanic
⟨W⟩ White
⟨S⟩ Something else
⟨R⟩ Refused/don't know

Desk #2–Desk #14

86. What is the lowest percentage of (R's Race) you would be willing to accept in your children's classroom?

87. Now I'm going to read a list of different types of people. For each category, tell me how close you feel to the people in terms of your ideas and feelings about things. A score of 0 means very distant and a score of 10 means very close.

0 Very distant . . . . 10 Very close

Whites
African Americans
Hispanics or Latinos
Asians

Religious, church-going whites
Religious, church-going African Americans
Religious, church-going Hispanics or Latinos
Religious, church-going Asians

Young white men
Young African American men
Young Hispanic or Latino men
Young Asian men

Young white women
Young African American women
Young Hispanic or Latino women
Young Asian women

Poor whites
Poor African Americans
Poor Hispanics or Latinos
Poor Asians

Middle-class whites
Middle-class African Americans
Middle-class Hispanics or Latinos
Middle-class Asians

Rich whites
Rich African Americans
Rich Hispanics or Latinos
Rich Asians

White elected officials
African Americans elected officials
Hispanic or Latino elected officials
Asian elected officials

White business owners
African American business owners
Hispanic or Latino business owners
Asian business owners

White newscasters
African American newscasters
Hispanic or Latino newscasters
Asian newscasters

White doctors, lawyers, and other professionals
African American doctors, lawyers, and other professionals
Hispanic or Latino doctors, lawyers, and other professionals
Asian doctors, lawyers, and other professionals

Whites with Caucasian first names
African Americans with African first names
Hispanics or Latinos with Spanish first names
Asians with Asian first names

White rappers and hip-hop artists
African American rappers and hip-hop artists
Hispanic or Latino rappers and hip-hop artists
Asian rappers and hip-hop artists

Whites who benefit from affirmative action
African Americans who benefit from affirmative action
Hispanics or Latinos who benefit from affirmative action
Asians who benefit from affirmative action

Perceptions of Prejudice

I am now going to read some statements about various situations that affect minorities in the United States. Please listen to statements carefully and, on a scale of 0 to 10, tell me how much you disagree or agree. If you completely disagree, say 0; if you completely agree, say 10; and if you are neutral, say 5. Feel free to use any number between 0 and 10.

0 Strongly disagree . . . . .10 Strongly agree

88. Any African American who is educated and does what is considered "proper" will be accepted and eventually get ahead.

89. Many African American have only themselves to blame for not doing better in life. If they tried harder, they would do better.

90. When two qualified people, one African American and one white, are considered for the same job, the African American won't get the job no matter how hard he or she tries.

91. The best way to overcome discrimination is for each individual African American person to be even better trained and more qualified than the most qualified white person.

92. The future looks very promising for educated African Americans.

93. Any Hispanic or Latino who is educated and does what is considered "proper" will be accepted and eventually get ahead.

94. Many Hispanic or Latino have only themselves to blame for not doing better in life. If they tried harder, they would do better.

95. When two qualified people, one Hispanic or Latino and one white, are considered for the same job, the Hispanic or Latino won't get the job no matter how hard he or she tries.

96. The best way to overcome discrimination is for each individual Hispanic or Latino person to be even better trained and more qualified than the most qualified white person.

97. The future looks very promising for educated Hispanics or Latinos.

98. Any Asian who is educated and does what is considered "proper" will be accepted and eventually get ahead.

99. Many Asian have only themselves to blame for not doing better in life. If they tried harder, they would do better.

100. When two qualified people, one Asian and one white, are considered for the same job, the Asian won't get the job no matter how hard he or she tries.

101. The best way to overcome discrimination is for each individual Asian person to be even better trained and more qualified than the most qualified white person.

102. The future looks very promising for educated Asians.

103. Thinking about the way things are today compared to how they were before the civil rights movement of the 1960s, would you say there is more, less, or about the same discrimination against:

    African Americans? _____
    Hispanics or Latinos? _____
    Asians? _____

104. Twenty years from now, do you think there will be more, less, or the same amount of discrimination against:

    African Americans? _____
    Hispanics or Latinos? _____
    Asians? _____

Common Fate Identity

105. What do you think should be more important to African Americans in the United States, being African American, being American, or should both identities be equally important?

106. What do you think should be more important to Hispanics or Latinos such as Mexicans—do you think it should be more important for them to be Hispanic or Latino, American, or should both identities be equally important?

107. And for Asian groups such as Chinese—do you think it should be more important for them to be Asian, American, or should both identities be equally important?

108. (HAND R CARD 9) To what extent do you think what happens to African Americans will affect what happens to you in your life? Would you say it will not affect you at all, affect you a little, affect you somewhat, or it affect you a lot?

	Will Not Affect Me at All	Will Affect Me a Little	Will Affect Me Somewhat	Will Affect Me a Lot
Hispanics or Latinos?				
Asians?				

Racial/Ethnic Identity

109. How much do you agree or disagree with each of the following statements:

	Strongly Agree	Somewhat Agree	Somewhat Disagree	Strongly Disagree	Neither
African American children should study an African language.					
African Americans should always vote for African American candidates.					
African American women should not date white men.					
African American men should not date white women.					
African Americans should marry other African Americans.					
African American children should have mostly African American friends.					

African American consumers should shop in African American–owned stores.

African American parents should give their children African names.

African American students should attend predominantly African American schools.

African American families should live in predominantly African American neighborhoods.

Predominantly African American schools should have African American teachers and administrators.

110. Again, how much do you agree or disagree with each of the following statements:

	Strongly Agree	Somewhat Agree	Somewhat Disagree	Strongly Disagree	Neither

Hispanics or Latinos should always vote for Hispanic or Latino candidates.

Hispanic or Latino women should not date white men.

Hispanic or Latino men should not date white women.

Hispanic or Latino should marry other Hispanics or Latinos.

Hispanic or Latino children should have mostly Hispanic or Latino friends.

Hispanic or Latino consumers should shop in Hispanic or Latino-owned stores.

Hispanic or Latino parents should give their children Spanish names.

Hispanic or Latino students should attend predominantly Hispanic or Latino schools.

Hispanic or Latino families should live in predominantly Hispanic or Latino neighborhoods.

Predominantly Hispanic or Latino schools should have Hispanic or Latino teachers and administrators.

111. Finally, consider Asians. How much do you agree or disagree with each of the following statements:

	Strongly Agree	Somewhat Agree	Somewhat Disagree	Strongly Disagree	Neither

Asian children should study Asian languages.

Hispanics or Latinos should always vote for Asian candidates.

Asian women should not date white men.

Asian men should not date white women.

Asian should marry other Asians.

Asian children should have mostly Asian friends.

Asian consumers should shop in Asian-owned stores.

Asian parents should give their children Asian names.

Asian students should attend predominantly Asian schools.

Asian families should live in predominantly Asian neighborhoods.

Predominantly Asian schools should have Asian teachers and administrators.

Self-esteem

112. The next items assess how you feel about yourself. Please tell me how much you agree or disagree with each of the following statements:

	Strongly Agree	Agree	Neither Agree or Disagree	Disagree
I feel that I am a person of worth, equal to others.				
I feel that I have a number of good qualities.				
All in all, I am inclined to feel that I am a failure.				
I am able to do things as well as most people.				
I feel that I do not have much to be proud of.				
I take a positive attitude toward myself.				
On the whole, I am satisfied with myself.				
I wish I could have more respect for myself.				
I feel useless at times.				
At times, I think I'm no good at all.				

Self-efficacy

113. Thinking about your life at the moment, how much do you agree or disagree with the following statements:

	Strongly Agree	Agree	Neither Agree or Disagree	Disagree	Strongly Disagree
I don't have control over the direction my life is taking.					
In life, good luck is more important than hard work for success.					
Every time I try to get ahead something or somebody stops me.					
When I make plans, I am almost certain I can make them work.					
I feel left out of things going on around me.					
If I work hard, I can do well.					

Demographic and Socioeconomic Background

114. What is the highest level of schooling achieved by your mother or the woman most responsible for raising you?

( ) Grade school
( ) Some high school

( ) High school graduate
( ) Some college
( ) College graduate
( ) Some postgraduate
( ) Graduate or professional degree

115. What is the highest level of schooling achieved by your father or the man most responsible for raising you?

( ) Grade school
( ) Some high school
( ) High school graduate
( ) Some college
( ) College graduate
( ) Some postgraduate
( ) Graduate or professional degree

116. Mother's occupation   _____

117. Has your mother or the woman most responsible for raising you ever worked?   Yes / No

118. Is your mother or the woman most responsible for raising you currently working?   Yes / No

(IF YES, CONTINUE; IF NO, SKIP TO 122.)

119. How many hours per week?

120. Is her/Was her most recent occupation the same one she had last year?   Yes / No

(IF YES, TAKE OCCUPATION FROM 116 AND SKIP TO 122. IF NO, CONTINUE.)

121. What is/was her occupation?

122. Father's occupation

123. Has your father or the man most responsible for raising you ever worked?   Yes / No

124. Is your father or the man most responsible for raising you currently working?   Yes / No

(IF YES, CONTINUE; IF NO, SKIP TO 128.)

125. How many hours per week?

126. Is his/Was his most recent occupation the same one he had last year?
                                                                Yes / No

(IF YES, TAKE OCCUPATION FROM 122 AND SKIP TO 128. IF NO, CONTINUE.)

127. What is/was his occupation?

128. How many of your siblings, including step-brothers, step-sisters, half-brothers and half-sisters are aged 18 or older?

129. How many have graduated from high school?

130. How many of your siblings, including step-brothers, step-sisters, half-brothers, and half-sisters, are aged 25 or older?

131. How many have graduated from college?

132. (HAND R CARD 11) Which term best describes your racial and ethnic origins? Just give me the number on the card.

⟨1⟩ White   ⟨2⟩ Non-Hispanic Black

Asian
⟨3⟩ Chinese   ⟨7⟩ Filipino
⟨4⟩ Japanese   ⟨8⟩ Indian
⟨5⟩ Vietnamese   ⟨9⟩ Asian, other
⟨6⟩ Korean

Hispanic Black
⟨10⟩ Mexican   ⟨13⟩ Dominican
⟨11⟩ Puerto Rican   ⟨14⟩ Central American
⟨12⟩ Cuban   ⟨15⟩ South American

Hispanic White

⟨16⟩ Mexican   ⟨19⟩ Dominican
⟨17⟩ Puerto Rican   ⟨20⟩ Central American
⟨18⟩ Cuban   ⟨21⟩ South American

⟨t⟩ Mixed race
⟨s⟩ Other
⟨98⟩ Don't know
⟨97⟩ Refused

133. Where was your biological or adoptive mother born?

134. Where was your biological or adoptive father born?

135. Where were you born?

   (IF OUTSIDE OF U.S., CONTINUE; IF U.S., SKIP TO 141.)

136. In what year did you first enter the United States?

137. How old were you when you first entered the United States?

138. Including your current stay, in total, how many visits have you made to the United States?

139. What is the total time you have spent in the United States (including all visits)?

140. Are you a citizen or a legal resident alien?

141. Is your religious background:

   ⟨1⟩ Catholic   ⟨8⟩ Protestant & other religion combined
   ⟨2⟩ Protestant   ⟨9⟩ Jainism
   ⟨3⟩ Jewish   ⟨10⟩ Unitarian
   ⟨4⟩ Muslim   ⟨11⟩ Jehovah's Witness
   ⟨5⟩ Hindu   ⟨12⟩ Jewish & Catholic
   ⟨6⟩ Buddhist   ⟨13⟩ Jewish & Protestant
   ⟨7⟩ Greek/Eastern Orthodox   ⟨14⟩ Seventh Day Adventist

⟨77⟩ Something else?
  [Do not read]
⟨94⟩ Other combination
⟨95⟩ No religious background
⟨96⟩ Agnostic
⟨98⟩ Don't know
⟨97⟩ Refused

142. On a scale of 0 to 10, how religious would you say you are? Zero indicates you are extremely unreligious and 10 indicates you are extremely religious. Feel free to use any number between 0 and 10.

143. On a scale of 0 to 10, how observant would you say you are of your religion's customs, ceremonies, and traditions? Zero is extremely unobservant and 10 is extremely observant.

144. Do you attend religious services:

  ( ) Never
  ( ) Rarely
  ( ) Often, but not every week
  ( ) Once a week
  ( ) More than once a week

145. Did your parent or parents own the home or apartment where you spent your senior year of high school?   Yes / No

  IF YES, CONTINUE; IF NO, SKIP TO 147.

146. How much do you think that home or apartment is worth? That is, how much do you think it would sell for if it were put up for sale?

147. (HAND R CARD 12) Please look at this card and tell me your estimate of the annual income of the household in which you spent your senior year of high school. In thinking about household income, you should include the wages and salaries of all household members, plus any self-employment income they may have had, along with interest, dividends, alimony payments, social security, pensions, and public assistance. You can just tell me the letter.

a. under $3,000
b. $3,000–$3,999
c. $4,000–$4,999
d. $5,000–$5,999
e. $6,000–$6,999
f. $7,000–$7,999
g. $8,000–$8,999
h. $9,000–$14,999
i. $15,000–$19,999
j. $20,000–$24,999
k. $25,000–$34,999
l. $35,000–$49,999
m. $50,000–$74,999
n. $75,000 or more

148. Since the time when you were 6 years old, has your family ever received public assistance?   Yes / No

149. Did you apply for financial aid when you sought admission to college?   Yes / No

Tracking Information

150. What is your current telephone number?

151. What is the name, address, and phone number of your mother?

152. What is the name, address, and phone number of your father?

153. Please give me the name, relationship, and phone number of at least two other people who do not live with you who would always know how to contact you. We will contact them only if we are unable to reach you for the follow-up interview this spring. We will not tell them anything about you or your answers to this interview.

	Name	Relationship	Phone Number
Person 1			
Person 2			

154. It would be very helpful for this study if we could link the information on your financial aid application to the information we collect from this survey. Would you be willing to give permission to use information from your application if we promised to take your name off of all the resulting data files and kept everything strictly confidential?   Yes / No

155. Would you be willing to allow access to your college application, so that that we could be connected with information from this survey? Again, this would significantly advance the goals of the study and we promise to strip all identifying information from the application form and keep all the data strictly confidential.   Yes / No

APPENDIX B

CONSTRUCTION OF SOCIAL SCALES

TABLE B1

Construction of index of parental involvement in human capital formation

Age and Item	Response Range	Scale Scores	
		Minimum	Maximum
Age 6			
Parent(s) Read to R	Never to always	0	4
Parent(s) Helped R with Homework	Never to always	0	4
Parent(s) Took R to Library	Never to always	0	4
Parent(s) Put R in Summer School	No or yes	0	1
Parent(s) Put R in Summer Educational Camp	No or yes	0	1
Parent(s) Put R in Summer Enrichment Program	No or yes	0	1
Age 13			
Parent(s) Helped R with Homework	Never to always	0	4
Parent(s) Took R to Library	Never to always	0	4
Parent(s) Put R in Summer Educational Camp	No or yes	0	1
Parent(s) Participated in PTA	Never to always	0	4

Age 18

		Low	High
Parent(s) Checked R's Homework	Never to always	0	4
Parent(s) Helped with R's Homework	Never to always	0	4
Parent(s) Met with R's Teachers	Never to always	0	4
Parent(s) Read Daily Newspaper	Never to always	0	4
Parent(s) Read Sunday Newspaper	Never to very often	0	4
Parent(s) Read Weekly News Magazine	Never to very often	0	4
Mother Pushed R to Do Best	Strongly disagree to strongly agree	0	4
Mother Helped with Schoolwork	Strongly disagree to strongly agree	0	4
Mother Encouraged R When Got Poor Grades	Strongly disagree to strongly agree	0	4
Father Pushed R to Do Best	Strongly disagree to strongly agree	0	4
Father Helped with Schoolwork	Strongly disagree to strongly agree	0	4
Father Encouraged R When Got Poor Grades	Strongly disagree to strongly agree	0	4
Index Range		0	104
Cronbach's Alpha			.830

TABLE B2

Construction of index of parental involvement in formation of cultural capital and social capital

		Scale Scores		
Age and Item	Response Range	Minimum	Maximum	
Cultural Capital				
Age 6				
Parent(s) Took R to Museum	Never to always	0	4	
Parent(s) Took R to Science Center	Never to always	0	4	
Parent(s) Took R to Zoo or Aquarium	Never to always	0	4	
Parent(s) Took R Traveling Abroad	Never to always	0	4	
Age 13				
Parent(s) Took R to Museum	Never to always	0	4	
Parent(s) Took R to Science Center	Never to always	0	4	
Parent(s) Took R to Plays or Concerts	Never to always	0	4	
Parent(s) Took R Traveling Abroad	Never to always	0	4	
Age 13				
Parent(s) Took R to Museum	Never to always	0	4	
Parent(s) Took R to Plays or Concerts	Never to always	0	4	
Parent(s) Took R Traveling Abroad	Never to always	0	4	
Total			44	
Cronbach's Alpha				.886
Social Capital				
Age 13				
Parent(s) Talked to R's Friends	Never to always	0	4	
Age 18				
Parent(s) Talked to R's Friends	Never to always	0	4	
Mother Knew Who R's Friends Were	Strongly disagree to strongly agree	0	4	
Father Knew Who R's Friends Were	Strongly disagree to strongly agree	0	4	
Total			18	
Cronbach's Alpha				.778

TABLE B3

Construction of index of parental cultivation of intellectual independence

Age and Item	Response Range	Scale Scores	
		Minimum	Maximum
Age 6			
Parent(s) Checked R's Homework	Never to always	0	4
Parent(s) Rewarded R for Good Grades	Never to always	0	4
Age 13			
Parent(s) Checked R's Homework	Never to always	0	4
Parent(s) Rewarded R for Good Grades	Never to always	0	4
Age 18			
Mother Thought You Should Give in on Arguments	Strongly agree to strongly disagree	0	4
Mother Pushed Me to Think Independently	Strongly disagree to strongly agree	0	4
Mother Explained Reasons for Decisions	Strongly disagree to strongly agree	0	4
Mother Thought You Shouldn't Argue with Adults	Strongly agree to strongly disagree	0	4
Mother Thought She Was Always Right	Strongly agree to strongly disagree	0	4
Mother Told R Would Understand When Grown Up	Strongly agree to strongly disagree	0	4
Father Thought You Should Give in on Arguments	Strongly agree to strongly disagree	0	4
Father Pushed Me to Think Independently	Strongly disagree to strongly agree	0	4
Father Explained Reasons for Decisions	Strongly disagree to strongly agree	0	4
Father Thought You Shouldn't Argue with Adults	Strongly agree to strongly disagree	0	4
Father Thought He Was Always Right	Strongly agree to strongly disagree	0	4
Father Told R Would Understand When Grown Up	Strongly agree to strongly disagree	0	4
Total		0	64
Cronbach's Alpha		.719	

TABLE B4

Construction of index of strictness of parental child-rearing practices

Age and Item	Response Range	Scale Scores	
		Minimum	Maximum
Strictness of Discipline			
Age 6			
Parent(s) Punished R for Bad Grades	Never to always	0	4
Parent(s) Punished R for Disobedience	Never to always	0	4
Age 13			
Parent(s) Punished R for Bad Grades	Never to always	0	4
Parent(s) Punished R for Disobedience	Never to always	0	4
Parent(s) Limited R's Time with Friends	Never to always	0	4
Age 18			
Parent(s) Punished R for Bad Grades	Never to always	0	4
Parent(s) Punished R for Disobedience	Never to always	0	4
Parent(s) Limited R's Time with Friends	Never to always	0	4
Mother Forbade R Things When Displeased	Strongly disagree to strongly agree	0	4

Item	Scale			Total	Cronbach's Alpha
Mother Made Life Miserable When Got Poor Grades	Strongly disagree to strongly agree	0	4		
Father Forbade R Things When Displeased	Strongly disagree to strongly agree	0	4		
Father Made Life Miserable When Got Poor Grades	Strongly disagree to strongly agree	0	4		
Total				56	
Cronbach's Alpha					.702
Use of Shame and Guilt					
Mother Acted Cold if I Displeased Her	Strongly disagree to strongly agree	0	4		
Mother Made Me Feel Guilty for Poor Grades	Strongly disagree to strongly agree	0	4		
Mother Did Fun Things with Me	Strongly agree to strongly disagre	0	4		
Mother Spent Lots of Time Just Talking to Me	Strongly agree to strongly disagree	0	4		
Father Acted Cold if I Displeased Him	Strongly disagree to strongly agree	0	4		
Father Made Me Feel Guilty for Poor Grades	Strongly disagree to strongly agree	0	4		
Father Did Fun Things with Me	Strongly agree to strongly disagree	0	4		
Father Spent Lots of Time Just Talking to Me	Strongly agree to strongly	0	4		
Total				32	
Cronbach's Alpha					.702

TABLE B5
Construction of index of exposure to neighborhood disorder

Age and Item	Wolfgang-Sellin Severity Index	Response Range	Scale Scores	
			Minimum	Maximum
Witnessed Aged 6				
Homeless People on Street	0.3	No or yes (0–1)	0	0.3
Prostitutes on Street	2.1	No or yes (0–1)	0	2.1
Drug Paraphernalia	1.3	No or yes (0–1)	0	1.3
Use of Illegal Drugs	6.5	No or yes (0–1)	0	6.5
Public Drunkenness on Street	0.8	No or yes (0–1)	0	0.8
Witnessed Aged 13				
Homeless People on Street	0.3	Never to very often (0–4)	0	1.2
Prostitutes on Street	2.1	Never to very often (0–4)	0	8.4
Drug Paraphernalia	1.3	Never to very often (0–4)	0	5.2
Use of Illegal Drugs	6.5	Never to very often (0–4)	0	26.0
Public Drunkenness on Street	0.8	Never to very often (0–4)	0	3.2
Witnessed Aged 13				
Homeless People on Street	0.3	Never to very often (0–4)	0	1.2
Prostitutes on Street	2.1	Never to very often (0–4)	0	8.4
Drug Paraphernalia	1.3	Never to very often (0–4)	0	5.2
Use of Illegal Drugs	6.5	Never to very often (0–4)	0	26.0
Public Drunkenness on Street	0.8	Never to very often (0–4)	0	3.2
Graffiti on Businesses	1.0	Never to very often (0–4)	0	4.0
Graffiti on Homes	1.0	Never to very often (0–4)	0	4.0
Total			0	107.0
Cronbach's Alpha			.780	

TABLE B6
Construction of index of exposure to neighborhood violence

Age and Item	Wolfgang-Sellin Severity Index	Response Range	Scale Scores	
			Minimum	Maximum
Witnessed Aged 6				
Gang Members on Street	1.1	No or yes (0–1)	0	1.1
Selling of Illegal Drugs	20.6	No or yes (0–1)	0	20.6
Physical Violence	6.9	No or yes (0–1)	0	6.9
Gunshots	2.1	No or yes (0–1)	0	2.1
Witnessed Aged 13				
Gang Members on Street	1.1	Never to very often (0–4)	0	4.4
Selling of Illegal Drugs	20.6	Never to very often (0–4)	0	82.4
Physical Violence	6.9	Never to very often (0–4)	0	27.6
Gunshots	2.1	Never to very often (0–4)	0	8.4
Witnessed Aged 13				
Gang Members on Street	1.1	Never to very often (0–4)	0	4.4
Selling of Illegal Drugs	20.6	Never to very often (0–4)	0	82.4
Physical Violence	6.9	Never to very often (0–4)	0	27.6
Gunshots	2.1	Never to very often (0–4)	0	8.4
Stabbings	18.0	Never to very often (0–4)	0	8.4
Shootings	24.8	Never to very often (0–4)	0	8.4
Muggings	4.9	Never to very often (0–4)	0	8.4
Total			0	467.1
Cronbach's Alpha			.779	

TABLE B7
Construction of index of exposure to school disorder

Age and Item	Wolfgang-Sellin Severity Index	Response Range	Scale Scores	
			Minimum	Maximum
Witnessed Aged 6				
Students Smoking	0.1	No or yes (0–1)	0	0.1
Students Cutting Classes	0.2	No or yes (0–1)	0	0.2
Students Cutting School	0.2	No or yes (0–1)	0	0.2
Verbal Abuse of Teacher	1.1	No or yes (0–1)	0	1.1
Vandalism of Property	3.8	No or yes (0–1)	0	3.8
Theft of Property	2.9	No or yes (0–1)	0	2.9
Students Using Alcohol	1.7	No or yes (0–1)	0	1.7
Students Using Illegal Drugs	1.4	No or yes (0–1)	0	1.4
Witnessed Aged 13				
Students Late for Class	0.1	Never to very often (0–4)	0	0.4
Students Cutting Class	0.1	Never to very often (0–4)	0	0.4
Students Cutting School	0.2	Never to very often (0–4)	0	0.8
Verbal Abuse of Teacher	1.1	Never to very often (0–4)	0	4.4
Vandalism of Property	3.8	Never to very often (0–4)	0	15.2
Theft of Property	2.9	Never to very often (0–4)	0	11.6
Students Using Alcohol	1.7	Never to very often (0–4)	0	6.8
Students Using Illegal Drugs	1.4	Never to very often (0–4)	0	5.6
Witnessed Aged 13				
Students Late for Class	0.1	Never to very often (0–4)	0	0.4
Students Cutting Class	0.1	Never to very often (0–4)	0	0.4
Students Cutting School	0.2	Never to very often (0–4)	0	0.8
Verbal Abuse of Teacher	1.1	Never to very often (0–4)	0	4.4
Vandalism of Property	3.8	Never to very often (0–4)	0	15.2
Theft of Property	2.9	Never to very often (0–4)	0	11.6
Students Using Alcohol	1.7	Never to very often (0–4)	0	6.8
Students Using Illegal Drugs	1.4	Never to very often (0–4)	0	5.6
Total			0	105.7
Cronbach's Alpha			.828	

TABLE B8
Construction of index of exposure to school violence

Age and Item	Wolfgang-Sellin Severity Index	Response Range	Scale Scores Minimum	Maximum
Witnessed Aged 6				
Students Fighting	7.3	No or yes (0–1)	0	7.3
Violence Directed at Teacher	9.3	No or yes (0–1)	0	9.3
Students Carrying Knives	2.4	No or yes (0–1)	0	2.4
Students with Guns	4.6	No or yes (0–1)	0	4.6
Witnessed Aged 13				
Students Fighting	7.3	Never to very often (0–4)	0	29.2
Violence Directed at Teacher	9.3	Never to very often (0–4)	0	37.2
Students Carrying Knives	2.4	Never to very often (0–4)	0	9.6
Students with Guns	4.6	Never to very often (0–4)	0	18.2
Robbery of Students	5.1	Never to very often (0–4)	0	20.4
Witnessed Aged 18				
Students Fighting	7.3	Never to very often (0–4)	0	29.2
Violence Directed at Teacher	9.3	Never to very often (0–4)	0	37.2
Students Carrying Knives	2.4	Never to very often (0–4)	0	9.6
Students with Guns	4.6	Never to very often (0–4)	0	18.4
Robbery of Students	5.1	Never to very often (0–4)	0	20.4
Gang Activities	0.8	Never to very often (0–4)	0	30.8
Uniformed Security Officers	0.8	Never to very often (0–4)	0	0.8
Metal Detectors at Entrance	0.7	Never to very often (0–4)	0	0.7
Total			0	285.5
Cronbach's Alpha			.801	

TABLE B9
Construction of indices of high school quality

Item	Response Range	Scale Scores	
		Minimum	Maximum
Quality of Infrastructure			
Had Library	No or yes	0	1
Had Foreign Language Laboratory	No or yes	0	1
Had Psychologist	No or yes	0	1
Had Computers for Student Use	No or yes	0	1
Had Guidance Counselor	No or yes	0	1
School Building	Poor to excellent	0	3
Classrooms	Poor to excellent	0	3
Audiovisual Equipment	Poor to excellent	0	3
Library	Poor to excellent	0	3
Computers	Poor to excellen	0	3
Total		0	20
Cronbach's Alpha		.759	
Quality of Teaching			
Teacher Interest	Poor to excellent	0	3
Teacher Preparation	Poor to excellent	0	3
Fairness of Discipline	Poor to excellent	0	3
Felt Encouraged to Think Independently	Never to always	0	5
Total		0	14
Cronbach's Alpha		.702	

TABLE B10

Construction of indices of peer support for academic effort

		Scale Scores	
Item	Response Range	Minimum	Maximum
Peer Support for Academic Effort			
Coolness to Friends of Studying Outside of Class	Very uncool to very cool	0	4
Coolness to Friends of Getting Good Grades	Very uncool to very cool	0	4
Coolness to Friends of Planning to Go to College	Very uncool to very coo	0	4
Importance to Friends of Attending Classes	Not important to very important	0	3
Importance to Friends of Studying Hard	Not important to very important	0	3
Importance to Friends of Getting Good Grades	Not important to very important	0	3
Importance to Friends of Going to College	Not important to very important	0	3
Best Friend Got Good Grades	Very untrue to very true	0	2
Best Friend Interested in School	Very untrue to very true	0	2
Best Friend Studied Hard	Very untrue to very true	0	2
Best Friend Attend Class Regularly	Very untrue to very true	0	2
Best Friend Planned to Go to College	Very untrue to very true	0	2
Best Friend Read a Lot	Very untrue to very true	0	2
Total		0	36
Cronbach's Alpha		.819	

(continued)

TABLE B10 (cont.)

Item	Response Range	Scale Scores	
		Minimum	Maximum
Peer Support for Academic Independence			
Coolness to Friends of Asking Challenging Questions	Very uncool to very cool	0	4
Coolness to Friends of Volunteering Information	Very uncool to very coo	10	4
Coolness to Friends of Answering Questions	Very uncool to very cool	0	4
Coolness to Friends of Helping Others	Very uncool to very cool	0	4
Coolness to Friends of Solving Problems	Very uncool to very cool	0	4
Total		0	20
Cronbach's Alpha			.814
Peer Support for Delinquency			
Importance of Friends to be Willing to Party	Not important to very important	0	3
Close Friends Got Drunk	Very untrue to very true	0	2
Close Friends Used Illegal Drugs	Very untrue to very true	0	2
Best Friend Got Drunk	Very untrue to very true02		
Best Friend Used Illegal Drugs	Very untrue to very true	0	2
Total		0	13
Cronbach's Alpha			.825

TABLE B11

Construction of indices of social preparation for college

Item	Response Range	Scale Scores	
		Minimum	Maximum
Susceptibility to Peer Influence			
Thought and Acted Like Others	Strongly disagree to strongly agree	0	4
Hung Out with Others	Strongly disagree to strongly agree	0	4
Felt Comfortable with Others	Strongly disagree to strongly agree	0	4
Valued Same Thing as Others	Strongly disagree to strongly agree	0	4
Worried about What Others Thought	Never to very often	0	4
Worried about Being Called Nerd or Brainiac	Never to very often	0	4
Did Things so Others Would Like Me	Never to very often	0	4
Total		0	28
Cronbach's Alpha		.592	
Social Distance from Minorities			
Perceived Closeness to Blacks in General	Very distant to very close	0	10
Perceived Closeness to Young Black Men	Very distant to very close	0	10
Perceived Closeness to Young Black Women	Very distant to very close	0	10
Perceived Closeness to Latinos in General	Very distant to very close	0	10
Perceived Closeness to Young Latino Men	Very distant to very close	0	10
Perceived Closeness to Young Latino Women	Very distant to very close	0	10
Total		0	60
Cronbach's Alpha		.905	
Social Distance from Whites			
Perceived Closeness to Whites in General	Very distant to very close	0	10
Perceived Closeness to Young White Men	Very distant to very close	0	10
Perceived Closeness to Young White Women	Very distant to very close	0	10
Total		0	30
Cronbach's Alpha		.874	

TABLE B12
Construction of indices of psychological preparation for college

Item	Response Range	Scale Scores	
		Minimum	Maximum
Self-Esteem			
Am Person of Worth Equal to Others	Strongly disagree to strongly agree	0	4
Have a Number of Good Qualities	Strongly disagree to strongly agree	0	4
Am Inclined to Feel I Am Failure	Strongly agree to strongly disagree	0	4
Able to Do Things as Well as Most People	Strongly disagree to strongly agree	0	4
Do Not Have Much to Be Proud of	Strongly agree to strongly disagree	0	4
Take Positive Attitude toward Self	Strongly disagree to strongly agree	0	4
Satisfied with Myself	Strongly disagree to strongly agree	0	4
Wish I Could Respect Self More	Strongly agree to strongly disagree	0	4
Feel Useless at Times	Strongly agree to strongly disagree	0	4
Think I'm No Good at All	Strongly agree to strongly disagree	0	4
Total		0	40
Cronbach's Alpha			.855

Self-Efficacy			
Don't Have Control Over Life	0	Strongly agree to strongly disagree	4
Good Luck More Important Than Hard Work	0	Strongly agree to strongly disagree	4
Something Stops Me from Getting Ahead	0	Strongly agree to strongly disagree	4
Certain I Can Make Plans Work	0	Strongly disagree to strongly agree	4
Feel Left Out of Things Going on Around Me	0	Strongly agree to strongly disagree	4
If I Work Hard I Can Do Well	0	Strongly disagree to strongly agree	4
Total	0		24
Cronbach's Alpha			.691
Self-Confidence			
Likelihood of Finishing Two Years of College	0	Very unlikely to very likely	10
Likelihood of Graduating from College	0	Very unlikely to very likely	10
Likelihood of Postgraduate Education	0	Very unlikely to very likely	10
Likelihood of Finishing Grad/Prof Degree	0	Very unlikely to very likely	10
Total	0		40
Cronbach's Alpha			.701

REFERENCES

Ainsworth-Darnell, James W., and Douglas B. Downey. 1998. "Assessing the Oppositional Culture Explanation for Racial/Ethnic Differences in School Performance." *American Sociological Review* 63:436–53.

Allport, Gordon W. 1954. *The Nature of Prejudice.* Cambridge: Addison-Wesley.

Anderson, Elijah. 1990. *Streetwise: Race, Class, and Change in an Urban Community.* Chicago: University of Chicago Press.

———. 1999. *Code of the Street: Decency, Violence, and the Moral Life of the Inner City.* New York: Norton.

Aronson, J., D. M. Quinn, and S. J. Spencer. 1998. "Stereotype Threat and the Academic Under-performance of Minorities and Women." Pp. 83–103 in *Prejudice: The Target's Perspective.* Edited by Janet K. Swim and Charles Stangor. San Diego: Academic Press.

Ashmore, Richard, and Francis Del Boca. 1981. "Conceptual Approaches to Stereotypes and Stereotyping." Pp. 1–36 in *Cognitive Processes in Stereotyping and Intergroup Behavior.* Edited by David L. Hamilton. Hillsdale, N.J.: Erlbaum.

Becker, Gary S. 1964. *Human Capital: A Theoretical and Empirical Analysis, with Special Reference to Education.* New York: Columbia University Press.

Blalock Hubert M. 1991. *Understanding Social Inequality: Modeling Allocation Processes.* Newbury Park, Calif.: Sage Publications.

Blumer, Herbert. 1958. "Race Prejudice as a Sense of Group Position." *Pacific Sociological Review* 1:3–7.

Bobo, Lawrence D., and Devon Johnson. 2000. "Racial Attitudes in a Prismatic Metropolis: Mapping Identity, Stereotypes, Competition, and Views on Affirmative Action." Pp. 81–166 in *Prismatic Metropolis: Inequality in Los Angeles.* Edited by Lawrence D. Bobo, Melvin L. Oliver, James H. Johnson Jr., and Abel Valenzuela. New York: Russell Sage.

Bobo, Lawrence D., Melvin L. Oliver, James H. Johnson Jr., and Abel Valenzuela. 2000. *Prismatic Metropolis: Inequality in Los Angeles.* New York: Russell Sage.

Bourdieu, Pierre. 1977. *Outline of a Theory of Practice.* New York: Cambridge University Press.

———. 1986. "The Forms of Capital." Pp. 241–58 in *Handbook of Theory and Research for the Sociology of Education.* Edited by John G. Richardson. New York: Greenwood Press

Bourdieu, Pierre, and Loic Wacquant. 1992. *An Invitation to Reflexive Sociology.* Chicago: University of Chicago Press.

Bowen, William G., and Derek Bok. 1998. *The Shape of the River: Long-Term Consequences of Considering Race in College and University Admissions.* Princeton: Princeton University Press.

Bowles, Samuel, and Herbert Gintis 1976. *Schooling in Capitalist America: Educational Reform and the Contradictions of Economic Life.* New York: Basic Books.

Bronfenbrenner, Urie. 1979. *The Ecology of Human Development: Experiments by Nature and Design.* Cambridge: Harvard University Press.

Brooks-Gunn, Jeanne, Greg J. Duncan, and J. Lawrence Aber. 1997. *Neighborhood Poverty.* Volume 1: Context and Consequences for Children. New York: Russell Sage.

Brooks-Gunn, Jeanne, and P. Lindsay Chase-Lansdale. 1991. "Children Having Children: Effects on the Family System." *Pediatric Annals* 20(9): 467–81.

Brooks-Gunn, Jeanne, K. Klebanov, and Greg J. Duncan. 1996. "Ethnic Differences in Children's Intelligence Test Scores: The Role of Economic Deprivation, Home Environment, and Maternal Characteristics." *Child Development* 67: 396–408.

Brown, B. Bradford. 1990. "Peer Groups and Peer Cultures." Pp. 157–86 in *At the Threshold: The Developing Adolescent.* Edited by S. Shirley Feldman and Glenn R. Elliot. Cambridge: Harvard University Press.

Burtless. Gary. 1996. *Does Money Matter? The Effect of School Resources on Student Achievement and Adult Success.* Washington, D.C.: Brookings Institution.

Carter, Prudence. 2001. "Low-Income Black and Latino Youths' Orientation to Mobility: Why School Success Is Not Perceived as 'Acting White.'" Ms., Department of Sociology, University of Michigan, Ann Arbor.

Chase-Lansdale, P. Lindsay, and R. A. Gordon. 1996. "Economic Hardship and the Development of Five- and Six-Year-Olds: Neighborhood and Regional Perspectives." *Child Development* 67:3338–67.

Cheryan, Spana, and Galen V. Bodenhausen. 2000. "When Positive Stereotypes Threaten Intellectual Performance." *Psychological Science* 11:399–402.

Coleman, James S. 1961. *The Adolescent Society: The Social Life of the Teenager and Its Impact on Education.* New York: Free Press.

———. 1966. *Equality of Educational Opportunity.* Washington, D.C.: U.S. Government Printing Office.

———. 1988. "Social Capital in the Creation of Human Capital." *American Journal of Sociology,* 94:S95–S120.

———. 1990. *Foundations of Social Theory.* Cambridge: Harvard University Press.

Coleman, James S., Thomas Hoffer, and Sally Kilgore. 1982. *High School Achievement: Public, Catholic, and Private Schools Compared.* New York: Basic Books.

Condition of Education. 2000. *Condition of Education.* Washington, D.C.: U.S. Department of Education.

Conley, Dalton. 1999. *Being Black, Living in the Red: Race, Wealth, and Social Policy in America.* Berkeley: University of California Press.

———. 2001. "Capital for College: Parental Assets and Post-secondary Schooling." *Sociology of Education* 74:59–72.

Connerly, Ward. 2000. *Creating Equal: My Fight against Race Preferences.* San Francisco: Encounter Books.

Cook, Philip J., and Jens Ludwig. 1998. "The Burden of 'Acting White': Do African American Adolescents Disparage Academic Achievement?" Pp. 375–400 in *The Black-White Test Score Gap.* Edited by Christopher Jencks and Meredith Phillips. Washington, D.C.: Brookings Institution Press.

Crocker, Jennifer, and Brenda Major. 1989. "Social Stigma and Self-Esteem: The Self-Protective Properties of Stigma. *Psychological Review* 96:608–30.

Crocker, Jennifer, and Diane Quinn. 1998. "Racism and Self-Esteem." Pp. 169–87 in *Confronting Racism: The Problem and the Response*. Edited by Jennifer L. Eberhardt and Susan T. Fiske. Thousand Oaks, Calif.: Sage Publications.

Crouse, James, and Dale Trusheim. 1988. *The Case against the SAT*. Chicago: University of Chicago Press.

Davies, Scott. 1995. "Leaps of Faith: Shifting Currents in Critical Sociology of Education." *American Journal of Sociology* 100:1448–78.

Denton, Nancy A., and Douglas S. Massey. 1989. "Racial Identity among Caribbean Hispanics: The Effect of Double Minority Status on Residential Segregation." *American Sociological Review* 54:790–808.

Devine, John. 1996. *Maximum Security: The Culture of Violence in Inner City Schools*. Chicago: University of Chicago Press.

Deyhle, Donna. 1995. "Navajo Youth and Anglo Racism: Cultural Integrity and Resistance." *Harvard Educational Review* 65(3): 403–44.

DiMaggio, Paul. 1982. "Cultural Capital and School Success: The Impact of Status Cultural Participation on the Grades of U.S. High School Students." *American Sociological Review* 47:189–201.

DiMaggio, Paul, and Francie Ostrower. 1990. "Participation in the Arts by Black and White Americans." *Social Forces* 68:753–78.

Downey, Douglas B., and James W. Ainsworth-Darnell. 2002. "The Search for Oppositional Culture among Black Students." *American Sociological Review* 61:156–64.

Duncan, Greg J., and Jeanne Brooks-Gunn. 1997. "Income Effects across the Life Span: Integration and Interpretation." Pp. 596–610 in *Consequences of Growing Up Poor*. Edited by Greg J. Duncan and Jeanne Brooks-Gunn. New York: Russell Sage.

Duncan, Otis D. 1969. "Inheritance of Poverty or Inheritance of Race?" Pp. 85–110 in *On Understanding Poverty: Perspectives from the Social Sciences*. Edited by Daniel P. Moynihan. New York: Basic Books.

Dunn, J. 1983. "Sibling Relationships in Early Childhood." *Child Development* 54:787–811.

Epstein, Joyce, and Nancy Karweit. 1983. *Friends in School*. New York: Academic Press.

Erikson, Erik H. 1975. *Life History and the Historical Moment*. New York: Norton.

Farkas, George. 1996. *Human Capital or Cultural Capital? Ethnicity and Poverty Groups in an Urban School District*. New York: Aldine de Gruyter.

Farkas, George, Christy Lleras, and Steve Maczuga. 2002. "Does Oppositional Culture Exist in Minority and Poverty Peer Groups?" *American Sociological Review* 61:149–55.

Farley, Reynolds. 1998. *The New American Reality: Who We Are, How We Got Here, Where We Are Going*. New York: Russell Sage.

Feagin, Joe R., Hernan Vera, and Nikitah O. Imani. 1996. *The Agony of Education: Black Students at White Colleges and Universities*. New York: Routledge.

Festinger, Leon. 1954. "A Theory of Social Comparison Processes." *Human Relations* 7:117–40.

Fischer, Claude S., Michael Hout, Martín Sánchez Jankowski, Samuel R. Lucas, Ann Swidler, and Kim Voss. 1996. *Inequality by Design: Cracking the Bell Curve Myth.* Princeton: Princeton University Press.

Fiske, Susan T., Amy J. C. Cuddy, Peter Glick, and Jun Xu. 2002. "A Model of (Often Mixed) Stereotype Content: Competence and Warmth Respectively Follow from Perceived Status and Competition." *Journal of Personality and Social Psychology,* forthcoming.

Fiske, Susan T., and Shelley E. Taylor. 1991. *Social Cognition.* New York: McGraw-Hill.

Fordham, Signithia. 1988. "Racelessness as a Factor in Black Students' School Success: Pragmatic Strategy or Pyrrhic Victory?" *Harvard Educational Review* 58:54–84.

———. 1996. *Blacked Out: Dilemmas of Race, Identity, and Success at Capital High.* Chicago: University of Chicago Press.

Fordham, Signithia, and John U. Ogbu. 1986. "Black Students' School Success: Coping with the 'Burden of Acting White.'" *The Urban Review* 18:176–206.

Furstenberg, Frank F. 1987. "Race Differences in Teenage Sexuality, Pregnancy, and Adolescent Childbearing." *The Milbank Quarterly* 65:S381–S403.

Furstenberg, Frank F., Jeanne Brooks-Gunn, and S. Philip Morgan. 1987. *Adolescent Mothers in Later Life.* New York: Cambridge University Press.

Furstenberg, Frank F., and Andrew J. Cherlin. 1991. *Divided Families: What Happens to Children When Parents Part.* Cambridge: Harvard University Press.

Furstenberg, Frank F., S. Philip Morgan, Kristin A. Moore, and James L. Peterson. 1987. "Race Differences in the Timing of Adolescent Intercourse." *American Sociological Review* 52:511–18.

Glazer, Nathan. 1997. *We Are All Multiculturalists Now.* Cambridge: Harvard University Press.

Guo, Guang, and Kathleen Mullan Harris. 2000. "The Mechanisms Mediating the Effects of Poverty on Children's Intellectual Development." *Demography* 37:431–48.

Hallinan, Maureen T. 1982. "The Peer Influence Process." *Studies in Educational Evaluation* 7(3): 285–306.

———. 1983. "Commentary: New Directions for Research on Peer Influences." Pp. 219–31 in *Friends in School.* Edited by Joyce Epstein and Nancy Karweit. New York: Academic Press.

Hanushek, Eric. 1989. "The Impact of Differential Expenditures on School Performance." *Educational Researcher* 18:48–52.

Hartup, W. 1989. "Social Relationships and Their Developmental Significance." *American Psychologist* 44(2): 120–26.

Hayes, Cheryl D., John L. Palmer, and Martha J. Zaslow. 1990. *Who Cares for America's Children? Child Care Policy for the 1990s.* Washington, D.C.: National Academy Press.

Herrnstein, Richard J., and Charles Murray. 1996. *The Bell Curve: Intelligence and Class Structure in American Life.* New York: Free Press.

Hochschild, Jennifer L. 1995. *Facing Up to the American Dream: Race, Class, and the Soul of the Nation.* Princeton: Princeton University Press.

Hofferth, Sandra L., and D. A. Phillips. 1991. "Child Care Policy Research." *Journal of Social Issues* 47:1013.

Jackman, Mary R. 1994. *The Velvet Glove: Paternalism and Conflict in Gender, Class, and Race.* Berkeley: University of California Press.

Jencks, Christopher, Susan Bartlett, Mary Corcoran, and Greg. J. Dunanc. 1979. *Who Gets Ahead? The Determinants of Economic Success in America.* New York: Basic Books.

Johnson, Monica Kirkpatrick, Robert Crosnoe, and Glen H. Elder Jr. 2001. "Students' Attachment and Academic Engagement: The Role of Race and Ethnicity." *Sociology of Education* 74:318–40.

Josephs, R., and D. Schroeder. 1997. "The Self-Protective Function of the Learning Curve. Ms., University of Texas at Austin.

Kandel, Denise. 1978. "Homophily, Selection, and Socialization in Adolescent Friendships." *American Journal of Sociology* 84:427–63.

Kane, Thomas J. 1998. Racial and Ethnic Preferences in College Admissions. Pp. 431–56 in *The Black-White Test Score Gap.* Edited by Christopher Jencks and Meredith Phillips. Washington, D.C.: Brookings Institution Press.

Kao, Grace. 1995. "Asian Americans as Model Minorities? A Look at Their Academic Performance." *American Journal of Education* 103:121–59.

———. 2001. "Race and Ethnic Differences in Peer Influences on Educational Achievement." Pp. 437–60 in *Problem of the Century: Racial Stratification in the United States.* Edited by Elijah Anderson and Douglas S. Massey. New York: Russell Sage.

Kao, Grace, and Marta Tienda. 1998. "Educational Aspirations among Minority Youth." *American Journal of Education* 106:349–84.

Kao, Grace, Marta Tienda, and Barbara Schneider. 1996. "Racial and Ethnic Variations in Academic Performance." *Research in Sociology of Education and Socialization* 11:263–98.

Kelley, Harold H. 1967. "Attribution Theory in Social Psychology." *Nebraska Symposium on Motivation* 15:192–238.

Kluegel, James R., and Eliot R. Smith. 1986. *Beliefs about Inequality: Americans' Views of What Is and What Ought to Be.* New York: Aldine de Gruyter.

Kohn, Melvin L. 1969. *Class and Conformity: A Study in Values.* Homewood, Ill.: Dorsey Press.

Kozol, Jonathan. 1991. *Savage Inequalities: Children in America's Schools.* New York: Crown Publishers.

Lamont, Michele. 1992. *Money, Morals, and Manners: The Culture of the French and American Upper-Middle Class.* Chicago: University of Chicago Press.

———. 1999. *The Cultural Territories of Race: Black and White Boundaries.* Chicago: University of Chicago Press.

Lamont, Michele, and Annette Lareau. 1988. "Cultural Capital: Allusions, Gaps and Glissandos in Recent Theoretical Developments." *Sociological Theory* 6(2): 153–68.

Lareau, Annette. 2000. *Home Advantage: Social Class and Parental Intervention in Elementary Education.* Oxford: Roman and Littlefield.

LeDoux, Joseph. 1986. "Sensory Systems and Emotion." *Integrative Psychiatry* 4:237–43.

Logan, John R., Richard D. Alba, Tom McNulty, and Brian Fischer. 1996. "Making a Place in the Metropolis: Locational Attainment in Cities and Suburbs." *Demography* 33:443–54.

MacLeod, Jay. 1995. *Ain't No Makin' It: Aspirations and Attainment in a Low-Income Neighborhood.* Boulder: Westview Press.

Major, Brenda, and Jennifer Crocker. 1993. "Social Stigma: The Affective Consequences of Attributional Ambiguity." Pp. 345–70 in *Affect, Cognition, and Stereotyping: Interactive Processes in Intergroup Perception.* Edited by Diane M. Mackie and David L. Hamilton. San Diego: Academic Press.

Massey, Douglas S., Rafael Alarcón, Jorge Durand, and Humberto González. 1987. *Return to Aztlan: The Social Process of International Migration from Western Mexico.* Berkeley: University of California Press.

Massey, Douglas S., and Brooks Bitterman. 1985. "Explaining the Paradox of Puerto Rican Segregation." *Social Forces* 64:306–31.

Massey, Douglas S., Gretchen A. Condran, and Nancy A. Denton. 1987. "The Effect of Residential Segregation on Black Social and Economic Well-Being." *Social Forces* 66:29–57.

Massey, Douglas S., and Nancy A. Denton. 1985. "Spatial Assimilation as a Socioeconomic Process." *American Sociological Review* 50:94–105.

———. 1989. "Hypersegregation in U.S. Metropolitan Areas: Black and Hispanic Segregation along Five Dimensions." *Demography* 26:373–93.

———. 1992. "Racial Identity and the Segregation of Mexicans in the United States." *Social Science Research* 21:235–60.

———. 1993. *American Apartheid: Segregation and the Making of the Underclass.* Cambridge: Harvard University Press.

Massey, Douglas S., and Mary J. Fischer. 1999. "Does Rising Income Bring Integration? New Results Blacks, Hispanics, and Asians in 1990." *Social Science Research* 28:316–26.

———. 2000. "How Segregation Concentrates Poverty." *Ethnic and Racial Studies* 23:670–91.

Massey, Douglas S., and Eric Fong. 1990. "Segregation and Neighborhood Quality: Blacks, Hispanics, and Asians in the San Francisco Metropolitan Area." *Social Forces* 69:15–32.

Matute-Bianchi, Maria, E. 1986. "Ethnic Identities and Patterns of School Success and Failure among Mexican-Descent and Japanese American Students in a California High School." *American Journal of Education* 95:233–55.

McLanahan, Sara, and Gary Sandefur 1994. *Growing Up with a Single Parent: What Hurts, What Helps.* Cambridge: Harvard University Press.

Merton, Robert K., and Alice S. Rossi. 1968. "Contributions to the Theory of Reference Group Behavior." Pp. 279–329 in *Social Theory and Social Structure.* Edited by Robert K. Merton. New York: Free Press.

Miller, Scott L. 1995. *American Imperative: Accelerating Minority Educational Advancement.* New Haven: Yale University Press.

Morenoff, Jeffrey, and Robert Sampson. 1997. "Ecological Perspectives on the Neighborhood Context of Poverty and Social Organization: Past and Present." In *Neighborhood Poverty: Context and Consequences for Children.* Volume 2:

Conceptual, Methodological, and Policy Approaches to Studying Neighbor-hoods. New York: Russell Sage.

Mruk, Christopher J. 1999. *Self-Esteem: Research, Theory, and Practice.* New York: Springer.

National Center for Education Statistics. 1995. *Degrees and Other Formal Awards Conferred.* Washington, D.C.: U.S. Department of Education.

———. 2001. *1997 Enrollment Survey.* At http://www.nsf.gov/sbe/srs/seind00/append/c4/at04-02.xls.

Nettles, Michael T. 1991. "Racial Similarities and Differences in the Predictors of College Student Achievement." Pp. 75–94 in *College in Black and White: African American Students in Predominantly White and in Historically Black Public Universities.* Edited by Walter Allen. Albany: State University of New York Press.

O'Connor, Carla. 1997. "Dispositions toward (Collective) Struggle and Educational Resilience in the Inner City: A Case Analysis of Six African-American High School Students." *American Educational Research Journal* 34:593–629.

Ogbu, John U. 1978. *Minority Education and Caste: The American System in Cross-Cultural Perspective.* New York: Academic Press.

———. 1981. "Education, Clientage, and Social Mobility: Caste and Social Change in the United States and Nigeria." Pp. 277–300 in *Social Inequality: Comparative and Developmental Approaches.* Edited by Gerald D. Berreman. New York: Academic Press.

———. 1991. "Minority Responses and School Experiences." *The Journal of Psychohistory* 18:433–56.

Oliver, Melvin L., and Thomas M. Shapiro. 1995. *Black Wealth/White Wealth: A New Perspective on Racial Inequality.* New York: Routledge.

Operario, Donald, and Susan T. Fiske. 2001. "Stereotypes: Processes, Structures, Content, and Context." Pp. 22–44 in *Blackwell Handbook in Social Psychology.* Volume 4: *Intergroup Processes.* Edited by Rupert Brown and Samuel L. Gaertner. Cambridge, Mass.: Blackwell.

Orfield, Gary. 1993. *The Growth of Segregation in American Schools: Changing Patterns of Separation and Poverty since 1968.* Alexandria, Va.: National School Boards Association.

Orfield, Gary, and Susan E. Eaton. 1996. *Dismantling Desegregation: The Quiet Reversal of Brown v. Board of Education.* New York: New Press, distributed by W.W. Norton.

Patillo-McCoy, Mary. 1999. *Black Picket Fences: Privilege and Peril among the Black Middle Class.* Chicago: University of Chicago Press.

Parcel, Toby L., and Micaela J. Dufur. 2001. "Capital at Home and at School: Effects on Student Achievement." *Social Forces* 79:881–912.

Rich, Judith. 1998. *The Nurture Assumption: Why Children Turn Out the Way They Do.* New York: Free Press.

Roscigno, Vincent J., and James W. Ainsworth-Darnell. 1999. "Race, Cultural Capital, and Educational Resources: Persistent Inequalities and Achievement Returns." *Sociology of Education* 72:158–78.

Sampson, Robert J., Jeffrey D. Morenoff, and Felton Earls. 1999. "Beyond Social

Capital: Social Dynamics of Collective Efficacy for Children." *American Sociological Review* 64:633–42.

Savin-Williams, Ritch C., and Thomas J. Berndt. 1990. "Friendship and Peer Relations." Pp. 277–307 in *At the Threshold: The Developing Adolescent.* Edited by S. Shirley Feldman and Glen R. Elliott. Cambridge: Harvard University Press.

Schultz, Theodore W. 1963. *The Economic Value of Education.* New York: Columbia University Press.

Sellin, Thorsten, and Marvin E. Wolfgang. 1964. *The Measurement of Delinquency.* New York: Wiley.

Sewell, William H., Archibald O. Haller, and Alejandro Portes. 1969. "The Educational and Early Occupational Attainment Process." *American Sociological Review* 34:83–92.

Skogan, Wesley G. 1990. *Disorder and Decline: Crime and the Spiral of Decay in American Neighborhoods.* New York: Free Press.

Smith, Sandra, and Mignon R. Moore. 2000. "Intraracial Diversity and Relations among African Americans: Closeness among Black Students at a Predominantly White University." *American Journal of Sociology* 106:1–39

Solomon, R. Patrick. 1992. *Black Resistance in High School: Forging a Separatist Culture.* Albany: SUNY-Albany.

South, Scott J., and Kyle D. Crowder. 1998. "Leaving the 'Hood: Residential Mobility between Blacks, White, and Integrated Neighborhoods." *American Sociological Review* 63:17–26.

Steele, Claude M. 1988. "The Psychology of Self-Affirmation: Sustaining the Integrity of the Self." Pp. 261–302 in *Advances in Experimental Social Psychology.* Edited by L. Berkowitz. New York: Academic Press.

———. 1992. "Race and the Schooling of Black Americans." *The Atlantic Monthly* 269(4): 68–78.

———. 1997. "A Threat in the Air: How Stereotypes Shape the Intellectual Identities and Performance of Women and African Americans." *American Psychologist* 52:613–29.

———. 1998. "A Threat in the Air: How Stereotypes Shape Intellectual Identity and Performance." Pp. 234–62 in *Confronting Racism: The Problem and the Response.* Edited by Jennifer L. Eberhardt and Susan T. Fiske. Thousand Oaks, Calif.: Sage Publications.

———. 1999. "Thin Ice: 'Stereotype Threat' and Black College Students." *The Atlantic Monthly,* 284(2): 44–47, 50–54.

Steele, Claude M., and J. Aronson. 1995. "Stereotype Threat and the Intellectual Test Performance of African-Americans." *Journal of Personality and Social Psychology* 69: 797–811.

Steele, Claude M., S. Spencer, R. Nisbett, M. Hummel, K. Harber, and D. Schoem. Forthcoming. "African American College Achievement: A 'Wise' Intervention." *Harvard Educational Review.*

Steinberg, Laurence. 1996. *Beyond the Classroom: Why School Reform Has Failed and What Parents Need To Do.* New York: Simon and Schuster.

Stephan, Walter G. 1985. "Intergroup Relations." Pp. 599–658 in *The Handbook of Social Psychology.* Volume 2. Edited by Gardner Linzey and Ellion Aronson. New York: Random House.

Suarez-Orozco, Marcelo M. 1991. "Migration, Minority Status, and Education: European Dilemmas and Responses in the 1990s." *Anthropology and Education Quarterly* 22:99–120.

Sue, Stanley, and Sumie Okazaki. 1990. "Asian-American Educational Achievement: A Phenomenon in Search of an Explanation." *American Psychologist* 45:913–20.

Swidler, Ann. 1986. "Culture in Action: Symbols and Strategies." *American Sociological Review* 51:273–86.

Tatum, Beverly Daniel. 1997. *Why Are All the Black Kids Sitting Together in the Cafeteria? And Other Conversations about Race.* New York: Basic Books.

Taylor, Howard F. 1980. *The IQ Game: A Methodological Inquiry into the Heredity-Environment Controversy.* New Brunswick, N.J.: Rutgers University Press.

Teachman, Jay D. 1987. "Family Background, Education Resources, and Educational Attainment." *American Sociological Review* 52:548–57.

Tinto, Vincent. 1993. *Leaving College: Rethinking the Causes and Cures of Student Attrition.* 2nd edition. Chicago: University of Chicago Press.

Tonry, Michael H. 1995. *Malign Neglect: Race, Crime, and Punishment in America.* New York: Oxford University Press.

Vars, Frederick, and William G. Bowen 1998. "SAT Scores, Race, and Academic Performance in Academically Selective Colleges and Universities." Pp. 401–30 in *The Black-White Test Score Gap.* Edited by Christopher Jencks and Meredith Phillips. Washington, D.C.: Brookings Institution Press.

Waters, Mary C. 1999. *Black Identities: West Indian Immigrant Dreams and American Realities.* Cambridge: Harvard University Press,

Willis, Paul E. 1977. *Learning to Labour: How Working-Class Kids Get Working-Class Jobs.* Westmead, England: Saxon House.

Wilson, James Q. 1983. *Thinking about Crime.* New York: Basic Books.

Wilson, William Julius. 1987. *The Truly Disadvantaged: The Inner City, the Underclass, and Public Policy.* Chicago: University of Chicago Press.

Wolfgang, Marvin E., Robert M. Figlio, Paul E. Tracy, and Simon I. Singer. 1985. *The National Survey of Crime Severity.* Washington, D.C.: U.S. Government Printing Office.

Yinger, John. 1995. *Closed Doors, Opportunities Lost: The Continuing Costs of Housing Discrimination.* New York: Russell Sage.

INDEX

adolescence: early (*see* early adolescence); late (*see* late adolescence)

Advanced Placement (AP) courses, 16–17, 104–5, 156, 159–61

affirmative action, 1, 142–43, 145

African Americans: aspirations of, 9–10; college, percentage of attending, 1; college experience of (*see* first semester experience); and college preparation (*see* preparation for college); demographic characteristics of, 39–41, 198–200; diversity and assumptions regarding, 199–201; educational experiences of (*see* educational experiences; high school); and gender ratio of the student cohort, 44–45, 201–2; graduation rate of, 2; home environment of (*see* child-rearing; families); as minority, 4–5, 7–8; neighborhood background of (*see* neighborhoods); oppositional identity of (*see* oppositional culture); overconfidence among, 129–32, 185; and peer influence (*see* peers and peer influence); and perceptions of self (*see* racial identity; self-confidence); and residential segregation (*see* neighborhoods); response rates of, 21–22, 35–36, 198; and SAT tests, 15–17; segregation and (*see* segregation); and separatism, 136; socioeconomic background of, 41–43; stereotype vulnerability of (*see* stereotype vulnerability); women, demographic problem confronting, 201–2

Ainsworth-Darnell, James W., 7, 9

Anderson, Elijah, 85

AP. *See* Advanced Placement credits

Asians: aspirations of, 10; college, percentage of attending, 1; college experience of (*see* first semester experience); and college preparation (*see* preparation for college); demographic characteristics of, 39–41, 198–99; educational experiences of (*see* educational experiences; high school); graduation rate of, 2; home environment of (*see* child-rearing; families); as minority, 4–5, 7; neighborhood

background of (*see* neighborhoods); participation rates of, 21–22, 35–36; and peer influence (*see* peers and peer influence); and perceptions of self (*see* racial identity; self-confidence); and SAT tests, 15–17; segregation and (*see* segregation); socioeconomic background of, 41–43

attachment theory, 13–14, 18

autonomous minorities, 7

blacks. *See* African Americans

blocked opportunities framework. *See* oppositional culture

Bok, Derek, 3, 28

Bourdieu, Pierre, 6

Bowen, William G., 3, 28

Bowles, Samuel, 14

California at Berkeley, University of, 28

capital deficiency, theory of, 5–7, 18, 205–6

Carter, Prudence, 9

caste theory of education. *See* oppositional culture

Catholic schools, 88

childhood (early): and home environment, 47–49 (*see also* child-rearing; families); and neighborhood background, 71–73 (*see also* neighborhoods); and schooling, 87–89 (*see also* educational experiences)

child-rearing, 52; consequences of differences in, 203–4; continuities and contrasts in, 66–69; and cultivation of intellectual independence, 59–62; and cultural capital formation, 56–58; and human capital formation, 53–56; and shame and guilt, use of, 65–66; and social capital formation, 58–59; and strictness of discipline, 62–64

Coleman, James S., 7, 15, 109

college experience. *See* first semester experience

college preparation. *See* preparation for college

contextual peer effects, 12